POCKET

NEW YORK CITY

TOP SIGHTS · LOCAL EXPERIENCES

Map Included

ALI LEMER, REGIS ST LOUIS,
ROBERT BALKOVICH, RAY BARTLETT

Contents

Plan Your Trip

Grand Central Terminal (p156)
OPUS1NY/GETTY IMAGES ©

Explore
New York City 37

Worth a Trip

Survival
Guide 237

Special Features

Welcome to New York City

Epicenter of the arts. Dining and shopping capital. Trendsetter. New York wears many crowns, spreading an irresistible feast for all. With seemingly infinite diversions in this round-the-clock town, NYC rewards diving right in and joining the flow – just hit the streets and see where the day (or night) takes you.

Top Sights

Empire State Building
It's all about the view. **p150**

PAWEL GAUL/GETTY IMAGES ©

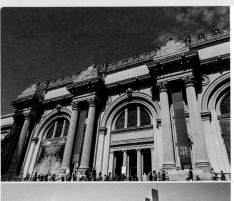

Metropolitan Museum of Art

A truly world-class art collection. **p176**

Central Park

NYC's most popular backyard. **p198**

Brooklyn Bridge

Iconic beauty and engineering marvel. **p42**

Times Square
The neon heart of NYC. **p148**

Statue of Liberty
NYC's most enduring national symbol. **p40**

LEFT: MARCIO JOSE BASTOS SILVA/SHUTTERSTOCK ©; RIGHT: CHECUBUS/SHUTTERSTOCK ©

LEFT: OSUGI/SHUTTERSTOCK ©; RIGHT: OSC AITY/SHUTTERSTOCK ©

MoMA PS1
Queens' top avant-garde art museum. **p218**

Museum of Modern Art
Mecca for modern art fans. **p152**

National September 11 Memorial & Museum
Commemoration of loss. **p44**

Guggenheim Museum
Modern art and singular architecture. **p180**

LEFT: MATTHEW T. CARROLL/GETTY IMAGES © RIGHT: GARDEL BERTRAND/GETTY IMAGES
© INTERIOR OF THE SOLOMON R. GUGGENHEIM MUSEUM, NEW YORK ©SRGF, NY. USED

LEFT: MATT MUNRO/LONELY PLANET ©; RIGHT: ALESSIO CATELLI/SHUTTERSTOCK ©

The High Line
Urban renewal at its best. **p104**

Coney Island
Old-fashioned fun on the boardwalk. **p234**

Eating

From inspired iterations of world cuisine to quintessentially local nibbles, New York City's dining scene is infinite, all-consuming and a proud testament to its kaleidoscope of citizens. Even if you're not an obsessive foodie hitting ethnic enclaves or the newest cult-chef openings, an outstanding meal is always only a block away.

To Market, To Market

Don't let the concrete streets and buildings fool you – New York City has a thriving greens scene. At the top of your list should be Chelsea Market (pictured; p112), packed with gourmet goodies of all kinds, with both shops (where you can assemble picnics) and food stands (where you can eat on-site). Nearby is the new Gansevoort Market (p116), with its countless temptations. For picnics, head to the Union Square Greenmarket (p143), open four days a week. Check Grow NYC (www.grownyc.org/greenmarket) for a list of NYC's other greenmarkets.

Food Trucks & Carts

Skip the hot-dog carts – mobile crews are dishing up unique fusion fare around town. Trucks stop around designated zones throughout the city – namely Union Square, Midtown and the Financial District – so if you're looking for a particular grub wagon, follow them on Twitter. Among our favorites are Mad Sq Eats (p136), Kimchi Taco (www.twitter.com/kimchitruck), MysttikMasaala (www.facebook.com/MysttikMasaala), King David Taco (p227) and Cool Haus (www.cool.haus/foodtrucks).

Best Fine Dining

Eleven Madison Park Arresting, cutting-edge cuisine laced with unexpected whimsy. (p135)

Le Bernardin One of Midtown's holy grails for fine dining, with dishes that shine with delicious complexity. (p160)

Degustation A tiny East Village eatery where you

ALREDOSAZ/SHUTTERSTOCK ©

can watch the chefs create edible works of art. (p90)

Bâtard Beautifully balanced food is the focus at this Michelin-starred spot in Lower Manhattan. (p52)

Best Vegan & Vegetarian

Nix Serving some of the best Michelin-starred, cruelty-free dishes in the city. (p114)

Hangawi Meat- (and shoe-) free Korean restaurant in Koreatown. (p163)

Candle Cafe West A candle-lit Upper West Side mainstay with a wide-ranging menu. (p206)

Two Boots Get your pizza fix with vegan and gluten-free options. (p187)

Best Old-School NYC

Barney Greengrass Perfect plates of smoked salmon and sturgeon for over 100 years in the Upper West Side. (p207)

Russ & Daughters A celebrated Jewish deli in the Lower East Side. (p99)

Zabar's Upper West Side store selling gourmet, kosher foods since the 1930s. (p206)

Margon Unfussy, unchanged Cuban lunch counter in Midtown. (p149)

Papaya King Serving cheap, tasty hot dogs (and papaya juice), an institution since 1932. (p188)

Worth a Trip

Hipster-saturated warehouse restaurant **Roberta's** (☏ 718-417-1118; www.robertaspizza. com; 261 Moore St, near Bogart St, East Williamsburg; pizzas $12-19; ⏱ 11am-midnight Mon-Fri, from 10am Sat & Sun; 🖍; Ⓢ L to Morgan Ave) consistently produces some of NYC's best pizza. The classic margherita is sublimely simple; more adventurous palates can opt for the seasonal hits like Speckenwolf (mozzarella, speck, crimini and onion).

New York City on a Plate
The Best Pizza Slice

The dough base is hand-tossed and baked into a thin crust.

The proper way to hold a NY slice is folded lengthwise.

The tomato sauce must perfectly balance acidity and sweetness.

Typical toppings include pepperoni, green peppers, onions and mushrooms. (Never pineapple!)

Grated mozzarella cheese is used (ricotta is added for a 'white pie').

★ Top Places for Pizza

Roberta's (p11)

Prince Street Pizza (p71)

Two Boots (p187)

Totonno's (p235)

Juliana's (☎718-596-6700; www.julianaspizza.com; 19 Old Fulton St, btwn Water & Front Sts, Brooklyn Heights; pizzas $18-32; ⏱11:30am-10pm, closed 3:15-4pm; ✈; ⓢA/C to High St)

A Slice of Heaven

Whether grabbed on the go as a slice or eaten whole at a sit-down restaurant, pizza is one of New York's most ubiquitous and beloved foods. The light, springy crunch of the thin NY-style crust combines with the slightly sweet tomato sauce and thick, melted mozzarella cheese to create a symphony in your mouth. Add on some meat or vegetable toppings for a classic New York meal.

Queuing for pizza at Juliana's

ANDRIY BLOKHIN/SHUTTERSTOCK ©

Drinking & Nightlife

You'll find all kinds of thirst-quenching venues here, from terminally hip cocktail lounges and historic dive bars to specialty taprooms and 'third wave' coffee shops. Then there's the legendary club scene, spanning everything from celebrity staples to gritty, indie hangouts. Head downtown or to Brooklyn for the parts of the city that, as they say, truly never sleep.

Coffee Culture

A boom in specialty coffee roasters is transforming New York's once-dismal caffeine culture. More locals are cluing into single-origin beans, different brewing techniques and cupping classes. Many are transplants, such as Portland's Stumptown and the Bay Area's Bluebottle. An antipodean influence is notable, with a growing number of top cafes claiming Australian roots.

Craft Beer

NYC's craft beer culture is increasingly dynamic, with an ever-expanding booty of breweries, bars and shops showcasing local artisan brews. Top local sud-makers include Brooklyn Brewery, Sixpoint, Coney Island Brewing Company and Single-Cut Beersmiths.

Prohibition Chic

Here in the land where the term 'cocktail' was born, mixed drinks are still stirred with the utmost gravitas. Often, it's a case of history in a glass; New York's obsession with rediscovered recipes, Prohibition-style 'speakeasies' and

Worth a Trip

Anything goes at warehouse venue **House of Yes** (pictured; www.houseofyes.org; 2 Wyckoff Ave, at Jefferson St, Bushwick; tickets free-$40; ☺hours vary by event, Tue-Sat; ⑤L to Jefferson St), which offers some of the most creative themed performance and dance nights in Brooklyn. Costumes or other glamwear highly encouraged.

GUILLAUME GAUDET/LONELY PLANET ©

1920s panache shows no signs of abating.

Best Coffee

Bluestone Lane Aussie brewing prowess in the shadow of Wall St. (p56)

Kaffe 1668 Caffeinated glory (and room to sit) in Tribeca. (p57)

Irving Farm Roasters Quality brews from beans roasted just upstate; found on the Upper East Side and other locations. (p190)

Stumptown Coffee Roasters The famous Portland coffee company's West Village outpost. (p120)

Best Spirits

Ghost Donkey Eclectic downtown space that specializes in mezcal and tequila. (p74)

Brandy Library Blue-blooded cognacs, brandies and more for Tribeca connoisseurs. (p55)

Rum House Unique, coveted rums and a pianist to boot in Midtown. (p165)

Dead Rabbit NYC's finest collection of rare Irish whiskeys in the Financial District. (p55)

Best Cocktails

Apothéke An atmospheric lounge and former opium den with great cocktails, hidden away in Chinatown. (p74)

Bar Goto Lower East Side icon under the helm of New York's most famous mixologist. (p93)

Employees Only Award-winning barkeeps and arresting

libations in the timeless West Village. (p117)

Lantern's Keep Classic, elegant libations in an historic Midtown hotel. (p165)

Rue B An appealing little East Village den with live jazz and a fun crowd. (p93)

Best Wines

Terroir Tribeca An enlightened, encyclopedic wine list in trendy Tribeca. (p56)

La Compagnie des Vins Surnaturels A love letter to Gallic wines, steps away from Little Italy. (p76)

Buvette A buzzing, candlelit wine bar on a tree-lined West Village street. (p116)

Immigrant Wonderful wines and service in a skinny East Village setting. (p95)

New York City in a Glass
Best Bloody Mary

Celery stick and a slice of lemon

Plenty of ice

Vodka

Celery salt

Tomato juice

Worcestershire sauce and Tabasco to taste

★ Top Spots for a Bloody Mary

Cookshop (☎212-924-4440; www.cookshopny.com; 156 Tenth Ave, btwn W 19th & 20th Sts, Chelsea; ◷8am-11pm Mon-Fri, from 10am Sat, 10am-10pm Sun; ⑤1, C/E to 23rd St)

Buttermilk Channel (☎718-852-8490; www.buttermilk channelnyc.com; 524 Court St, at Huntington St, Carroll Gardens; ◷lunch 11:30am-3pm Mon-Fri, brunch 10am-3pm Sat & Sun, dinner 5-10pm Sun-Thu, to 11:30pm Fri & Sat; ⑤F, G to Smith-9th Sts)

Pine Box Rock Shop (☎718-366-6311; www.pineboxrockshop.com; 12 Grattan St, btwn Morgan Ave & Bogart St, East Williamsburg; ◷4pm-2am Mon & Tue, to 4am Wed-Fri, 2pm-4am Sat, noon-2am Sun; ⑤L to Morgan Ave)

Prune (☎212-677-6221; www.prunerestaurant.com; 54 E 1st St, btwn First & Second Aves, East Village; ◷5:30-11pm, also 10am-3:30pm Sat & Sun; ⑤F to 2nd Ave)

History of a Classic

The classic Bloody Mary – considered a true hangover remedy by many – is a staple of weekend brunches in NYC. The modern version of this drink was invented at the St Regis Hotel's King Cole Bar in 1934 (it's still their signature drink). Garnishes range from vegetables like pickles, olives, chili peppers, lemon and celery to outrageous sculptures teetering with bacon, salami or even shrimp.

Bloody Mary topped with red pepper

MARIA BOCHAROVA/SHUTTERSTOCK ©

Shopping

Not surprisingly for a capital of commercialism, creativity and fashion, New York City is quite simply one of the best shopping destinations on the planet. Every niche is filled. From indie designer-driven boutiques to landmark department stores, thrift shops to haute couture, record stores to the Apple store, street-eats to gourmet groceries, it's quite easy to blow one's budget.

Flea Markets & Vintage Adventures

As much as New Yorkers gravitate towards all that's shiny and new, it can be infinitely fun to riffle through unwanted wares and threads. The most popular flea market is the **Brooklyn Flea** (www.brooklynflea.com; 80 Pearl St, Manhattan Bridge Archway, Anchorage Pl at Water St, Dumbo; ⏰10am-6pm Sun Apr-Oct; 👣; 🚇B67 to York/Jay Sts, Ⓢ F to York St), found in different locations on different days, April through October. The

East Village is the city's go-to neighborhood for secondhand and vintage stores – the uniform of the unwavering legion of hipsters.

Sample Sales

While clothing sales happen year-round – usually when seasons change and old stock must be moved out – sample sales are held frequently, mostly in the huge warehouses in the Fashion District of Midtown or in SoHo. While the original sample sale was a way for designers to get rid of one-of-a-kind prototypes that

weren't quite up to snuff, most sample sales these days are for high-end labels to get rid of overstock at wonderfully deep discounts.

Best Department Stores

Barneys Serious fashionistas shop at Barneys for its spot-on collections of in-the-know labels. (p172)

Bergdorf Goodman Exclusive labels, lunching ladies, and brilliant Christmas window installations. (p172)

Century 21 A giant wonderland of cut-price fashion, kicks and more. (pictured; p60)

KRISTI BLOKHIN/SHUTTERSTOCK ©

Best Fashion & Accessories

Rag & Bone Beautifully tailored clothes for men and women, in SoHo and elsewhere. (p77)

Opening Ceremony Head-turning, cutting-edge threads and kicks in SoHo. (p78)

Shinola Unusual accessories from a cutting-edge Detroit design house in Tribeca. (p60)

Best Bookshops

Strand Book Store Handsdown NYC's best indie bookstore. (p98)

McNally Jackson Great SoHo spot for book browsing and author readings. (p65)

Idlewild Books An inspiring place for travelers with titles spanning the globe. (p126)

Best Vintage

Beacon's Closet Get a new outfit without breaking the bank at this great vintage shop. (p125)

Housing Works Thrift Shop Always a fun place to browse, with locations around the city. (p127)

Screaming Mimi's Lots of appealing clothes from decades past. (p125)

Best Museum Stores

Lower East Side Tenement Museum Books, jewelry, bags, scarves and more. (p86)

MoMA Design & Book Store Beautiful tomes on art and architecture. (p172)

Museum of the City of New York Quality NYC-themed gifts from the eye-catching store. (p185)

Top Tip

Clothing and footwear that costs less than $110 is exempt from sales tax. For everything else, you'll pay 8.875% retail sales tax on every purchase.

Top New York City Souvenirs

DROP OF LIGHT/SHUTTERSTOCK ©

Strand Book Store Totes & Tees

Stop into NYC's largest independent bookstore (p98) to get their iconic logo on a canvas tote bag or T-shirt.

Old Prints & Photographs

Frame a piece of old New York with a reproduction of an old lithograph or photo, available at Bowne & Co Stationers (p60).

IMAGE COURTESTY OF BOWNE & CO STATIONERS.
GABRIEL ELLISON-SCOWCROFT ©

MoMA Skyline Mug

Both beautiful and functional, this mug from the MoMA Design & Book Store (p172) features some of NYC's most iconic buildings.

Sports Merch

Show your love for New York teams with a classic baseball cap or vintage jersey found at No Relation Vintage (p230).

Local Wears

Add something NYC-made to your wardrobe, like some rugged outerwear from By Robert James (p21).

Museums

The M

The Met, MoMA and the Guggenheim are just the beginning of a dizzying list of New York museums. You'll find institutions devoted to everything from fin de siècle Vienna to immigrant life in the Lower East Side, and sprawling galleries filled with Japanese sculpture, postmodern American painting, Himalayan textiles and New York City lore.

Planning

Most museums close at least one day a week, usually Monday (though the Guggenheim shutters on Thursdays). Many stay open late one or more nights a week – often a Thursday or Friday.

You can save time at the most popular museums by purchasing tickets online.

Galleries

Chelsea is home to the highest concentration of art galleries in the entire city (see p106). Most lie in the 20s, on the blocks between Tenth and Eleventh Aves. For a complete guide and map, pick up Art Info's Gallery Guide, available for free at most galleries, or visit www.chelseagallerymap.com. Wine-fueled openings for new shows are typically held on Thursday evenings, while most art houses tend to close their doors on Sundays and Mondays.

For Free

Many museums offer free or reduced admission once a week – check the websites to

Worth a Trip

Overlooking the Hudson River, the **Cloisters Museum & Gardens** (📞212-923-3700; www.metmuseum.org/cloisters; 99 Margaret Corbin Dr, Fort Tryon Park; adult/senior/child $25/$17/free; ⏲10am-5:15pm; 🚇A to 190th St) is a curious mishmash of European monasteries. Built in the 1930s to house the Metropolitan Museum of Art's medieval treasures, it also contains the beguiling 16th-century tapestry The Hunt of the Unicorn.

seum of Modern Art

find out when. Most gallery openings are on Thursdays, but you'll find gratis events throughout the week.

Best Art Museums

Museum of Modern Art (MoMA) Brilliantly curated galleries feature no shortage of iconic modern works. (pictured; p152)

Metropolitan Museum of Art Heavyweight of the Americas, the Met even comes with its own Egyptian temple. (p176)

Whitney Museum of American Art World-class contemporary shows in a grand new space designed by Renzo Piano. (p110)

Guggenheim Museum The architecture is the real star at this Frank Lloyd Wright creation. (p180)

New Museum of Contemporary Art A cutting-edge temple to contemporary art in all its forms. (p86)

Best New York Museums

Lower East Side Tenement Museum Fascinating glimpse of lifeas an immigrant during the 19th and early 20th centuries. (p86)

Merchant's House Museum Step back in time at this perfectly preserved Federal home from well over a century ago. (p68)

New-York Historical Society NYC's oldest museum runs historical exhibits filled with artifacts. (p205)

Museum of the City of New York Details of the city's past abound in this refurbished Georgian mansion. (p185)

Best Less-Known Treasures

MoMA PS1 Across the river in Queens are some of NYC's most cutting-edge exhibitions. (p218)

Frick Collection A Gilded Age mansion sparkling with Vermeers, El Grecos, Goyas, and a courtyard fountain. (p183)

Morgan Library & Museum Rare manuscripts, books, drawings and paintings in a lavish steel magnate's mansion. (p159)

Neue Galerie An exquisite collection in a former Rockefeller mansion. (p183)

With Kids

New York City has loads of activities for young ones, including imaginative playgrounds and leafy parks where kids can run free, plus lots of kid-friendly museums and sights. Other highs: carousel rides, puppet shows, and noshing at markets around town.

Eating Out

Restaurants in the most touristy corners of the city are ready at a moment's notice to bust out the high chairs and kiddie menus. In general, however, dining venues are small, and eating at popular joints can be a hassle with the little ones in tow. Early dinners can alleviate some of the stress, as most locals tend to eat between 7:30pm and 9:30pm. In good weather, we recommend grabbing a blanket and food from one of the city's excellent grocers and heading to Central Park or one of the many other green spaces for a picnic.

Resources

If you're hitting the Big Apple with kids, you can check for upcoming events online at **Time Out New York Kids** (www.timeoutnewyorkkids.com) and **Mommy Poppins** (www.mommypoppins.com). For an insight into New York aimed directly at kids, pick up a copy of Lonely Planet's *Not for Parents: New York*. Perfect for children aged eight and up, it opens up a world of intriguing stories and fascinating facts about New York's people, places, history and culture.

Best Family Outings

American Museum of Natural History Dinosaurs, butterflies, a planetarium and IMAX, oh my! (p204)

Metropolitan Museum of Art A fun trip back in time – make sure to stop at the Egyptian Wing. (p176)

Coney Island Spend a day on the oceanside boardwalk and thrilling amusement-park rides. (pictured; p234)

Best Shopping

Flying Tiger Copenhagen Quirky objects under $5 make for a kid-friendly shopping spree. (p192)

CHRISTIAN MUELLER/SHUTTERSTOCK ©

Books of Wonder Storybooks, teen novels, NYC-themed gifts and in-house storytime make this rainy-day perfection. (p145)

Mary Arnold Toys A neighborhood toy store stuffed to the brim with toys and games, plus free monthly events. (p192)

Best Parks

Central Park Row a boat, visit the zoo and hit Heckscher playground, the best of the park's 21 playgrounds. (p198)

Hudson River Park Choose from mini-golf, a fun playground, a carousel, water features and a science-themed play. (p110)

Prospect Park Brooklyn's 585-acre park has a zoo and an ice-skating rink that's

a water park in summer. (p224)

Best Food

Smorgasburg A great family spot to grab snacks in Prospect Park. (p226)

Chelsea Market Limitless temptations – assemble a

picnic then munch in the nearby Hudson River Park or on the High Line. (p112)

Ample Hills Creamery Watch the ice cream being made as you choose from their singular flavors. (p226)

Worth a Trip

The city has several zoos, but the best by far is the 265-acre **Bronx Zoo** (☎718-220-5100; www.bronxzoo.com; 2300 Southern Blvd; full experience tickets adult/child $37/27, suggested donation Wed; ☺10am-5pm Mon-Fri, to 5:30pm Sat & Sun Apr-Oct, to 4:30pm Nov-Mar; ⑤2, 5 to West Farms Sq-E Tremont Ave), the country's biggest and oldest, with over 6000 animals and re-created habitats from around the world, from African plains to Asian rainforests.

Festivals

SONGQUAN DENG/SHUTTERSTOCK ©

Lunar (Chinese) New Year Festival (www.betterchinatown.com; ⊘late January/early February) This display of fireworks and dancing dragons is one of the biggest in the country.

St Patrick's Day Parade (☎718-231-4400; www.nycstpatricksparade.org; ⊘Mar 17) A massive audience lines Fifth Ave for this popular parade of bagpipers and floats.

Tribeca Film Festival (☎212-941-2400; www.tribecafilm.com; ⊘Apr) A major star of the indie movie circuit.

Cherry Blossom Festival (☎718-623-7200; www.bbg.org; Brooklyn Botanic Garden, Prospect Park; ⊘Apr or May) A celebration of pink flowering cherry trees in Brooklyn.

NYC Pride (www.nycpride.org; ⊘late Jun) Gay Pride Month culminates in a major march down Fifth Ave on the last Sunday in June.

HBO Bryant Park Summer Film Festival (www.bryantpark.org; ⊘mid-Jun–Aug) On Monday nights in summer, classic films are shown on a huge outdoor screen in Bryant Park.

Celebrate Brooklyn! (☎718-683-5600; www.bricartsmedia.org; near Prospect Park W & 11th St, Prospect Park Bandshell, Park Slope; ⊘Jun-Aug) A beloved open-air summer concert and events series.

July Fourth Fireworks (pictured; www.macys.com; ⊘Jul 4) The USA's Independence Day is celebrated with fireworks over the East River, starting at 9pm.

SummerStage (www.cityparksfoundation.org/summerstage; Rumsey Playfield, Central Park, access via Fifth Ave & 69th St; ⊘Jun-Sep; ⋒; Ⓢ6 to 68th St-Hunter College) A series of outdoor concerts in Central Park with a wide mix of cultural fare.

Village Halloween Parade (www.halloween-nyc.com; Sixth Ave, from Spring St to 16th St; ⊘7-11pm Oct 31) The country's largest, a mix of Mardi Gras and art project.

Thanksgiving Day Parade (www.macys.com; ⊘4th Thu in Nov) Massive helium-filled cartoon balloons soar overhead at this cold-weather event.

NYC Marathon (www.nycmarathon.org; ⊘Nov) This annual 26-mile run through the five boroughs on the first Sunday in November draws thousands of athletes from around the world.

Rockefeller Center Christmas Tree Lighting (www.rockefellercenter.com; ⊘Dec) The massive Christmas tree in Rockefeller Center gets bedecked with more than 25,000 lights.

New Year's Eve (www.timessquarenyc.org/nye) A raucous, freezing party to watch the famous ball drop in Times Square.

For Free

The Big Apple isn't exactly the world's cheapest destination. Nevertheless, there are many ways to kick open the NYC treasure chest without spending a dime – free concerts, theater and film screenings, pay-what-you-wish nights at legendary museums, city festivals, free ferry rides and kayaking, plus loads of green space.

F11PHOTO/SHUTTERSTOCK ©

Staten Island Ferry Hop on the free ferry bound for Staten Island for postcard-perfect views of southern Manhattan. (p242)

Chelsea Galleries More than 300 galleries are open to the public along Manhattan's West 20s. (p106)

New Museum Ethereal tooth-white boxes house a serious stash of contemporary art that's (almost) free for visitors on Thursday evenings after 7pm; minimum suggested donation $2. (p86)

Central Park New York's giant backyard, with acre after acre of tree-lined bliss. Go for a jog; relax on the lawn; or throw bread crumbs at the ducks in the pond. (pictured; p198)

The High Line This catwalk of parkland is great for a stroll and skyline ogling. (p104)

New York Public Library This grand beaux-arts gem merits a visit for its sumptuous architecture and free exhibitions. (p157)

MoMA The glorious Museum of Modern Art is free from 4pm to 8pm on Fridays – be prepared for massive crowds and long lines. (p152)

National September 11 Memorial The largest artificial waterfalls in North America are a spectacular tribute to the victims of terrorism. (p44)

SummerStage Free summertime concerts and dance performances in Central Park. (p26)

Neue Galerie This under-the-radar beauty is gratis from 6pm to 8pm on the first Friday of the month. (p183)

National Museum of the American Indian Beautiful textiles, objects and art are a vivid testament to Native American cultures at this gem. (p50)

African Burial Ground National Monument A moving memorial to the legacy of enslaved Africans in colonial New York. (p50)

Frick Collection Gaze at works by European masters for a pay-as-you-wish donation on Sundays from 11am to 1pm. (p183)

Green-Wood Cemetery Also a gorgeous park, with historical battle sites and high harbor views. (p224)

LGBTIQ+

ANDREI ORLOV/SHUTTERSTOCK ©

Weekdays Are the New Weekend

In NYC, any night of the week is fair game to paint the town rouge – especially for the LGBTIQ+ community. Wednesdays and Thursdays roar with a steady stream of parties, and locals love raging on Sundays (particularly in summer).

In the Know

Tons of websites are dedicated to the city's LGBT scene. Check out what's on around town with **Get Out!** (www.getoutmag. com). One of the best ways to be in on the party scene is to follow your favorite promoter.

Best Promoters

BoiParty (www.boiparty. com) Throws impressive weekly, monthly and annual dance parties.

Hot Rabbit (www.hotrabbit. com) Throws women-friendly queer dance parties every weekend in Manhattan and Brooklyn.

The Saint at Large (www. saintatlarge.com) Throws the annual Black Party, a massive circuit event in March.

Daniel Nardicio (www.dan ielnardicio.com) Notorious party promoter, famed for his often hedonistic events.

Josh Wood (www.josh woodproductions.com) Well-established promoter increasingly known for gala events, celebrity guests and philanthropic causes.

Best Classics

Marie's Crisis Show-tune singalongs at this West Village piano bar. (p118)

Duplex Camp quips, smooth crooners and riotously fun drag queens at a Village institution. (p124)

Best for Dancing Queens

Eagle NYC You'll find dancing, carousing and plenty of leather at this two-story club with a roof deck. (p118)

Industry At night this turns from a buzzing Hell's Kitchen bar into a thumping club. (p165)

Best Lesbian Bars

Henrietta Hudson Theme nights with different DJs at this Village staple draw queer women from all around the NYC area. (p119)

Cubbyhole Friendly bartenders and a great jukebox at an easygoing West Village dive. (p118)

Sports & Activities

Although hailing cabs in New York City can feel like a blood sport, and waiting on subway platforms in summer heat is steamier than a sauna, New Yorkers love to stay active in their spare time.

ALEX GOODLETT/STRINGER/GETTY IMAGES ©

Running & Cycling

The 1.6-mile path surrounding the Jacqueline Kennedy Onassis Reservoir (where Jackie O used to run) is for runners and walkers only; also try the paths along the Hudson River in Lower Manhattan or FDR Dr and the East River in the UES. Brooklyn's Prospect Park (p224) has plenty of paths.

NYC has added more than 250 miles of bike lanes in the last decade, but the uninitiated should stick to the less hectic trails in parks and along rivers.

Indoor Sports & Activities

Yoga and Pilates studios dot the city. For a gym workout, try scoring a complimentary pass from one of the major chains.

Best Spectator Sports

NY Yankees (☎718-293-4300; www.mlb.com/yankees; ⑤B/D, 4 to 161st St-Yankee Stadium) Major League Baseball (MLB).

NY Mets (www.mlb.com/mets; 120-01 Roosevelt Ave, Flushing; ⑤7 to Mets-Willets Point) MLB.

NY Knicks (see Madison Square Garden, p169) NBA basketball.

Brooklyn Nets (Barclays Center; ☎917-618-6100; www.barclayscenter.com; ⑤B/D, N/Q/R, 2/3, 4/5 to Atlantic Ave-Barclays Ctr) NBA basketball.

NY Rangers (see Madison Square Garden, p169) NHL ice hockey.

Top Tip
Aside from **Ticketmaster** (www.ticketmaster.com), the other major buy/sell outlet is **StubHub** (www.stubhub.com).

Four Perfect Days

Day 1

MICHAEL URMANN/SHUTTERSTOCK ©

First, wander through **Central Park** (p198), from **Columbus Circle** to **Central Park Zoo** (p201), up **the Mall** to **Bethesda Fountain** and then to **Strawberry Fields**. Stop for a rowboat paddle at the **Loeb Boathouse** (pictured; p199).

Next, take in **Grand Central Terminal** (p156), the **Chrysler Building** (p159), and the **New York Public Library** (p157). Round it off with a visit to **MoMA** (p152).

Later, soak up the atmosphere of **Times Square** (p148) from above the **TKTS Booth** (p170). Pick up a ticket for a blockbuster **Broadway** (p167) show, or go check out something ahead of the curve at **Playwrights Horizon** (p170) or **Second Stage Theatre** (p167). Then swig cocktails at **Rum House** (p165), and bid the city goodnight from the **Top of the Rock** (p156).

Day 2

LITTLENYSTOCK/SHUTTERSTOCK ©

Start at the **Metropolitan Museum of Art** (p176) for the Egyptian and Roman collections and the European masters, then head up to the rooftop (in summer) for Central Park views. Afterwards, visit nearby **Neue Galerie** (p183).

Head down to SoHo for shopping along **Prince** and **Spring Streets**. Next stop is Chinatown's **Mulberry St** (south of Canal St). Stroll by the neighborhood's **Buddhist temples**, stopping for custard tarts and almond ice cream.

Head to a pre-theater dinner at **Cafe Luxembourg** (p206), then walk down Broadway to the **Lincoln Center** (p204) for opera at the **Metropolitan Opera House** (pictured; p210) or to see the **New York Philharmonic** (p212). Later, grab a drink (book ahead) at the fabulously original **Manhattan Cricket Club** (p209).

Day 3

DROP OF LIGHT/SHUTTERSTOCK ©

Catch an early-morning **Staten Island Ferry** (p242) and watch the sun rise over Lower Manhattan. Then head skyward for a marvelous view from the **One World Observatory** (pictured; p48). Afterwards, visit the moving **National September 11 Memorial and Museum** (p44).

Head up to the Meatpacking District and the new **Whitney Museum of American Art** (p110). Then wander along the **High Line** (p104). Along the way stop for snacks, coffee breaks and intriguing views over the streetscape.

Stroll the lovely streets of Greenwich Village and delve into its soul-filled roots for an evening of intimate jazz at **Smalls** (p121) or the **Village Vanguard** (p122). Afterwards, stop by for wine and snacks at buzzing **Buvette** (p116), then head over to **Cielo** (p118) for dancing.

Day 4

KRISTI BLOKHIN/SHUTTERSTOCK ©

Hop over to Brooklyn's **Prospect Park** (p224), grabbing a breakfast burrito at **Grand Army Plaza** (p225) on your way. Kids will enjoy the small **Prospect Park Zoo** (p225) or **Lefferts Historic House** (p225).

Head west to stroll around **Park Slope** (p221). Further west is up-and-coming **Gowanus** (p228); its huge **No Relation Vintage** (p230) store is perfect for rummaging through for some Brooklyn fashion. Stop by **Four & Twenty Blackbirds** (p227) for some melt-in-your-mouth pie.

Jump in a green Boro Taxi up to **Williamsburg** (p232). Browse **Artists & Fleas** (p233) and **Buffalo Exchange** (p233), then hit up **Maison Premiere** (p233) for dinner and cocktails. Walk over to the **East River State Park** (p233) for Manhattan views, then take the **NYC Ferry** (pictured; p242) back across the water.

Need to Know

For detailed information, see Survival Guide (p236)

Currency
US dollar (US$)

Language
English

Visas
Nationals of 38 countries can enter the US without a visa, but must fill out an ESTA application.

Cell Phones
International travelers can use local SIM cards in an unlocked phone (or else buy a cheap US phone and load it with prepaid minutes).

Time
Eastern Standard Time (GMT/UTC minus five hours)

Plugs & Adaptors
The US electric current is 110V to 120V, 60Hz AC, using flat two-prong plugs (there's sometimes a third, round prong for grounding).

Tipping
Restaurant servers 18–20%, bartenders $1 per beer or $2 per specialty cocktail, taxi drivers 10–15%, and hotel housekeepers $3–5 per day.

Daily Budget

Budget: Less than $100
Dorm bed: $40–70
Food-truck taco: from $3
Slice of pizza: around $4
Bus or subway ride: $3

Midrange: $100–350
Double room in a midrange hotel: from around $200
Dinner for two at a midrange eatery: $130
Craft cocktail at a lounge: $14–19
Discount ticket to a Broadway show: $80

Top End: More than $350
Luxury stay at the NoMad Hotel: $325–850
Tasting menu at a top-end restaurant: $90–325
A 1½-hour massage at the Great Jones Spa: $200
Metropolitan Opera orchestra seats: $100–390

Useful Websites

Lonely Planet (www.lonelyplanet.com/usa/new-york-city) Destination information, hotel bookings, traveler forum and more.

NYC: The Official Guide (www.nycgo.com) New York City's official tourism portal.

New York Magazine (www.nymag.com) Comprehensive, current listings for bars, restaurants and entertainment.

Advance Planning

Two months before Book hotel reservations and tickets to a Broadway blockbuster.

Three weeks before Reserve a table at your top-choice high-end restaurant.

One week before Scan the web for the latest restaurant and bar openings, plus upcoming art exhibitions.

Arriving in NYC

✈ John F Kennedy International Airport (JFK)

The AirTrain ($5) links to the subway ($2.75), which makes the one-hour journey into Manhattan. Express bus to Grand Central or Port Authority costs $18. Taxis cost a flat $52 excluding tolls, tip and rush-hour surcharge.

✈ LaGuardia Airport (LGA)

The closest airport to Manhattan but least accessible by public transit: take the Q70 express bus from the airport to the 74th St–Broadway subway station. Express bus to Midtown costs $15. Taxis range from $34 to $53, excluding tolls and tip.

✈ Newark Liberty International Airport (EWR)

Take the AirTrain to Newark Airport rail station, then board any train bound for NYC's Penn Station ($13). From Midtown, hop on a subway to reach your final destination. Shared shuttles and buses are also available. Taxis range from $60 to $80 (plus $15 toll and tip).

Getting Around

Ⓢ Subway

The New York subway system (www.mta.info) is iconic, cheap ($2.75 per ride, regardless of the distance traveled) and open round the clock. It's also safer and (a bit) cleaner than it used to be. Download a useful smartphone app like Citymapper for a map, arrival countdowns and service changes.

🚌 Bus

Convenient especially for riding between Manhattan's eastern and western sides and between some areas in Brooklyn. Uses the Metro-Card ($2.75 per ride), and you get one free transfer to the subway or another bus.

🚕 Taxi

Outside of rush hours, taxi travel can be the fastest and most convenient way to get around; it's a good option when you'd rather stay above ground. (But it can be quite difficult to get a cab in inclement weather.) Ride-share programs like Uber, Lyft and Via are also popular.

🚲 Bicycle

New York's excellent bike-sharing network **Citi Bike** (www.citibikenyc. com; 24hr/7 days $11/27) has hundreds of kiosks around Manhattan and sections of Brooklyn and Queens. Find nearby docks with the Citi Bike app.

⚓ Boat

There are free rides to Staten Island, while the new **NYC Ferry** (www.ferry.nyc; one-way $2.75) services link Manhattan, Brooklyn and Queens for the price of a subway ride. There's also the pricey hop-on, hop-off **New York Water Taxi** (☎212-742-1969; www.nywatertaxi. com; all-day pass $35).

New York City Neighborhoods

Upper West Side & Central Park (p197)

Home to Lincoln Center and Central Park – the city's antidote to the endless stretches of concrete.

West Village, Chelsea & the Meatpacking District (p103)

Quaint streets and well-preserved brick townhouses lead to neighborhood cafes mixed with trendy nightlife options.

Lower Manhattan & the Financial District (p39)

Home to the National September 11 Memorial & Museum, the Brooklyn Bridge and the Statue of Liberty.

Brooklyn: Park Slope, Gowanus & Green-Wood Cemetery (p221)

Two of NYC's most popular residential areas and home to one of its best parks. Hidden treasure Green-Wood Cemetery is nearby.

Museum of Modern Art

Times Square

Empire State Building

The High Line

National September 11 Memorial & Museum

Brooklyn Bridge

Statue of Liberty

Central Park

Guggenheim Museum

Metropolitan Museum of Art

MoMA PS1

Upper East Side (p175)
High-end boutiques and sophisticated mansions culminate in the architectural flourish of Museum Mile.

Midtown (p147)
This is the NYC you're thinking of: Times Square, Broadway theaters, canyons of skyscrapers and bustling crowds.

Union Square, Flatiron District & Gramercy (p131)
The tie that binds the colorful menagerie of surrounding areas. It's short on sights but big on buzz-worthy restaurants.

East Village & Lower East Side (p81)
Old meets new on every block of this downtown duo – two of the city's hottest 'hoods for nightlife and cheap eats.

SoHo & Chinatown (p63)
Hidden temples and steaming dumpling houses dot Chinatown. Next door are SoHo's streamlined streets and high-end shopping.

Explore
New York City

Worth a Trip 👀

New York City's Walking Tours 🥾

Grand Central Terminal (p156) MACH PHOTOS/SHUTTERSTOCK ©

Explore ◈

Lower Manhattan & the Financial District

Gleaming with bold, architectural icons, eateries and a booming residential population, Manhattan's southern tip is no longer strictly business. It's also home to the National September 11 Memorial and Museum, One World Observatory and Wall Street and, just offshore, Ellis Island and Lady Liberty herself. To the north is Tribeca, with its vibrant restaurants and bars.

Start the day early with a sunrise stroll across the Brooklyn Bridge (p42) from the Brooklyn side. Grab a few snacks then head out on the ferry to visit the Statue of Liberty (p40), followed by a stroll through history on Ellis Island (p51). Head back to Manhattan and stop for French pastries and a perfectly pulled espresso at Le District (p53). Then take to the skies at the One World Observatory (p48). Nearby is the moving National September 11 Memorial and Museum (p44), which tells the story of the tragic events that transpired here that day. In the evening, go early to Michelin-starred Bâtard (p52) before catching an innovative production at Soho Rep (p58), a venerable Off-Broadway venue. End the night with a tasting flight of single-malt whiskies at the Brandy Library (p55).

Getting There & Around

Ⓢ The Financial District is well serviced by subway lines; main interchange Fulton St connects the A/C, J/Z, 2/3 and 4/5 lines. Take the 1 train to South Ferry to access the ferries to Staten Island or the Statue of Liberty and Ellis Island.

Neighborhood Map on p46

Top Sight 📷
Statue of Liberty

Lady Liberty has been gazing sternly toward 'unenlightened Europe' since 1886. Dubbed the 'Mother of Exiles,' the statue symbolically admonishes the rigid social structures of the old world. 'Give me your tired, your poor, your huddled masses yearning to breathe free, the wretched refuse of your teeming shore,' she declares in Emma Lazarus' famous 1883 poem 'The New Colossus.'

◉ **MAP P46, C8**

www.nps.gov/stli

adult/child incl Ellis Island
$18.50/9

⊘8:30am-5:30pm, hours
vary by season

Ⓢ1 to South Ferry or 4/5
to Bowling Green, then
🚢to Liberty Island

From the Suez to the City

Sculptor Frédéric-Auguste Bartholdi originally intended a colossal statue to guard the entrance to the Suez Canal in Egypt, one of France's greatest 19th-century engineering achievements, but the ambitious monument failed to attract serious funding. A French writer, Édouard de Laboulaye, proposed a gift to America as a symbol of the democratic values that underpinned both France and the US. Bartholdi tweaked his vision and turned his Suez flop into 'Liberty Enlightening the World'.

Creating the Lady

The artist spent nearly two decades turning his dream into reality. Hindered by serious financial problems, the statue's creation was helped by the fund-raising efforts of newspaper publisher Joseph Pulitzer and poet Emma Lazarus, whose ode to Lady Liberty is now inscribed on the statue's pedestal. Finally completed in 1884, it was shipped to NYC as 350 pieces packed into 214 crates, then reassembled over a span of four months and placed on the US-made granite pedestal. Its spectacular October 1886 dedication included New York's first ticker-tape parade and a flotilla of almost 300 vessels.

Visiting Liberty Today

Folks who reserve their tickets in advance are able to climb the (steep) 393 steps to Lady Liberty's crown, from where the city and harbor views are breathtaking. That said, crown access is extremely limited; the further in advance you can reserve, the better (up to six months before). If you miss out on crown tickets, you may have better luck with tickets to the pedestal, which also offers commanding views.

All ferry tickets to Liberty Island offer basic access to the grounds, including guided ranger tours or self-guided audio tours.

★ Top Tips

o If you want to see both the Statue of Liberty and Ellis Island, you'll have to get a ferry before 2pm.

o Security screening at the ferry terminal is airport-style – leave the pocket knives at home – and can take up to 90 minutes in high season.

o Advance ticket purchase is strongly recommended: it guarantees you a specific time to visit, plus allows you to skip the insanely long queues of people who didn't plan ahead.

✕ Take a Break

Skip the mediocre cafeteria fare at Lady Liberty and pack a picnic lunch to bring with you. Or visit early and return to Lower Manhattan for the gastronomic delights of French food emporium Le District (p53).

Top Sight 📷
Brooklyn Bridge

The Brooklyn Bridge, one of NYC's undisputed architectural masterpieces, opened in 1883. With a record-breaking span of 1596ft, it became the first land connection between Brooklyn and Manhattan, as well as the world's first steel suspension bridge. This magnificent example of urban design has inspired poets, writers and painters – and even today, the Brooklyn Bridge continues to dazzle.

◉ **MAP P46, F4**

⑤ 4/5/6 to Brooklyn Bridge-City Hall; J/Z to Chambers St; R/W to City Hall

The Bridge's Heavy Toll

A German-born engineer named John Roebling designed the bridge, but contracted tetanus in an 1869 accident and died before work even began. His son, Washington Roebling, supervised construction of the bridge, which lasted 14 years, though a few years in he suffered a paralyzing injury from the bends while helping to excavate the riverbed for the western tower, and remained bedridden for much of the project. His wife, Emily Warren Roebling, studied higher mathematics and civil engineering and acted in his stead, also dealing with budget overruns and unhappy politicians. Some 20 to 30 workers died during the bridge's construction, and there was one final tragedy to come in 1883, six days after the official opening: a massive crowd of pedestrians was bottle-necked at a stairway, causing a young woman to trip and fall down the stairs – the resulting shrieks set off a mad rush (people apparently thought the bridge was giving way), and 12 people were trampled to death in the ensuing stampede.

Crossing the Bridge

A stroll across the Brooklyn Bridge usually figures quite high on NYC 'must-do' lists. The pedestrian walkway affords a wonderful vista of Lower Manhattan; observation points under the support towers offer brass 'panorama' histories of the waterfront. It's about a mile across the bridge, which can take 20 to 40 minutes to walk, depending on how often you stop to admire the view.

The Manhattan entrance is directly off the eastern edge of City Hall Park; on the other side you'll find yourself on the border of two Brooklyn neighborhoods: leafy, residential Brooklyn Heights and hip shopping-and-dining destination Dumbo.

★ **Top Tips**

o Take care to stay on the pedestrian-signed side of the walkway – the other half is designated for cyclists, who use it for both commuting and leisure and get frustrated when oblivious tourists wander out in front.

o To beat the crowds, come early in the morning, when you'll have those views largely to yourself.

✕ **Take a Break**

For some post-walk fuel, get a tasty pizza from Juliana's (www.julianaspizza.com) or Grimaldi's (www.grimaldis-pizza.com), two pizzerias just under the bridge in Brooklyn Heights.

On the Manhattan side, the wonderful Arcade Bakery (p53) is only about a 10-minute walk away; cut through City Hall Park to Church St and walk north.

Top Sight 📷
National September 11 Memorial & Museum

The National September 11 Memorial and Museum is a dignified tribute to the victims of the worst terrorist attack to occur on American soil. Titled Reflecting Absence, the memorial's two massive reflecting pools feature the names of the thousands who lost their lives. Beside them stands the Memorial Museum, a striking, solemn space documenting that fateful fall day in 2001.

◎ MAP P46, C5

www.911memorial.org/ museum

memorial free, museum adult/child $24/15

🕙9am-8pm Sun-Thu, to 9pm Fri & Sat, last entry 2hr before close

Ⓢ E to World Trade Center; R/W to Cortlandt St; 2/3 to Park Pl

Reflecting Pools

Surrounded by a plaza planted with 400 swamp white oak trees, the 9/11 Memorial's striking and deeply poignant reflecting pools occupy the original footprints of the ill-fated Twin Towers. From their rim, a steady cascade of water pours 30ft down toward a central void. Bronze framing panels are inscribed with the names of those who died in the terrorist attacks of September 11, 2001, and in the World Trade Center car bombing on February 26, 1993.

Memorial Museum

The contemplative energy of the monument is further enhanced by the National September 11 Memorial Museum (p44). Standing between the reflective pools, the museum's glass entrance pavilion eerily evokes a toppled tower. Inside, an escalator leads down to the museum's subterranean main lobby. On the descent, visitors stand in the shadow of two steel tridents, originally embedded in the bedrock at the base of the North Tower. The moving In Memoriam gallery is lined with the photographs and names of those who perished, with details of their lives relayed through interactive touch screens.

A destroyed fire engine is testament to the inferno faced by those at the scene. The main exhibit's collection of videos, real-time audio recordings, images, objects and testimonies provide a rich, meditative exploration of the tragedy and the stories of grief, resilience and hope that followed. The last steel column removed during the clean-up is also on display, adorned with the messages and mementos of recovery workers, first-responders and loved ones of the victims.

★ Top Tips

o In the museum, look for the so-called 'Angel of 9/11,' the eerie outline of a woman's face on a twisted girder.

o Outside, take a moment to appreciate Santiago Calatrava's huge white Oculus, inspired by a dove's wings.

o Last entry is two hours before closing time.

o Entry is free from 5pm to 8pm on Tuesdays.

✕ Take a Break

Escape the swarm of restaurants serving the lunching Wall St crowd and head to Tribeca for a variety of in-demand eateries, such as Locanda Verde (p52). A good alternative for less-expensive dining is Two Hands (p54).

Lower Manhattan & the Financial District

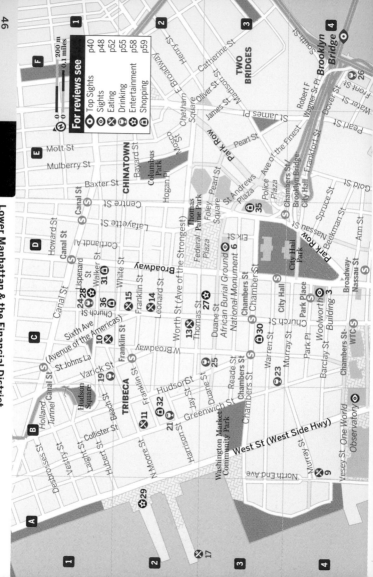

For reviews see

◉ Top Sights	p40
● Sights	p48
✖ Eating	p52
◕ Drinking	p55
★ Entertainment	p58
● Shopping	p59

0 ⸻ 200 m
0 ⸻ 0.1 miles

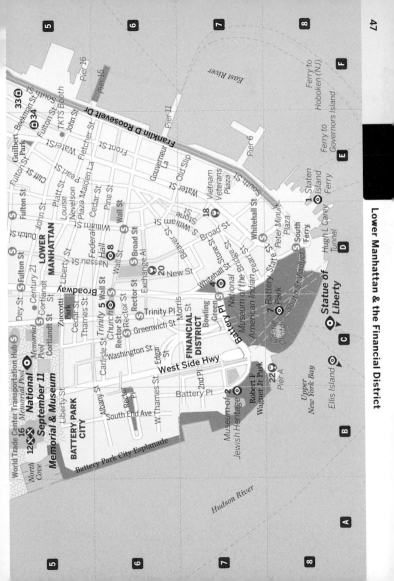

Sights

Staten Island Ferry

CRUISE

1 ⊚ MAP P46, D8

Staten Islanders know these hulking, orange ferryboats as commuter vehicles, while Manhattanites like to think of them as their secret, romantic vessels for a spring-day escape. Yet many tourists (at last count, two million a year) are clued into the charms of the Staten Island Ferry, whose 25-minute, 5.2-mile journey across the harbor between lower Manhattan and the Staten Island neighborhood of St George is one of NYC's finest free adventures. (www.siferry.com; Whitehall Terminal, 4 South St, at Whitehall St; admission free; ⏰24hr; S1 to South Ferry; R/W to Whitehall St; 4/5 to Bowling Green)

Museum of Jewish Heritage

MUSEUM

2 ⊚ MAP P46, B7

An evocative waterfront museum exploring all aspects of modern Jewish identity and culture, from

One World Trade Center

Filling what was a sore and glaring gap in the Lower Manhattan skyline, One World Trade Center symbolizes rebirth, determination and resilience; it's a richly symbolic giant, well aware of the past yet firmly focused on the future. For lovers of New York, it's also the best stop for dizzying, unforgettable urban views.

Leaping up from the northwest corner of the World Trade Center site, the 104-floor tower is architect David M Childs' redesign of Daniel Libeskind's original 2002 concept. This tapered giant is currently the tallest building in the Western Hemisphere – not to mention the fourth tallest in the world by pinnacle height. The tower soars skywards with chamfered edges, resulting in a series of isosceles triangles that, seen from the base, seem to reach to infinity. Crowning the structure is a 408ft cabled-stayed spire that brings the building's total height to 1776ft, a symbolic reference to the year of American independence.

The skyscraper is home to **One World Observatory** (⊚See map p46, B4; ☏844-696-1776; www.oneworldobservatory.com; cnr West & Vesey Sts; adult/child $34/28; ⏰9am-8pm, last ticket sold at 7:15pm; SE to World Trade Center; 2/3 to Park Pl; A/C, J/Z, 4/5 to Fulton St; R/W to Cortlandt St), the city's loftiest observation deck, spanning the 100th to 102nd floors. On a clear day you'll be able to see all five boroughs and some surrounding states. Not surprisingly, it's a hugely popular attraction. Purchase tickets online in advance; you'll need to choose the date and time of your visit.

LITTLENYSTOCK/SHUTTERSTOCK ©

Woolworth Building

religious traditions to artistic accomplishments. The museum's core exhibition includes a detailed exploration of the Holocaust, with personal artifacts, photographs and documentary films providing a personal, moving experience. Outdoors is the **Garden of Stones** installation. Created by artist Andy Goldsworthy and dedicated to those who lost loved ones in the Holocaust, its 18 boulders form a narrow pathway for contemplating the fragility of life. (☏646-437-4202; www.mjhnyc.org; 36 Battery Pl; adult/child $12/free, 4-8pm Wed free; ◷10am-6pm Sun-Tue, to 8pm Wed & Thu, to 5pm Fri mid-Mar–mid-Nov, to 3pm Fri rest of year, closed Sat; ♿; ⑤4/5 to Bowling Green; R/W to Whitehall St)

Woolworth Building

NOTABLE BUILDING

3 ◉ MAP P46, D4

The world's tallest building upon completion in 1913, Cass Gilbert's 60-story, 792ft-tall Woolworth Building is a neo-Gothic marvel, elegantly clad in masonry and terracotta. (It was surpassed in height by the Chrysler Building in 1930.) The breathtaking lobby – a spectacle of dazzling, Byzantine-like mosaics – is accessible only on prebooked guided tours, which also offer insight into the building's more curious original features, among them a dedicated subway entrance and a secret swimming pool. (☏203-966-9663; www.woolworthtours.com; 233 Broadway, at Park Pl; 30/60/90min tours $20/30/45;

$\boxed{S}$R/W to City Hall; 2/3 to Park Pl;
4/5/6 to Brooklyn Bridge-City Hall)

National Museum of the American Indian
MUSEUM

4 ◉ MAP P46, D7

An affiliate of the Smithsonian Institution, this elegant tribute to Native American culture is set in Cass Gilbert's spectacular 1907 **Custom House**, one of NYC's finest beaux-arts buildings. Beyond a vast elliptical rotunda, sleek galleries play host to changing exhibitions documenting Native American art, culture, life and beliefs. The museum's permanent collection includes stunning decorative arts, textiles and ceremonial objects that document the diverse native cultures across the Americas. (📞212-514-3700; www.nmai.si.edu; 1 Bowling Green; admission free; 🕙10am-5pm Fri-Wed, to 8pm Thu; $\boxed{S}$4/5 to Bowling Green; R/W to Whitehall St)

Trinity Church
CHURCH

5 ◉ MAP P46, C6

New York City's tallest building upon completion in 1846, Trinity Church features a 280ft-high bell tower and a richly colored stained-glass window over the altar. Famous residents of its serene cemetery include Founding Father and first Secretary of the Treasury (and now Broadway superstar) Alexander Hamilton, while its excellent music series includes Concerts at One (1pm Thursdays) and magnificent choir concerts,

including an annual December rendition of Handel's *Messiah*. (📞212-602-0800; www.trinitywallstreet.org; 75 Broadway, at Wall St; 🕙7am-6pm; $\boxed{S}$1, R/W to Rector St; 2/3, 4/5 to Wall St)

African Burial Ground National Monument
MEMORIAL

6 ◉ MAP P46, D3

In 1991, construction workers here uncovered more than 400 stacked wooden caskets, just 16ft to 28ft below street level. The boxes contained the remains of both enslaved and free African Americans from the 17th and 18th centuries (nearby Trinity Church would not allow them to be buried in its graveyard). Today, a poignant **memorial site** and a **visitor center** with educational displays honor the estimated 15,000 men, women and children buried here. (📞212-637-2019; www.nps.gov/afbg; 290 Broadway, btwn Duane & Reade Sts; admission free; 🕙memorial 10am-4pm Tue-Sat Apr-Oct, visitor center 10am-4pm Tue-Sat year-round; $\boxed{S}$J/Z to Chambers St; R/W to City Hall; 4/5/6 to Brooklyn Bridge-City Hall)

Battery Park
PARK

7 ◉ MAP P46, C8

Skirting the southern edge of Manhattan, this 12-acre oasis lures with public artworks, meandering walkways and perennial gardens, as well as memorials to the Holocaust and the Irish Famine. It was here that the Dutch settled in 1623, with the first 'battery' of cannons

Ellis Island

America's most famous and historically important gateway, **Ellis Island** (◉See map p46, C8; ☎212-363-3200, tickets 877-523-9849; www.nps.gov/elis; Ellis Island; ferry incl Statue of Liberty adult/child $18.50/9; ⏱8:30am-6pm, hours vary by season; Ⓢ1 to South Ferry or 4/5 to Bowling Green, then 🚢to Ellis Island) is where old-world despair met new-world promise. Between 1892 and 1924, over 12 million immigrants passed through this processing station, dreams in tow; an estimated 40% of Americans today have at least one ancestor who was processed here. The journey from Ellis Island led straight to the Lower East Side, where streets reflected these myriad origins with shop signs in Yiddish, Italian, German and Chinese.

An Irish Debut

The very first immigrant to be processed at Ellis Island was 17-year-old Anna 'Annie' Moore. After a 12-day journey in steerage from County Cork, Ireland, Annie arrived on January 1, 1892, accompanied by her brothers Philip and Anthony; they were joining their parents, who had migrated to New York City four years earlier. She later married German immigrant Joseph Augustus Schayer and gave birth to at least 10 children, only five of whom survived. Annie died on December 6, 1924, and was buried at Calvary Cemetery, Queens.

The Main Building

After the original wooden building burnt down in 1897, architects Edward Lippincott Tilton and William A Boring created a suitably impressive and imposing 'prologue' to America. The beaux-arts Main Building has majestic triple-arched entrances, decorative Flemish bond brickwork, and granite cornerstones and belvederes. Under the beautiful vaulted herringbone-tiled ceiling of the 338ft-long **Registry Room**, the newly arrived lined up to have their documents checked (polygamists, paupers, criminals and anarchists were turned back).

A Modern Restoration

After a $160 million restoration, the island's Main Building was reopened to the public as the **Ellis Island Immigration Museum** (p39) in 1990. Now after you ride the ferry to the island you experience a cleaned-up, modern version of the historic new-arrival experience, with the museum's interactive exhibits paying homage to the hope, jubilation and sometimes bitter disappointment of the millions who came here in search of a new beginning. Always purchase your tickets online in advance (at www.statuecruises.com) to avoid the soul-crushingly long queues.

erected here to defend the fledgling settlement of New Amsterdam. You'll also find historic **Castle Clinton** and the ferry service to Ellis Island and the Statue of Liberty. (www.nycgovparks.org; Broadway, at Battery Pl; ☺ sunrise-1am; ⑤ 4/5 to Bowling Green; R/W to Whitehall St; 1 to South Ferry)

Federal Hall
MUSEUM

8 ◉ MAP P46, D6

A Greek Revival masterpiece, Federal Hall houses a museum dedicated to postcolonial New York. Themes include George Washington's inauguration, Alexander Hamilton's relationship with the city, and the struggles of John Peter Zenger, a printer who on this site in 1734 was jailed, tried and eventually acquitted of libel for exposing government corruption in his newspaper. There's also a visitor information hall with city maps and brochures. (☎ 212-825-6990; www.nps.gov/feha; 26 Wall St; admission free; ☺ 9am-5pm Mon-Fri year-round, plus 9am-5pm Sat Jul-Oct; ⑤ J/Z to Broad St; 2/3, 4/5 to Wall St)

Eating

North End Grill
AMERICAN $$$

9 ✖ MAP P46, B4

Handsome, smart and friendly, this is celeb chef Danny Meyer's take on the American grill. Top-tier produce (including herbs and vegetables from the restaurant's own rooftop garden) forms the basis for modern takes on comfort grub, happily devoured by suited business-people and a scattering of more casual passersby. (☎ 646-747-1600; www.northendgrillnyc.com; 104 North End Ave, at Murray St; mains lunch $27-36, dinner $36-48; ☺ 11:30am-10pm Mon-Thu, to 10:30pm Fri, 11am-10:30pm Sat, 11am-8pm Sun; ☎; ⑤ 1/2/3, A/C to Chambers St; E to World Trade Center)

Bâtard
MODERN AMERICAN $$$

10 ✖ MAP P46, C1

Austrian chef Markus Glocker heads this warm, Michelin-starred hot spot, where a pared-back interior puts the focus squarely on the food. Glocker's dishes are beautifully balanced and textured, whether it's a crispy *branzino* (sea bass) with cherry tomatoes, basil and asparagus; risotto with rabbit sausage, broccoli spigarello and preserved lemon; or scallop crudo with avocado mousse, lime, radish and black sesame. (☎ 212-219-2777; www.batardtribeca.com; 239 W Broadway, btwn Walker & White Sts; 2/3/4 courses $58/75/85; ☺ 5:30-10:30pm Mon-Sat, plus noon-2:30pm Fri; ⑤ 1 to Franklin St; A/C/E to Canal St)

Locanda Verde
ITALIAN $$$

11 ✖ MAP P46, B2

Step through the velvet curtains into a scene of loosened button-downs, black dresses and slick bar staff behind a long, crowded bar. This celebrated brasserie showcases modern, Italo-inspired fare like housemade rigatoni with rabbit *genovese* or grilled swordfish with eggplant caponata. Weekend brunch is no less creative: try scampi and grits or lemon ricotta pancakes with blueberries. Bookings recommended. (☏212-925-3797; www.locandaverdenyc.com; 377 Greenwich St, at N Moore St; mains lunch $23-34, dinner $25-38; ☺7am-11pm Mon-Thu, to 11:30pm Fri, 8am-11:30pm Sat, to 11pm Sun; Ⓢ A/C/E to Canal St; 1 to Franklin St)

Le District
FRENCH, FOOD HALL $$$

12 ⊗ MAP P46, B5

Paris on the Hudson reigns at this sprawling French food emporium selling everything from high-gloss pastries and pretty *tartines* to stinky cheese and savory steak *frites*. Main restaurant **Beaubourg** has a large bistro menu, but for a quick sit-down feed, head to the **Market District** counter for a burger or the **Cafe District** for a savory crepe. (☏212-981-8588; www.ledistrict.com; Brookfield Place, 225 Liberty St, at West St; market mains $12-30, Beaubourg dinner mains $25-37; ☺Beaubourg 7:30am-11pm Mon-Fri, from 8am Sat & Sun, other hours vary; 🛜; Ⓢ E to World Trade Center; 2/3 to Park Place; R/W to Cortlandt St; 4/5 to Fulton St; A/C to Chambers St)

Arcade Bakery
BAKERY $

13 ⊗ MAP P46, C2

It's easy to miss this little treasure in the vaulted lobby of a 1920s office building, with a counter trading in beautiful, just-baked goods. Edibles include artful sandwiches and (between noon and 4pm) a small selection of puff-crust pizzas

Le District

with combos like mushroom, caramelized onion and goat's cheese. Top of the lot is one of the city's finest almond croissants. (📞212-227-7895; www.arcadebakery.com; 220 Church St, btwn Worth & Thomas Sts; pastries from $3, sandwiches $9, pizzas $9-13; 🕑8am-4pm Mon-Fri; 🚇1 to Franklin St)

Two Hands   AUSTRALIAN $$

14 🍴 MAP P46, C2

A palette of pale blues and whitewashed brick walls gives this modern cafe-restaurant an appealing, airy feel. The menu offers light dishes from granola, smashed avocado or mushroom toast to an Aussie-style burger (with cheese, fried egg and beet relish). The coffee's top-notch, too. (www.twohandsnyc.com; 251 Church St, btwn Franklin & Leonard Sts; lunch & brunch mains $14-19; 🕑8am-5pm; 🍴; 🚇1 to Franklin St; N/Q/R/W, 6 to Canal St)

Da Mikele   PIZZA $$

15 🍴 MAP P46, C2

An Italo-Tribeca hybrid where pressed tin and recycled wood meet retro Vespa, Da Mikele channels the *dolce vita* (sweet life) with its weeknight *aperitivo* (5pm to 7pm), where your drink includes a complimentary spread of lip-smacking bar bites. However, pizzas are the specialty. We're talking light, beautifully charred revelations, simultaneously crisp and chewy, and good enough to make a Neapolitan weep. (📞212-925-8800; www.luzzosgroup.

com/about-us-damikele; 275 Church St, btwn White & Franklin Sts; pizzas $17-21; 🕑noon-10:30pm Sun-Wed, to 11:30pm Thu-Sat; 🚇1 to Franklin St; A/C/E, N/Q/R, J/Z, 6 to Canal St)

Hudson Eats   FOOD HALL $

16 🍴 MAP P46, B5

Renovated office and retail complex **Brookfield Place** is home to Hudson Eats, a sleek and upmarket food hall. Decked out in terrazzo floors, marble counter tops and floor-to-ceiling windows with expansive views of Jersey City and the Hudson River, its string of respected, chef-driven eateries includes Blue Ribbon Sushi, Umami Burger and Dos Toros Taqueria. (📞212-417-2445; www.brookfieldplaceny.com/directory/food; Brookfield Place, 230 Vesey St, at West St; dishes from $7; 🕑10am-9pm Mon-Sat, noon-7pm Sun; 🛜; 🚇E to World Trade Center; 2/3 to Park Place; R/W to Cortlandt St; 4/5 to Fulton St; A/C to Chambers St)

Grand Banks   SEAFOOD $$

17 🍴 MAP P46, A3

Chef Kerry Heffernan's menu features sustainably harvested seafood at this restaurant on the *Sherman Zwicker,* a 1942 schooner moored on the Hudson, with the spotlight on Atlantic Ocean oysters (alternatively, try the ceviche, lobster rolls or soft-shell crab). It's mobbed with dressy crowds after work and on weekends; come for a late-dinner sundowner and enjoy the stupendous sunset views.

South Street Seaport 👍

The South Street Seaport is east of the financial district along the river, but a whole world away. This neighborhood of cobblestone and heritage buildings proudly carries on the traditions of its nautical past. Bars and restaurants have a funky, carefree vibe, and those looking to exercise their shopping muscle will be in heaven with the number of stores spread out across the neighborhood.

Before Hurricane Sandy flooded this enclave of cobbled streets, maritime warehouses and tourist-oriented shops in 2012, locals tended to leave this area to the tourists, as its nautical and historic importance was diluted by the manufactured 'Main Street' feel, street performers and poor-quality, often-mobbed restaurants. Revitalization and redevelopment have been slow, but recently momentum has picked up. A glossy, four-story mall on Pier 17, with a massive food court and rooftop entertainment, was scheduled at time of research to open by summer 2018.

(📞212-660-6312; www.grandbanks. org; Pier 25, near N Moore St; oysters $3-4, mains $23-27; ⏱3pm-midnight Mon & Tue, from noon Wed-Fri, from 11am Sat & Sun May–mid-Oct; Ⓢ1 to Franklin St; A/C/E to Canal St)

Drinking

Dead Rabbit COCKTAIL BAR

18 Ⓜ MAP P46, D7

Named in honor of a dreaded Irish-American gang, this most-wanted rabbit is regularly voted one of the world's best bars. Hit the sawdust-sprinkled Taproom for specialty beers, historic punches and pop-inns (lightly soured ale spiked with different flavors). Come evening, scurry upstairs to the cozy Parlor for meticulously researched cocktails. The Wall St crowd packs the place after work. (📞646-422-7906; www.deadrabbitnyc.com; 30 Water St, btwn Broad St & Coenties Slip; ⏱Taproom 11am-4am, Parlor 5pm-2am Mon-Sat, to midnight Sun; ⓈR/W to Whitehall St; 1 to South Ferry)

Brandy Library COCKTAIL BAR

19 Ⓜ MAP P46, C1

When sipping means serious business, settle in at this uber-luxe 'library', its handsome club chairs facing floor-to-ceiling, bottle-lined shelves. Go for top-shelf cognac, malt Scotch or vintage brandies, expertly paired with nibbles such as Gruyère-cheese puffs and a wonderful tartare made to order. Saturday nights are generally quieter than weeknights, making it a civilized spot for a weekend tête-à-tête. (📞212-226-5545; www. brandylibrary.com; 25 N Moore St, near Varick St; ⏱5pm-1am Sun-Wed, 4pm-2am Thu, 4pm-4am Fri & Sat; Ⓢ1 to Franklin St)

Bluestone Lane

COFFEE

20 🕒 MAP P46, D6

While the NYSE busies itself with stocks, its Aussie neighbor does a roaring trade in killer coffee. The second location of Bluestone Lane's expanding empire of coffee shops, this tiny outpost is littered with retro Melbourne memorabilia and squeezed into the corner of an art-deco office block. It's never short of smooth suits and homesick antipodeans craving a decent, velvety flat white. (📞646-684-3771; www.bluestonelaneny.com; 30 Broad St, entrance on New St; 🕒7am-5:30pm Mon-Fri, 8am-4:30pm Sat & Sun; Ⓢ J/Z to Broad St; 2/3, 4/5 to Wall St)

Terroir Tribeca

WINE BAR

21 🕒 MAP P46, B2

Award-winning Terroir gratifies oenophiles with its well-versed, well-priced wine list (the offbeat, entertaining menu book is a must-read). Drops span the Old World and the New, among them natural wines and inspired offerings from smaller producers. A generous selection of wines by the glass makes your global wine tour a whole lot easier. Offers early *and* late happy hours. (📞212-625-9463; www.wineisterroir.com; 24 Harrison St, at Greenwich St; 🕒4pm-midnight Mon & Tue, to 1am Wed-Sat, to 11pm Sun; Ⓢ 1 to Franklin St)

Pier A Harbor House

ARTYOORAN/SHUTTERSTOCK ©

Pier A Harbor House BAR

22 ⊜ MAP P46, C8

Looking dashing after a major restoration, Pier A is a super-spacious, casual eating and drinking house right on New York Harbor. If the weather's fine, try for a seat on the waterside deck – picnic benches, sun umbrellas and an eyeful of New York skyline offer a brilliant spot for sipping craft beers or one of the house cocktails on tap. (☏212-785-0153; www.piera.com; 22 Battery Pl, Battery Park; ⊙11am-2am Mon-Wed, to 4am Thu-Sat, to midnight Sun; �🛜; Ⓢ4/5 to Bowling Green; R/W to Whitehall St; 1 to South Ferry)

Kaffe 1668 South COFFEE

23 ⊜ MAP P46, C3

A coffee-geek mecca, with dual Synesso espresso machines pumping out single-origin magic. There's a large communal table speckled with suits and laptop-tapping creatives, and more seating downstairs. (☏212-693-3750; www.kaffe1668.com; 275 Greenwich St, btwn Warren & Murray Sts; ⊙6:30am-9pm Mon-Thu, to 8:30pm Fri, 7am-8pm Sat & Sun; 🛜; Ⓢ A/C, 1/2/3 to Chambers St)

Macao Trading Co COCKTAIL BAR

24 ⊜ MAP P46, C1

Though we love the 1940s-style 'gambling parlor' bar/restaurant, it's the downstairs 'opium den' (open Thursday to Saturday) that gets our hearts racing. A Chinese-Portuguese fusion of grub and liquor, both floors are solid locales for late-night sipping and snacking, especially if you've got a soft spot for sizzle-on-the-tongue libations. (☏212-431-8642; www.macaonyc.com; 311 Church St, btwn Lispenard & Walker Sts; ⊙bar 5pm-2am Sun-Wed, to 4am Thu-Sat; Ⓢ A/C/E to Canal St)

Weather Up COCKTAIL BAR

25 ⊜ MAP P46, C3

Simultaneously cool and classy: softly lit subway tiles, amiable and attractive barkeeps and seductive cocktails make for a bewitching trio at Weather Up. Sweet-talk the staff over a Fancy Free (bourbon, maraschino, orange and Ango-stura Bitters). Failing that, comfort yourself with some satisfying bites like oysters and steak tartare. There's a Brooklyn branch in **Pros-pect Heights** (www.weatherupnyc. com; 589 Vanderbilt Ave, at Dean St, Prospect Heights; ⊙5:30pm-midnight Sun-Thu, to 2am Fri & Sat). (☏212-766-3202; www.weatherupnyc.com; 159 Duane St, btwn Hudson St & W Broadway; ⊙5pm-1am Mon-Wed, to 2am Thu-Sat, to 10pm Sun; Ⓢ1/2/3 to Chambers St)

Cowgirl SeaHorse BAR

26 ⊜ MAP P46, F4

In a sea of very serious bars and restaurants, Cowgirl SeaHorse is a party ship. Its nautical theme and perfect bar fare – giant plates of nachos piled with steaming meat, and frozen margaritas so sweet and tangy you won't be able to say no to a second round – make this dive a can't-miss for those looking to let loose. (📞212-608-7873; www.cowgirlseahorse.com; 259 Front St, at Dover St; 🕐11am-11pm Mon-Thu, 11am-late Fri, 10am-late Sat, 10am-11pm Sun; ⑤A/C, J/Z, 2/3, 4/5 to Fulton St)

Entertainment

Flea Theater THEATER

27 ⭐ MAP P46, C3

One of NYC's top off-off-Broadway companies, Flea is famous for staging innovative and timely new works. A brand-new location offers three performance spaces, including one named for devoted alum Sigourney Weaver. The year-round program also includes music and dance productions, as well as shows for young audiences (aged five and up) and a rollicking late-night competition series of 10-minute plays. (📞tickets 212-226-0051; www.theflea.org; 20 Thomas St, btwn Church St & Broadway; ♿; ⑤A/C, 1/2/3 to Chambers St; R/W to City Hall)

Soho Rep THEATER

28 ⭐ MAP P46, C1

This is one of New York's finest off-Broadway companies, wowing theater fans and critics with its annual trio of sharp, innovative new works. Allison Janney, Ed O'Neill and John C Reilly all made their professional debuts here, and the company's productions have

Downtown Discounts

Looking for discounted tickets to Broadway shows? Skip the long lines at the TKTS Booth in Times Sqare for the much quieter **TKTS Booth** (Map p46, E5; www.tdf.org; cnr Front & John Sts; 🕐11am-6pm Mon-Sat, to 4pm Sun; ⑤A/C, 2/3, 4/5, J/Z to Fulton St; R/W to Cortlandt St) at South Street Seaport. Queues usually move a little faster and you can also purchase tickets for next-day matinees (something you can't do at Times Square). The TKTS smartphone app offers real-time listings of what's on sale.

garnered more than a dozen Obie (Off-Broadway Theater) Awards. Check the website for current or upcoming shows. (Soho Repertory Theatre; 📞212-941-8632; www.sohorep.org; 46 Walker St, btwn Church St & Broadway; ⑤A/C/E, 1 to Canal St)

City Vineyard LIVE MUSIC

29 ⭐ MAP P46, A2

This waterside bar-restaurant has an intimate, 233-seat cabaret-style theater that features live music nightly. The calendar tends toward emerging singer-songwriters, folk superstars and occasionally indie rock bands; past performers include notables such as Suzanne Vega, Squirrel Nut Zippers, Shawn Colvin, Robyn Hitchcock, Los Lobos, Aimee Mann, Billy Bragg and Yo La Tengo. (www.citywinery.com; Pier 26, near N Moore St; S 1 to Franklin St; A/C/E to Canal St)

Shopping

Philip Williams Posters

VINTAGE

30 🔒 MAP P46, C3

You'll find nearly half a million posters in this cavernous treasure trove, from oversized French advertisements for perfume and cognac to Eastern European film posters and retro-fab promos for TWA. Prices range from $15 for small reproductions to thousands of dollars for rare, showpiece originals like an AM Cassandre. There's a second entrance at 52 Warren St. (✆212-513-0313; www.postermuseum.com; 122 Chambers St, btwn Church St & W Broadway; ⊙10am-7pm Mon-Sat; S A/C, 1/2/3 to Chambers St)

Pearl River Mart

DEPARTMENT STORE

31 🔒 MAP P46, D1

Pearl River has been a downtown shopping staple for 40 years, chock-full of a dizzying array of Asian gifts, housewares, clothing and accessories: silk men's pajamas, cheongsam dresses, blue-and-white Japanese ceramic tableware, clever kitchen gadgets, paper lanterns, origami and calligraphy kits, bamboo plants and more lucky-cat figurines than you can wave a paw at. A great place for gifts. (✆212-431-4770; www.pearlriver.com; 395 Broadway, at Walker St; ⊙10am-7:20pm; S N/Q/R/W, J/M/Z, 6 to Canal St)

Cowgirl SeaHorse (p57)

Shinola
FASHION & ACCESSORIES

32 MAP P46, B2

Well known for its coveted wrist-watches, Detroit-based Shinola branches out with a super-cool selection of Made-in-USA life props. Bag anything from leather iPad cases and journal covers to grooming products, jewelry and limited-edition bicycles with customized bags. Added bonuses include complimentary monogramming of leather goods and stationery and an in-house espresso bar. (☏917-728-3000; www.shinola.com; 177 Franklin St, btwn Greenwich & Hudson Sts; ☺11am-7pm

Where New Yorkers Shop

For penny-pinching NYC fashionistas, the giant cut-price department store **Century 21** (Map p46, C5; ☏212-227-9092; www.c21stores.com; 22 Cortlandt St, btwn Church St & Broadway; ☺7:45am-9pm Mon-Wed, to 9:30pm Thu & Fri, 10am-9pm Sat, 11am-8pm Sun; ⑤A/C, J/Z, 2/3, 4/5 to Fulton St; R/W to Cortlandt St) is dangerously addictive. Physically dangerous as well, considering the elbows you might have to throw to ward off the competition bee-lining for the same rack. Not everything is a knockout or a bargain, but persistence pays off. You'll also find accessories, shoes, cosmetics and homewares.

Mon-Sat, noon-6pm Sun; ⑤1 to Franklin St)

Pasanella & Son
WINE

33 MAP P46, F5

A savvy wine peddler, with 400-plus drops both inspired and affordable. The focus is on small producers, with a number of bio-dynamic and organic winemakers in the mix. It offers free wine-tastings of the week's new arrivals on Sundays, and themed wine-and-cheese tastings throughout the year. Also houses an impressive choice of American whiskeys. (☏212-233-8383; www.pasanella andson.com; 115 South St, btwn Peck Slip & Beekman St; ☺10am-9pm Mon-Sat, noon-7pm Sun; ⑤A/C, J/Z, 2/3, 4/5 to Fulton St; R/W to Cortlandt St)

Bowne & Co Stationers
GIFTS & SOUVENIRS

34 MAP P46, E5

Suitably set in cobbled South Street Seaport (p55), this 18th-century veteran stocks reproduction vintage New York posters and NYC-themed notepads, pencil cases, cards, stamps and wrapping paper. At the **printing workshop** you can order customized business cards or hone your printing skills in monthly classes. For information see the **South Street Seaport Museum** website's Events page. (☏646-628-2707; www.southstreetseaportmuseum.org; 211 Water St, btwn Beekman & Fulton Sts; ☺11am-7pm; ⑤2/3, 4/5, A/C, J/Z to Fulton St)

Bowne & Co Stationers

CityStore
GIFTS & SOUVENIRS

35 🔒 MAP P46, D3

Score all manner of officially-produced New York City memorabilia here, from authentic-looking taxi medallions, sewerhole-cover coasters and borough-themed T-shirts to NYPD baseball caps, subway station signs and books about NYC. (Curious, though less relevant for the average visitor, are the municipal building codes and other regulatory guides for sale.) (📞212-386-0007; www.nyc.gov/citystore; North Plaza, Municipal Bldg, 1 Centre St, at Chambers St; 🕙10am-5pm Mon-Fri; 🚇4/5/6 to Brooklyn Bridge-City Hall; R/W to City Hall; J/Z to Chambers St)

Best Made Company
FASHION & ACCESSORIES

36 🔒 MAP P46, C1

Give your next camping trip a Manhattan makeover at this store/design-studio hybrid. Pick up cool handcrafted axes, leather duffel bags, sunglasses, enamel camping mugs and even designer dartboards and first-aid kits, many emblazoned with their signature 'X' logo. A small, smart collection of men's threads includes designer flannel shirts and pullovers, sweatshirts and rugged knitwear from Portland's Dehen Knitting Mills. (📞646-478-7092; www.bestmadeco.com; 36 White St, at Church St; 🕙noon-7pm Mon-Sat, 11am-7pm Sat, 11am-6pm Sun; 🚇A/C/E to Canal St; 1 to Franklin St)

Explore ◈

SoHo & Chinatown

SoHo (South of Houston), NoHo (North of Houston) and Nolita (North of Little Italy) are among Manhattan's trendiest neighborhoods, known for boutiques, bars and eateries. South, bustling Chinatown and a nostalgic sliver of Little Italy lure with idiosyncratic street life. These neighborhoods offer a delicious, contradictory jumble of cast-iron architecture, strutting fashionistas and hook-hung ducks and salami.

Spend the morning walking through the open-air market that is Chinatown (p68), with a people-watching break in Columbus Park (p69). Step back in time at the Merchant's House Museum (p68) or take in the heady scent of the New York Earth Room (p69). Tuck into lunch at Nom Wah Tea Parlor (p73) or Prince Street Pizza (p71), then pick up a creamy gelato at M'O (p73). Rummage through vintage goodies at Resurrection (p79) or discover new fashion talent at Opening Ceremony (p78). For dinner, go for some local flavor at Il Buco (p72) or Xi'an Famous Foods (p72), or for something different try the world fusion cuisine at Chefs Club (p72). Grab some bespoke cocktails at Pegu Club (p75) or Apothéke (p74), then catch the late show at Joe's Pub (p77) for some live music, cabaret or comedy.

Getting There & Around

S Various subway lines hit Canal St (J/Z, N/Q/R/W and 6); once there it's best to explore on foot.

🚗 Avoid taking cabs here – especially in Chinatown, as the area is small and the traffic full-on. For SoHo, have your taxi let you off along Broadway and walk from there.

Neighborhood Map on p66

Walking Tour 🥾

An Artisanal Afternoon in SoHo

Shopaholics across the world lust for SoHo and its sharp, trendy whirlwind of flagship stores, coveted labels and strutting fashionistas. Look beyond the giant global brands, however, and you'll discover a whole other retail scene, one where talented artisans and independent, one-off enterprises keep things local, unique and utterly inspiring. Welcome to SoHo at its homegrown best.

Walk Facts

Start Café Integral;
Ⓢ N/Q/R, J/Z, 6 to
Canal St

End McNally Jackson;
Ⓢ N/R to Prince St, 6 to
Spring St

Length 1.2 miles;
two to three hours
depending on stops

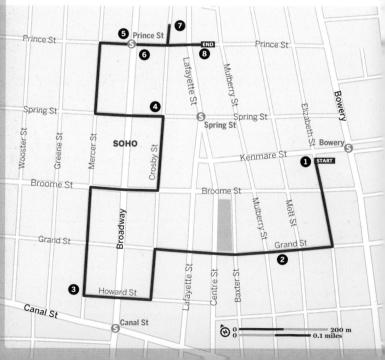

❶ A Shop with Single Origin

Charge up with a cup of single-origin coffee from **Café Integral** (📞646-801-5747; www.cafeintegral.com; 149 Elizabeth St, btwn Broome & Kenmare Sts; ⏰7am-6pm Mon-Fri, from 8am Sat & Sun). Add a croissant and you're ready to go.

❷ Top-notch Tiramisu

Ferrara Cafe & Bakery (📞212-226-6150; www.ferraranyc.com; 195 Grand St, btwn Mulberry & Mott Sts; pastries $7-9; ⏰8am-midnight, to 1am Fri & Sat) has a huge selection, but don't pass up the chance to have a world-class tiramisu (best eaten on the spot).

❸ Perfect Jeans

3x1 (📞212-391-6969; www.3x1.us; 15 Mercer St, btwn Howard & Grand Sts; ⏰11am-7pm Mon-Sat, noon-6pm Sun) lets you design your perfect pair of jeans. Choose hems and customize fabric and detailing on existing cuts, or create your most flattering pair from scratch.

❹ Modern Art

This branch of the hugely popular **MoMA Design Store** (📞646-613-1367; http://store.moma.org; 81 Spring St, at Crosby St; ⏰10am-8pm Mon-Sat, 11am-7pm Sun) has stylish, unique gifts, souvenirs and clothing. Trash cans, skateboards and mah-jongg art-inspired flatware can all be yours.

❺ Curbside Culture

The sidewalk engraving on the northwest corner of Prince St and Broadway is by Japanese-born sculptor Ken Hiratsuka, who has carved almost 40 sidewalks since moving to NYC in 1982. Although only about five hours of work, it took two years (1983–84) to complete: Hiratsuka's illegal nighttime chiseling was often disrupted by pesky police patrols.

❻ A Gourmet Nibble

NYC loves its luxe grocers and **Dean & DeLuca** (📞212-226-6800; www.deananddeluca.com; 560 Broadway, at Prince St; pastries from $3, sandwiches $11; ⏰7am-9pm Mon-Fri, 8am-9pm Sat & Sun) is one of the biggest names around. Feeling peckish? Ready-to-eat delectables include gourmet quesadillas and sugar-dusted almond croissants.

❼ Fragrance Flights

Drop into library-like apothecary **MiN New York** (📞212-206-6366; www.min.com; 117 Crosby St, btwn Jersey & Prince Sts; ⏰11am-7pm Tue-Sat, noon-6pm Mon & Sun) and request a free 'fragrance flight', a guided exploration of the store's extraordinary collection of tantalizing 'stories' told in scent.

❽ Books & Conversation

Browse the shelves at **McNally Jackson** (Map p66, E4; 📞212-274-1160; www.mcnallyjackson.com; 52 Prince St, btwn Lafayette & Mulberry Sts; ⏰10am-10pm Mon-Sat, to 9pm Sun), one of the city's best-loved independent bookstores, stocked with cognoscenti magazines and books, and an in-house cafe for a post-walk coffee.

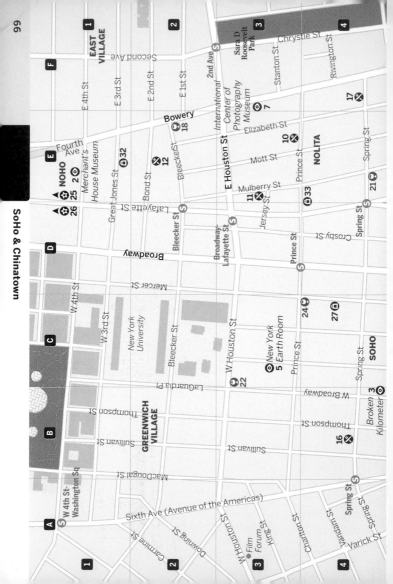

SoHo & Chinatown

EAST VILLAGE

NOHO

NOLITA

SOHO

GREENWICH VILLAGE

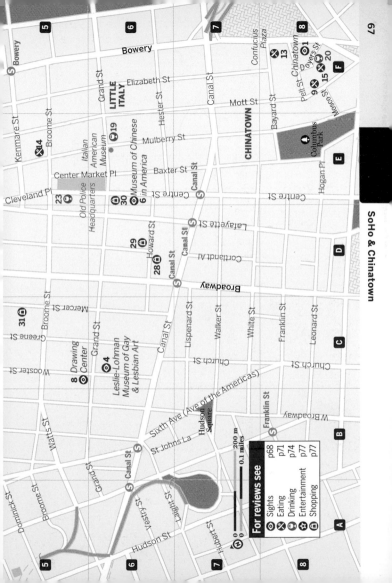

Bowery

LITTLE ITALY

CHINATOWN

5

6

7

8

Bowery
Kenmare St
Broome St
Grand St
Elizabeth St
Hester St
Canal St
Mott St
Confucius Plaza
Chinatown
Doyers St
Pell St
Bayard St
Mosco St
Bowery
Grand St
Mulberry St
Baxter St
Bayard St

Italian American Museum

Center Market Pl

Museum of Chinese 6 in America

Columbus Park

Hogan Pl

Cleveland Pl

Old Police Headquarters

Centre St

Lafayette St

Canal St

Howard St

Cortlandt Al

Centre St

Broadway

Mercer St

Grand St

Canal St

Lispenard St

Walker St

White St

Franklin St

Leonard St

Church St

Greene St

Wooster St

Broome St

Drawing Center

Leslie-Lohman Museum of Gay & Lesbian Art

Sixth Ave (Ave of the Americas)

St Johns La

Hudson Square

Franklin St

Church St

W Broadway

Watts St

Domick St

Broome St

Grand St

Canal St

Vestry St

Laight St

Hubert St

Hudson St

St Johns La

14

19

23

30

29

28

31

8

4

9

13

15

20

1

For reviews see	
⊙ Sights	p68
⊗ Eating	p71
⊗ Drinking	p74
⊗ Entertainment	p77
⊙ Shopping	p77

200 m
0.1 miles

A B C D E F

Sights

Chinatown AREA

1  MAP P66, F8

A walk through Manhattan's most colorful, cramped neighborhood is never the same, no matter how many times you hit the pavement. Peek inside temples and strange storefronts. Catch the whiff of ripe persimmons, hear the clacking of mah-jongg tiles on makeshift tables, eye dangling duck roasts swinging in store windows and shop for anything from rice-paper lanterns and 'faux-lex' watches to tire irons and a pound of pressed nutmeg. America's largest congregation of Chinese immigrants is your oyster. (www.explorechinatown.com; south of Broome St & east of Broadway; S N/Q/R/W, J/Z, 6 to Canal St; B/D to Grand St; F to East Broadway)

Merchant's House Museum MUSEUM

2  MAP P66, E1

Built in 1832 and purchased by merchant Seabury Tredwell three years later, this red-brick mansion remains the most authentic Federal house in town. It's as much about the city's mercantile past as it is a showcase of 19th-century high-end domestic furnishings. Everything in the house is a testament to what money could buy, from the bronze gasoliers and marble mantelpieces, to the elegant parlor chairs, attributed to noted furniture designer Duncan

Lunar New Year Parade in Chinatown

PHOTO SPIRIT/SHUTTERSTOCK ©

Phyfe. Even the multilevel call bells for the servants work to this day. (☏212-777-1089; www.merchants house.org; 29 E 4th St, btwn Lafayette St & Bowery, NoHo; adult/child $15/ free; ☉noon-5pm Fri-Mon, to 8pm Thu, guided tours 2pm Thu-Mon & 6:30pm Thu; Ⓢ6 to Bleecker St; B/D/F/M to Broadway-Lafayette St)

Broken Kilometer   GALLERY

3 ◉ MAP P66, B4

Occupying a cavernous ground-floor space in SoHo is this 1979 installation by the late American artist Walter De Maria. The work consists of 500 solid brass rods, positioned in five parallel rows, with the space between the rods increasing by 5mm with each consecutive space, from front to back. The result: a playful subversion of spacial perception. The rods appear to be identically spaced, even though at the back they're as much as 2ft apart. No photos allowed. (☏212-989-5566; www.diaart.org; 393 W Broadway, btwn Spring & Broome Sts, SoHo; admission free; ☉noon-3pm & 3:30-6pm Wed-Sun, closed mid-Jun–mid-Sep; Ⓢ N/R to Prince St, C/E to Spring St)

Leslie-Lohman Museum of Gay & Lesbian Art   MUSEUM

4 ◉ MAP P66, C6

Newly expanded in 2017, the world's first museum dedicated to LGBT themes stages six to eight annual exhibitions of both homegrown and international art. Offerings have included solo-artist

Columbus Park

Mah-jongg masters, slow-motion tai-chi practitioners and old aunties gossiping over homemade dumplings: it might feel like Shanghai, but the leafy oasis of **Columbus Park** (Map p66, E8; Mulberry & Bayard Sts, Chinatown; Ⓢ J/Z, N/Q/R, 6 to Canal St) serves up an intriguing slice of multicultural life that's core to NYC history. In the 19th century, this was part of the infamous Five Points neighborhood, the city's first tenement slums and the inspiration for Martin Scorsese's *Gangs of New York*.

retrospectives as well as themed shows exploring the likes of 'art and sex along the New York waterfront'. Much of the work on display is from the museum's own collection, which consists of over 24,000 works. The space also hosts queer-centric lectures, readings, film screenings and performances; check the website for updates. (☏212-431-2609; www.leslielohman. org; 26 Wooster St, btwn Grand & Canal Sts, Little Italy; suggested donation $8; ☉noon-6pm Wed & Fri-Sun, to 8pm Thu; Ⓢ A/C/E, N/Q/R, 1 to Canal St)

New York Earth Room   GALLERY

5 ◉ MAP P66, C3

Since 1980 the oddity of the New York Earth Room, the work of artist Walter De Maria, has been wooing the curious with something not easily found in the city: dirt (250 cu yd, or 280,000lb, of it, to be exact). Walking into the small space is a heady experience, as the scent will make you feel like you've entered a wet forest; the sight of such beautiful, pure earth in the midst of this crazy city is surprisingly moving. (☎212-989-5566; www.earthroom.org; 141 Wooster St, btwn Prince & W Houston Sts, SoHo; admission free; �)noon-3pm & 3:30-6pm Wed-Sun, closed mid-Jun–mid-Sep; Ⓢ N/R to Prince St)

Museum of Chinese in America

MUSEUM

6 ◉ MAP P66, E6

In this space designed by architect Maya Lin (designer of the famed Vietnam Memorial in Washington DC) is a multifaceted museum whose engaging permanent and temporary exhibitions shed light on Chinese American life, both past and present. Browse through interactive multimedia exhibits, maps, timelines, photos, letters, films and artifacts.The museum's anchor exhibit, 'With a Single Step: Stories in the Making of America', provides an often intimate glimpse into topics that include immigration, cultural identity and racial stereotyping. (MOCA; ☎212-619-4785; www.mocanyc.org; 215 Centre St, btwn Grand & Howard Sts, Chinatown; adult/child $10/5, first Thu of month free; ☉11am-6pm Tue, Wed & Fri-Sun, to 9pm Thu; Ⓢ N/Q/R/W, J/Z, 6 to Canal St)

International Center of Photography Museum

GALLERY

7 ◉ MAP P66, F3

ICP is New York's paramount platform for photography, with a strong emphasis on photojournalism and changing exhibitions on a wide range of themes. Past shows have included work by Sebastião Salgado, Henri Cartier-Bresson, Man Ray and Robert Capa. Its 11,000-sq-ft home on the Bowery, which opened in 2016 (formerly, it was in Midtown), places it close to the epicenter of the downtown art scene. (ICP; ☎212-857-0003; www.icp.org; 250 Bowery, btwn Houston & Prince, Nolita; adult/child $14/free, by donation Thu 6-9pm; ☉10am-6pm Tue-Sun, until 9pm Thu; Ⓢ F to 2nd Ave; J/Z to Bowery)

Drawing Center

GALLERY

8 ◉ MAP P66, C5

America's only nonprofit institute focused solely on drawings, the Drawing Center uses work by masters as well as unknowns to juxtapose the medium's various styles. Historical exhibitions have included work by Michelangelo, James Ensor and Marcel Duchamp, while contemporary shows have showcased heavyweights such as Richard Serra, Ellsworth Kelly and Richard Tuttle. As to the themes themselves, expect anything from the whimsical to the politically controversial. (☎212-219-2166; www.drawingcenter.org; 35 Wooster St, btwn Grand &

Broome Sts, SoHo; adult/child $5/free; ⏰noon-6pm Wed & Fri-Sun, to 8pm Thu; Ⓢ A/C/E, 1, N/Q/R to Canal St)

Eating

Peking Duck House   CHINESE $$$

9 ❌ MAP P66, F8

Offering arguably the best Peking duck in the region, the eponymous restaurant has a variety of set menus that include the house specialty. The space is fancier than some Chinatown spots, making it great to come with someone special. Do have the duck: perfectly crispy skin and moist meat make the slices ideal for a pancake, scallion strips and sauce. (☎212-227-1810; www.pekingduckhousenyc.com; 28a Mott St, Chinatown; Peking duck per person $45; ⏰11:30am-10:30pm

Sun-Thu, 11:45am-11pm Fri & Sat; Ⓢ J/Z to Chambers St, 6 to Canal St)

Prince Street Pizza   PIZZA $

10 ❌ MAP P66, E3

It's a miracle the oven door hasn't come off its hinges at this classic slice joint, its brick walls hung with shots of B-list celebrity fans. Ditch the average cheese slice for the exceptional square varieties (the pepperoni will blow your socks off, Tony). The sauces, mozzarella and ricotta are made in-house and while the queues can get long, they usually move fast. (☎212-966-4100; 27 Prince St, btwn Mott & Elizabeth Sts, Nolita; pizza slices from $2.95; ⏰11:45am-11pm Sun-Thu, to 2am Fri & Sat; Ⓢ N/R to Prince St; 6 to Spring St)

SoHo & Chinatown Eating

Eating in Chinatown   🍽️

The most rewarding experience for Chinatown neophytes is to access this wild and wonderful world through their taste buds. More than any other area of Manhattan, Chinatown's menus sport wonderfully low prices, uninflated by ambience, hype or reputation. But more than cheap eats, the neighborhood is rife with family recipes passed across generations and continents. Food displays and preparation remain unchanged and untempered by American norms; it's not unusual to walk by storefronts sporting a tangled array of glazed animals – chickens, rabbit and duck, in particular – ready to be chopped up and served at a family banquet. Steaming street stalls clang down the sidewalk serving pork buns and other finger-friendly food. Hit Chinatown's bustling dining dens with a handful of friends and eat 'family style' (order a ton of dishes and sample spoonfuls of each). You'll think the waiter left a zero off the bill. Finally, don't forget to wander down the back alleys for a Technicolor assortment of spices and herbs to perfect your own dishes.

Chefs Club   FUSION $$$

11  MAP P66, E3

In a building used in part for the show *Will & Grace*, Chefs Club sounds more like a discount warehouse than the spectacular dining spot it really is: visiting chefs prepare a menu for anywhere from three weeks to three months, offering their finest selections in menus that span the flavors of the globe. (☏212-941-1100; www.chefsclub.com; 275 Mulberry St, Nolita; mains $19-68; ⏰6-10:30pm Mon-Thu, to 11:30pm Fri & Sat)

Il Buco   ITALIAN $$$

12 MAP P66, E2

It's hard to resist this Italian charmer, nostalgically cluttered with copper pots, kerosene lamps and antique furniture. Sink your teeth into seasonal, sophisticated beauties such as Vermont *burrata* (soft Italian cheese) with celery essence, Serrano peppers, crisp Japanese eggplant and *bottarga di muggine* (cured gray mullet roe); or slow-roasted beef strip loin with Brussels sprouts, onion marmalade and shaved Gorgonzola. (☏212-533-1932; www.ilbuco.com; 47 Bond St, btwn Bowery & Lafayette St, Nolita; mains $24-40; ⏰noon-11pm Mon-Thu, noon-midnight Fri & Sat, 5-10:30pm Sun; Ⓢ B/D/F/M to Broadway-Lafayette St; 6 to Bleecker St)

Xi'an Famous Foods   CHINESE $

13 MAP P66, F8

Food bloggers hyperventilate at the mere mention of this small

Dominique Ansel Bakery

PERRY VAN MUNSTER/ALAMY STOCK PHOTO ©

chain's hand-pulled noodles. Another star menu item is the spicy cumin lamb burger – tender lamb sautéed with ground cumin, toasted chili seeds, peppers, red onions and scallions. (www.xianfoods.com; 45 Bayard St, btwn Elizabeth St & Bowery, Chinatown; dishes $3-12; 🕑11:30am-9pm Sun-Thu, to 9:30pm Fri & Sat; Ⓢ N/Q/R/W, J/Z, 6 to Canal St, B/D to Grand St)

M'O ICE CREAM $

14 ✖ MAP P66, E5

Little M'O gives tongues a solid workout with its dense, silky gelato. In addition to normal flavors, M'O offers dairy-free options, such as fresh mango and dark chocolate. If you're in no mood to cool down, warm up with creamy Sicilian cannoli, biscotti and a *tazza* (cup) of espresso. (☑ 212-226-6758; www.mogelato.com; 178 Mulberry St, at Broome St, Nolita; gelato from $4.75; 🕑noon-12:30am; Ⓢ B/D to Grand St; J/Z to Bowery)

Nom Wah Tea Parlor CHINESE $

15 ✖ MAP P66, F8

Hidden down a narrow lane, Nom Wah Tea Parlor might look like an old-school American diner, but it's actually the oldest dim-sum place in town. Grab a table or seat at one of the red banquettes or counter stools and point at the mouthwatering (and often greasy) delicacies pushed around on carts. (☑ 212-962-6047; www.nomwah.com; 13 Doyers St, Chinatown; dim sum from $3.75; 🕑10:30am-9pm Sun-Thu, to

10pm Fri & Sat; Ⓢ J/Z to Chambers St; 4/5/6 to Brooklyn Bridge-City Hall)

Dominique Ansel Bakery BAKERY $

16 ✖ MAP P66, B4

One of NYC's best and most well-known patisseries has much more up its sleeve than just cronuts (its world-famous donut-croissant hybrid), including buttery *kouign-amman* (a Breton cake), gleaming berry tarts, and the Paris-New York, a chocolate/caramel/peanut twist on the traditional Paris-Brest. If you do insist on scoffing a cronut, head in by 7:30am on weekdays (earlier on weekends) to beat the 'sold out' sign. (☑ 212-219-2773; www.dominiqueansel.com; 189 Spring St, btwn Sullivan & Thompson Sts, SoHo; desserts $6-7; 🕑8am-7pm Mon-Sat, 9am-7pm Sun; Ⓢ C/E to Spring St)

Uncle Boons THAI $$

17 ✖ MAP P66, F4

Michelin-starred Thai food served up in a fun, tongue-in-cheek combo of retro wood-paneled dining room with Thai film posters and old family snaps. Spanning the old and the new, zesty, tangy dishes include fantastically crunchy *mieng kum* (betel-leaf wrap with ginger, lime, toasted coconut, dried shrimp, peanuts and chili; $12), *kao pat puu* (crab fried rice; $26) and banana blossom salad ($15). (☑ 646-370-6650; www.uncleboons.com; 7 Spring St, btwn Elizabeth St & Bowery, Nolita;

small plates $12-16, large plates $21-29; ⏰5:30-11pm Mon-Thu, to midnight Fri & Sat, to 10pm Sun; 📶; 🚇J/Z to Bowery; 6 to Spring St)

Drinking

Ghost Donkey
BAR

18 🚇 MAP P66, E2

Laid-back meets trippy meets craft at this one-of-a-kind, classy mezcal house that gives vibes of Mexico, the Middle East and the Wild West. If the moon had a saloon, this place would fit right in. Dark and dim, yet pink, with low-cushioned couches encircling lower coffee tables, this bar also serves excellent craft cocktails. (Try the frozen house margarita! Tasty, right?) (📞212-254-0350; www.ghostdonkey.com; 4 Bleecker St, NoHo; ⏰5pm-2am; 🚇6 to Bleecker St; B/D/F/M to Broadway-Lafayette St)

Genuine Liquorette
COCKTAIL BAR

19 🚇 MAP P66, E6

What's not to love about a jamming basement bar with canned cocktails and a Farrah Fawcett–themed restroom? You're even free to grab bottles and mixers and make your own drinks. At the helm is Ashlee, the beverage director, who regularly invites New York's finest barkeeps to create cocktails using less-celebrated hooch. (📞212-726-4633; www.genuine liquorette.com; 191 Grand St, at Mulberry St, Little Italy; ⏰6pm-midnight Sun, Tue & Wed, to 2am Thu-Sat, from 5pm Fri; 🚇J/Z, N/Q/R/W, 6 to Canal St; B/D to Grand St)

Apothéke
COCKTAIL BAR

20 🚇 MAP P66, F8

It takes a little effort to track down this former opium-den-turned-apothecary bar on Doyers St. Inside, skilled barkeeps work like careful chemists, using local, seasonal produce from Greenmarkets to produce intense, flavorful 'prescriptions.' Their cocktail ingredient ratio is always on point, such as the pineapple-cilantro blend in the Sitting Buddha, one of the best drinks on the menu. (📞212-406-0400; www.apothekenyc.com; 9 Doyers St, Chinatown; ⏰6:30pm-2am Mon-Sat, from 8pm Sun; 🚇J/Z to Chambers St; 4/5/6 to Brooklyn Bridge-City Hall)

Spring Lounge
BAR

21 🚇 MAP P66, E4

This neon-red rebel has never let anything get in the way of a good time. In Prohibition days, it peddled buckets of beer. In the '60s its basement was a gambling den. These days, it's best known for its kooky stuffed sharks, early-start regulars and come-one, come-all late-night revelry. Perfect last stop on a bar-hopping tour of the neighborhood. (📞212-965-1774; www.thespringlounge.com; 48 Spring St, at Mulberry St, Nolita; ⏰8am-4am Mon-Fri, from noon Sat & Sun; 🚇6 to Spring St; R/W to Prince St)

Little Italy

In the last 50 years, New York's Little Italy has shrunk from a big, brash boot to an ultra-slim sandal. A mid-century exodus to the suburbs of Brooklyn and beyond would see this once-strong Italian neighborhood turn into a micro pastiche of its former self, with the most authentic Italian restaurants now found along Arthur Ave, up in the Bronx. But a stroll around the area still offers up 19th-century tenement architecture, fresh pizza by the slice, gelato by the cone and some of the best tiramisu in town.

Mulberry Street

Little Italy is little more than **Mulberry Street** (Little Italy; S N/Q/R, J/Z, 6 to Canal St; B/D to Grand St) these days, an endearingly kitsch strip of gingham-tablecloths, mandolin muzak and nostalgia for the old country. It's also on Mulberry St that you'll find the tiny **Italian American Museum** (Map p66, E6; 212-965-9000; www. italianamericanmuseum.org; 155 Mulberry St, at Grand St, Little Italy; suggested donation $7; noon-6pm Fri-Sun; S J/Z, N/Q/R/W, 6 to Canal St; B/D to Grand St), a random mishmash of historical objects documenting early Italian life in NYC, from Sicilian marionettes to old Italian comics starring New York's famous mafia-busting cop, Giuseppe 'Joe' Petrosino. Between 1885 and 1932, the building was occupied by the Banca Stabile, which helped immigrants sort their monetary needs as well as providing a lifeline back to the homeland. Among the artifacts belonging to the former Stabile bank is the giant 19th-century safe.

The Feast of San Gennaro

Come late September, the street turns into a raucous, 11-day block party for the **San Gennaro Festival** (www.sangennaro.org; Sep), a celebration honoring the patron saint of Naples. It's a loud, convivial affair, with food and carnival stalls, free entertainment, and more big hair than MTV's *Jersey Shore*. The streets get packed with locals from around town as well as visitors, so throw yourself into the throngs and revel in this holdover from Little Italy's golden days.

Pegu Club

COCKTAIL BAR

22 MAP P66, C3

Dark, elegant Pegu Club (named after a legendary gentleman's club in colonial-era Rangoon) is an obligatory stop for cocktail connoisseurs. Sink into a velvet lounge and savor seamless libations such as the silky-smooth Earl Grey

MarTEAni (tea-infused gin, lemon juice and raw egg white). Grazing options are suitably Asianesque, among them duck wontons and Mandalay shrimp. (📞212-473-7348; www.peguclub.com; 77 W Houston St, btwn W Broadway & Wooster St, SoHo; ⏱5pm-2am Sun-Wed, to 4am Thu-Sat; 🚇B/D/F/M to Broadway-Lafayette St; C/E to Spring St)

La Compagnie des Vins Surnaturels

WINE BAR

23 📍 MAP P66, E5

A snug melange of Gallic-themed wallpaper, svelte armchairs and tea lights, La Compagnie des Vins Surnaturels is an offshoot of a Paris bar by the same name. Head sommelier Theo Lieberman steers an impressive, French-heavy wine list, with some 600 drops and no shortage of arresting labels by the glass. A short, sophisticated menu includes housemade charcuterie and chicken rillettes. (📞212-343-3660; www.compagnienyc.com; 249 Centre St, btwn Broome & Grand Sts, Nolita; ⏱5pm-1am Mon-Wed, to 2am Thu & Fri, 3pm-2am Sat, to 1am Sun; 🚇6 to Spring St; R/W to Prince St)

Fanelli's Cafe

BAR

24 📍 MAP P66, C4

Cozy, convivial Fanelli's is the consummate soak, pouring drinks on this corner since 1847. And while SoHo may have changed over the years, Fanelli's remains true to its earthy roots – tinted mirrors, hanging pugilists and all. Skip the average food; you're here to swill and reminisce among friends, new

Joe's Pub

and old. (☎212-226-9412; 94 Prince St, at Mercer St, SoHo; ⏰10am-1am Mon-Thu, to 2am Fri & Sat, to midnight Sun; ⓢN/R to Prince St)

Entertainment

Joe's Pub
LIVE MUSIC

25 ⭐ MAP P66, E1

Part bar, part cabaret and performance venue, intimate Joe's serves up both emerging acts and top-shelf performers. Past entertainers have included Patti LuPone, Amy Schumer, the late Leonard Cohen and British songstress Adele (in fact, it was right here that Adele gave her very first American performance, back in 2008). (☎212-539-8778, tickets 212-967-7555; www.joespub.com; Public Theater, 425 Lafayette St, btwn Astor Pl & 4th St, NoHo; ⓢ6 to Astor Pl; R/W to 8th St-NYU)

Public Theater
LIVE PERFORMANCE

26 ⭐ MAP P66, D1

This legendary theater was founded as the Shakespeare Workshop back in 1954 and has launched some of New York's big hits, including *Hamilton* back in 2015. Today, you'll find a lineup of innovative programming as well as reimagined classics from the past, with Shakespeare in heavy rotation. Speaking of the bard, the Public also stages star-studded Shakespeare in the Park performances during the summer. (☎212-539-8500; www.publictheater. org; 425 Lafayette St, btwn Astor Pl &

Film Forum

A three-screen nonprofit cinema, **Film Forum** (Map p66, A3; ☎212-727-8110; www. filmforum.com; 209 W Houston St, btwn Varick St & Sixth Ave, SoHo; ⏰noon-midnight; ⓢ1 to Houston St) shows an astounding array of independent films, revivals and career retrospectives from greats such as Orson Welles. Theaters are small, so get there early for a good viewing spot. Showings often include director talks or other film-themed discussions for hardcore cinephiles.

4th St, NoHo; ⓢ6 to Astor Pl; R/W to 8th St-NYU)

Shopping

Rag & Bone
FASHION & ACCESSORIES

27 🔒 MAP P66, C4

Downtown label Rag & Bone is a hit with many of New York's coolest, sharpest dressers – both men and women. Detail-oriented pieces range from clean-cut shirts and blazers and graphic tees to monochromatic sweaters, feather-light strappy dresses, leather goods and Rag & Bone's highly prized jeans. The tailoring is generally impeccable, with accessories including shoes, hats, bags and wallets. (☎212-219-2204; www.rag-bone.com; 117-119 Mercer St, btwn Prince & Spring Sts, SoHo; ⏰11am-9pm Mon-Sat, 11am-7pm Sun; ⓢN/R to Prince St)

Opening Ceremony
FASHION & ACCESSORIES,

28 🔒 MAP P66, D6

Unisex Opening Ceremony is famed for its never-boring edit of A-list indie labels. It showcases a changing roster of names from across the globe, both established and emerging; complementing them are Opening Ceremony's own avant-garde creations. No matter who's hanging on the racks, you can always expect showstopping, 'where-did-you-get-that?!' threads that are street smart, bold and refreshingly unexpected. (📞212-219-2688; www.openingceremony.com; 35 Howard St, btwn Broadway & Lafayette St, SoHo; ⏱11am-8pm Mon-Sat, noon-7pm Sun; Ⓢ N/Q/R/W, J/Z, 6 to Canal St)

De Vera
ANTIQUES

29 🔒 MAP P66, D6

Federico de Vera travels the globe in search of exquisite jewelry, carvings, lacquerware and other *objets d'art* for this jewel-box of a store. Illuminated vitrines display works such as 200-year-old Buddhas, Venetian glassware and gilded boxes from the Meiji period, while oil paintings and carvings along the walls complete the museum-like experience. (📞212-625-0838; www.deveraobjects.com; 1 Crosby St, at Howard St, SoHo; ⏱11am-7pm Tue-Sat; Ⓢ N/Q/R/W, J/Z, 6 to Canal St)

Odin
FASHION & ACCESSORIES

30 🔒 MAP P66, E6

Odin's flagship men's boutique carries hip downtown labels, and a select edit of imports, among

Shopping in SoHo & Chinatown

SoHo bursts at its fashionable seams with stores big and small. Hit Broadway for Main St chains, shoe shops and jean outlets, or the streets to the west for higher-end fashion and accessories. Over on Lafayette, shops cater to the DJ and skate crowds with indie labels and vintage thrown into the mix. Style fiends hyperventilate over SoHo's fashion-conscious streets but serious shopaholics should consult the city's in-the-know retail blogs before hitting SoHo and surrounds – there's always some sort of 'sample sale' or offer going on, or a new boutique showcasing fresh talent. Try www.racked.com, www.thecut.com and www.the12ishstyle.com.

If indie-chic is your thing, continue east to Nolita, home of tiny jewel-box boutiques selling unique threads, kicks and accessories. Mott St is best for browsing, followed by Mulberry and Elizabeth.

For medicinal herbs, exotic fruits, woks and Chinese teapots, scour the frenetic streets of Chinatown.

EUGENE GOLOGURSKY/STRINGER/GETTY IMAGES ©

Opening Ceremony

them Nordic labels Acne. Other in-store tempters include jewelry from Brooklyn creatives such as Naval Yard and Uhuru, and footwear from cult labels like Common Projects. (☏212-966-0026; www.odinnewyork.com; 161 Grand St, btwn Lafayette & Centre Sts, Nolita; ⏱11am-8pm Mon-Sat, noon-7pm Sun; Ⓢ6 to Spring St; N/R to Prince St)

Joe's Jeans FASHION & ACCESSORIES

31 🔒 MAP P66, C5

Sex up your pins with a pair of jeans from this cult LA label. Options include 'Flawless' denim, which has stretch fabric to flatter your form, as well as skinny jeans designed to fit more shapes than just 'supermodel.' Mix and match with super-comfy shirts, hoodies, sweaters and the ever-popular denim jacket. (☏212-925-5727; www.joesjeans.com; 77 Mercer St, btwn Spring & Broome Sts, SoHo; ⏱11am-7pm Mon-Sat, noon-6pm Sun; Ⓢ N/R to Prince St; 6 to Spring St)

Resurrection VINTAGE

32 🔒 MAP P66, E1

Resurrection gives new life to cutting-edge designs from past decades. Striking, mint-condition pieces cover the eras of mod, glam-rock and new-wave design, and design deities such as Marc Jacobs have dropped by for inspiration. Top picks include Halston dresses and Courrèges coats and jackets. (☏212-625-1374; www.resurrectionvintage.com; 45 Great Jones St, btwn Lafayette & Bowery Sts, NoHo; ⏱11am-7pm Mon-Sat; Ⓢ6 to Spring St; N/R to Prince St)

Explore ✦

East Village & Lower East Side

The East Village and the Lower East Side are two of the city's hottest 'hoods for cramming into low-lit lounges; clubs for live music and cheap eats lure students, bankers and scruffier types alike. Luxury high-rise condominiums and hip boutique hotels coexist within blocks of tenement-style buildings. They're inspiring, lively and the perfect place to feel young.

Start with a classic New York breakfast of bagels and lox at Russ & Daughters Cafe (p91), then hit the not-to-be-missed Tenement Museum (p86). Stroll around the Lower East Side, browsing its boutiques, such as Tictail Market (p98) and Reformation (p100). For lunch, hit up Katz's Delicatessen (p89). Explore the current art scene at the New Museum of Contemporary Art (p86), or else weave through the eclectic stores of the East Village, especially punk-rock stalwart Trash & Vaudeville (p83) and A-1 Records (p100). Splash out for dinner at Prune (p90) or Motorino (p89), then pop into a hidden bar like Angel's Share (p93) or Berlin (p93). Drop into Rockwood Music Hall (p96) for some local live music – or make some yourself at Sing Sing Karaoke (p98). Grab a late-night pierogi snack at 24-hour Veselka (p90).

Getting There & Around

S In the East Village the L train runs along 14th St stopping at 1st and 3rd Aves, while the F stops on Houston St at Second Ave. The 6 to Astor Pl lets you off right near St Marks Pl. For the Lower East Side take the B/D to Grand St or F/M and J/Z to Delancey–Essex Sts.

Neighborhood Map on p84

Katz's Delicatessen (p89) TOMMY LIGGETT/SHUTTERSTOCK ©

Walking Tour 🚶

East Village Nostalgia

Gentrification is taming the beast but few neigh-borhoods exude old-school NYC cool like the East Village. For decades an epicenter of counter-culture, its streets sizzle with tales of drugs, drag and punk rock. Countless musicians got their break here: Patti Smith, the Ramones, Blondie, Madonna and more. Times have changed, but clues to the Village's rocking golden days can still be found.

Walk Facts

Start CBGB; **S** F/M to 2nd Ave, 6 to Bleecker St

End Tompkins Square Park; **S** 6 to Astor Pl

Length 1.5 miles; two to three hours depending on stops

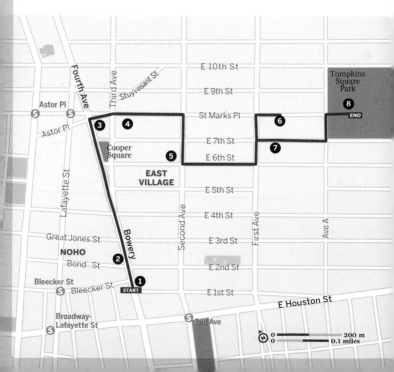

❶ Remembering CBGBs

At the intersection where leafy Bleecker St meets the Bowery is a John Varvatos boutique, formerly the home of the legendary music venue **CBGB**. Other than the fading posters and graffitied walls little remains of the concert hall, but it's still a pilgrimage for music enthusiasts.

❷ Joey Ramone Place

The corner just north of here marks the block-long **Joey Ramone Place**, named after the late Ramones' singer. A native of Queens, he and his band first played at CBGB in 1974.

❸ Cooper Union

A few blocks north on the Bowery – formerly one of Manhattan's most notorious streets, filled with flophouses and seedy hotels – is the **Cooper Union**, a public college founded by glue millionaire Peter Cooper in 1859. In its Great Hall in 1860, presidential hopeful Abraham Lincoln rocked a skeptical New York crowd with a rousing anti-slavery speech.

❹ St Marks Place

To the east is **St Marks Place** (St Marks Pl, Ave A to Third Ave; ⓢ N/R/W to 8th St-NYU; 6 to Astor Pl), a block full of tattoo parlors, vape shops and cheap eateries. Rising rents have pushed out many of the establishments that made this street famous, but you can still get a feeling of the lawless spirit that once inhabited this stretch.

❺ Fillmore East

The bank at 105 Second Ave (near the E 6th St corner) was once the **Fillmore East**, a 2000-seat live-music venue run by promoter Bill Graham from 1968 to 1971. In the '80s it was transformed into the Saint – the legendary club that kicked off a joyous, drug-fueled, gay nightclub culture.

❻ Album Art

Just off First Ave and E 8th St, a row of tenements is the site of **Led Zeppelin's Physical Graffiti cover** (96–98 St Marks Pl), and where Mick and Keith sat in 1981 in the Rolling Stones' hilarious video for 'Waiting on a Friend.'

❼ Trash & Vaudeville

A couple of blocks away is legendary punk-rock shop **Trash & Vaudeville** (☎ 212-982-3590; www.trashandvaudeville.com; 96 East 7th St, btwn First Ave & Ave A; ⊗ noon-8pm Mon-Sat, 1-7:30pm Sun; ⓢ 6 to Astor Pl), which relocated from St Marks Pl due to rising rents. You'll find everyone from drag queens to theme-partygoers here.

❽ Tompkins Square Park

End your stroll at **Tompkins Square Park** (www.nycgovparks.org; E 7th & 10th Sts, btwn Aves A & B; ⊗ 6am-midnight; ⓢ 6 to Astor Pl), a 10.5-acre park that's like a friendly town square for locals. In the 1980s, drag queens started the Wigstock summer festival at the bandshell where Jimi Hendrix played in the 1960s.

East Village & Lower East Side

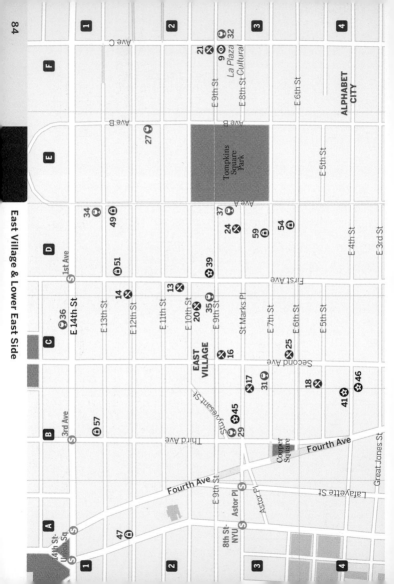

A **B** **C** **D** **E** **F**

1

2

3

4

14th St-Union Sq

3rd Ave

E 14th St

1st Ave

Ave B

Ave C

E 13th St

E 12th St

E 11th St

E 10th St

E 9th St

St Marks Pl

E 7th St

E 6th St

E 5th St

E 4th St

E 3rd St

Ave A

Ave B

E 9th St

E 8th St Cultural

E 6th St

E 5th St

Tompkins Square Park

ALPHABET CITY

EAST VILLAGE

Second Ave

First Ave

Stuyvesant St

Third Ave

Cooper Square

Fourth Ave

Fourth Ave

E 9th St

Astor Pl

Astor Pl

8th St-NYU

Lafayette St

Great Jones St

La Plaza

57

36

47

14

34

49

51

13

20

35

39

37

24

59

54

16

25

17

31

45

29

18

41

46

21

9

32

27

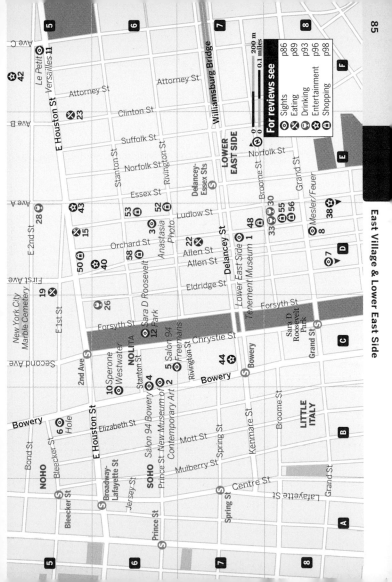

Sights

Lower East Side Tenement Museum
MUSEUM

1 ◎ MAP P84, D7

This museum puts the neighborhood's heartbreaking but inspiring heritage on full display in three re-created turn-of-the-20th-century tenement apartments, including the late-19th-century home and garment shop of the Levine family from Poland, and two immigrant dwellings from the Great Depressions of 1873 and 1929. Visits to the tenement building are available only as part of scheduled guided tours, with many departures each day. (📞877-975-3786; www.tenement.org; 103 Orchard St, btwn Broome & Delancey Sts, Lower East Side; tours adult/student & senior $25/20; ⏱10am-6:30pm Fri-Wed, to 8:30pm Thu; Ⓢ B/D to Grand St; J/M/Z to Essex St; F to Delancey St)

New Museum of Contemporary Art
MUSEUM

2 ◎ MAP P84, C6

Rising above the neighborhood, the New Museum of Contemporary Art is a sight to behold: a seven-story stack of off-kilter, white, ethereal boxes designed by Tokyo-based architects Kazuyo Sejima and Ryue Nishizawa of SANAA and the New York–based firm Gensler. It is a long-awaited breath of fresh air along what was a completely gritty Bowery strip when it arrived back in 2007 – though since the museum's opening, many glossy new constructions have joined it, quickly transforming this once down-and-out avenue. (📞212-219-1222; www.newmuseum.org; 235 Bowery, btwn Stanton & Rivington Sts, Lower East Side; adult/child $18/free, 7-9pm Thu by donation; ⏱11am-6pm Tue, Wed & Fri-Sun, to 9pm Thu; Ⓢ R/W to Prince St; F to 2nd Ave; J/Z to Bowery; 6 to Spring St)

Anastasia Photo
GALLERY

3 ◎ MAP P84, D6

This small gallery specializes in documentary photography and photojournalism. Expect evocative, thought-provoking works covering subjects such as poverty in rural America, the ravages of war and disappearing cultures in Africa. Works are beautifully shot, and the staff member on hand can give a meaningful context to the images. (www.anastasia-photo.com; 143 Ludlow St, btwn Stanton & Rivington Sts, Lower East Side; ⏱11am-7pm Tue-Sun; Ⓢ F to Delancey St; J/M/Z to Essex St)

Salon 94 Bowery
GALLERY

4 ◎ MAP P84, C6

This raw space is the Bowery branch of an Upper East Side gallery and its location beside the New Museum makes it a key player in the downtown art scene. Don't miss the video wall (a 20ft LCD screen) in front of the gallery broadcasting short- and long-form works from a wide range of video artists. (📞212-979-0001; www.salon94.com; 243 Bowery, cnr Stanton

St, Lower East Side; ⊙11am-6pm Tue-Sat; **S** F to 2nd Ave; J/Z/M to Bowery)

Salon 94 Freemans   GALLERY

5 ◎ MAP P84, C6

Tucked down a narrow alley, this small gallery feels like a well-kept secret, and it hosts intriguing and unconventional shows by emerging artists. Visits are by appointment only. (www.salon94.com; 1 Freeman Alley, off Rivington, Lower East Side; **S** F to 2nd Ave; J/Z/M to Bowery)

Hole   GALLERY

6 ◎ MAP P84, B5

Known for its excellent installations, this 4000-sq-ft gallery is an anchor of the downtown art scene with monthly solo and group shows. (📞212-466-1100;

www.theholenyc.com; 312 Bowery, at Bleecker, East Village; ⊙noon-7pm Wed-Sun; **S** 6 to Bleeker St; B/D/F/M to Broadway-Lafayette St)

Museum at Eldridge Street Synagogue   MUSEUM

7 ◎ MAP P84, D8

This landmark house of worship, built in 1887, was once a center of Jewish life before falling into squalor in the 1920s. Left to rot, the synagogue was restored following a 20-year-long, $20-million restoration that was completed in 2007, and it now shines with original splendor. Museum admission includes a **guided tour** of the synagogue, which departs hourly, with the last one starting at 4pm. (📞212-219-0302; www.eldridgestreet. org; 12 Eldridge St, btwn Canal &

Lower East Side Tenement Museum

DW LABS INCORPORATED/SHUTTERSTOCK ©

East Village & Lower East Side Sights

Lower East Side Art Scene

Though Chelsea may be the heavy hitter when it comes to the New York gallery scene, the Lower East Side has dozens of quality showplaces. An early pioneer, the **Sperone Westwater gallery** (p88) (opened in 1975) represents art-world darlings such as William Wegman and Richard Long. Nearby the avant-garde **Salon 94** has two Lower East Side outposts: one secreted away on **Freeman Alley** (p87) and another on **Bowery** (p86) near the New Museum of Contemporary Art. The latter has a 20ft LCD video wall that broadcasts video art out into the street. A few blocks north is the 4000-sq-ft **Hole** (p87) – known as much for its art as for its rowdy openings that gather both scenesters of the downtown art circuit and well-known faces.

Broome St between Chrystie and Bowery is quickly becoming the nexus of the Lower East Side art scene, with galleries such as **White Box**, **Canada** and **Jack Hanley** right next door to one another. Another buzzing strip of galleries runs south down Orchard St between Rivington and Canal Sts.

Division Sts, Lower East Side; adult/child $14/8, Mon by suggested donation; ⏲10am-5pm Sun-Thu, to 3pm Fri; Ⓢ F to East Broadway)

Mesler/Feuer
GALLERY

8 ⊙ MAP P84, D8

A dynamic downtown gallery that's forever pushing the envelope. It's now in a new location on bustling Grand St. (www.meslerfeuer.com; 319 Grand St, 2nd fl, btwn Allen & Orchard Sts, Lower East Side; ⏲11am-6pm Wed-Sun; Ⓢ J/M/Z/F to Delancey/Essex St; B/D to Grand St)

La Plaza Cultural
GARDENS

9 ⊙ MAP P84, F3

Three dramatic weeping willows, an odd sight in the city, grace La Plaza Cultural, one of the loveliest public gardens in the East Village. The verdant, flower-filled space forms the backdrop to art installations, theater, dance and musical performances throughout the warmer months. (www.laplazacultural.com; E 9th St, at Ave C, East Village; ⏲10am-7pm Sat & Sun Apr-Oct; Ⓢ F to 2nd Ave; L to 1st Ave)

Sperone Westwater
GALLERY

10 ⊙ MAP P84, B6

The Sperone Westwater gallery represents heavy hitters such as William Wegman and Richard Long. Its new home was designed by the famed Norman Foster, who's already made a big impact on NYC with his designs for the Hearst Building and the Avery Fisher Hall at Lincoln Center. (☎212-999-7337; www.speronewestwater.com; 257

Bowery, btwn E Houston & Stanton Sts, Lower East Side; ⏰10am-6pm Tue-Sat; 🅂F to 2nd Ave)

Le Petit Versailles GARDENS

11 ◎ MAP P84, F5

Le Petit Versailles is a unique marriage of a verdant oasis and electrifying arts organization, offering a range of quirky performances and screenings to the public. (www.alliedproductions.org; 346 E Houston St, at Ave C, East Village; ⏰2-7pm Thu-Sun; 🅂F to Delancey St; J/M/Z to Essex St)

Sara D Roosevelt Park PARK

12 ◎ MAP P84, C6

Spiffed up in recent years, this three-block-long park is a hive of activity on weekends, with basketball courts, a small soccer pitch (with synthetic turf) and a well-loved playground (just north of Hester St). Tai-chi practitioners, vegetable sellers (on the nearby cross streets) and strollers of all ages and ethnic backgrounds add to the ever-evolving scene. (Houston St, at Chrystie St, Lower East Side; 🅂F to Delancey-Essex Sts)

Eating

Momofuku
Noodle Bar NOODLES $$

13 🍴 MAP P84, D2

With just 30 stools and a no-reservations policy, you'll always have to wait to cram into this bustling phenomenon. Queue for the namesake special: homemade ramen noodles in broth, served with poached egg and pork belly or some interesting combos. The menu changes daily and includes buns (such as brisket and horseradish), snacks (smoked chicken wings) and desserts. (☎212-777-7773; www.noodlebar-ny.momofuku.com; 171 First Ave, btwn E 10th & 11th Sts, East Village; mains $16; ⏰noon-11pm Sun-Thu, to 1am Fri & Sat; 🅂L to 1st Ave; 6 to Astor Pl)

Motorino PIZZA $$

14 🍴 MAP P84, D1

On a restaurant-lined strip of the East Village, this intimate eatery serves up excellent pizzas with perfect pillowy crusts. (☎212-777-2644; www.motorinopizza.com; 349 E 12th St, btwn First & Second Aves, East Village; individual pizza $16-19; ⏰11am-midnight Sun-Thu, to 1am Fri & Sat; 🍴; 🅂L to First Ave)

Katz's Delicatessen DELI $$

15 🍴 MAP P84, D5

Though visitors won't find many remnants of the classic, old-world Jewish LES dining scene, there are a few stellar holdouts, among them Katz's Delicatessen, where Meg Ryan faked her famous orgasm in the 1989 movie *When Harry Met Sally*. If you love classic deli grub like pastrami and salami on rye, it just might have the same effect on you. (☎212-254-2246; www.katzsdelicatessen.com; 205 E Houston St, at Ludlow St, Lower East Side; sandwiches $15-22; ⏰8am-10:45pm Mon-Wed & Sun, to 2:45am Thu, from 8am Fri, 24hr Sat; 🅂F to 2nd Ave)

East Village & Lower East Side Eating

Making Dinner Plans 🍴

A lot of the restaurants in this neck of the woods don't take reservations, so stop by the restaurant of your choosing in the early afternoon (2pm should do the trick) and place your name on the roster for the evening meal – chances are high that they'll take your name and you'll get seated right away when you return for dinner later on.

Veselka   EASTERN EUROPEAN $

16 🍽 MAP P84, C3

A bustling tribute to the area's Ukrainian past, Veselka dishes out pierogi (handmade dumplings) and veal goulash amid the usual suspects of greasy comfort food. The cluttered spread of tables is available to loungers and carb-loaders all night long, though it's a favorite any time of day, and a regular haunt for writers, actors and East Village characters. (☎212-228-9682; www. veselka.com; 144 Second Ave, at 9th St, East Village; mains $10-19; ⏱24hr; Ⓢ L to 3rd Ave; 6 to Astor Pl)

Mamoun's   MIDDLE EASTERN $

17 🍽 MAP P84, C3

This former grab-and-go outpost of the beloved NYC falafel chain has expanded its iconic St Marks storefront with more seating. Come late on a weekend to find a line of inebriated bar hoppers ending the night with a juicy shawarma covered in Mamoun's famous hot sauce. (☎646-870-5785; www.mamouns.com; 30 St Marks Pl, btwn Second & Third Aves, East Village; sandwiches $4-7, plates $7-12; ⏱11am-2am Mon-Wed, to 3am Thu, to 5am Fri & Sat, to 1am Sun; Ⓢ 6 to Astor Pl; L to 3rd Ave)

Degustation   MODERN EUROPEAN $$$

18 🍽 MAP P84, C4

Blending Iberian, French and new-world recipes, Degustation does a beautiful array of tapas-style plates at this narrow, 19-seat eatery. It's an intimate setting, with guests seated around a long wooden counter while chef Oscar Islas Díaz and his team are center stage, firing up mole octopus and oyster tacos, among other inventive dishes. (☎212-979-1012; www. degustation-nyc.com; 239 E 5th St, btwn Second & Third Aves, East Village; small plates $12-22, tasting menu $85; ⏱6-11:30pm Tue-Sat; Ⓢ 6 to Astor Pl)

Prune   AMERICAN $$$

19 🍽 MAP P84, D5

Expect lines around the block on the weekend, when the hungover show up to cure their ills with Prune's brunches and excellent Bloody Marys. The small room is always busy as diners pour in for grilled trout with mint and almond salsa, seared duck breast and rich sweetbreads. Reservations available for dinner only. (☎212-677-6221; www.prunerestaurant.com; 54 E 1st St, btwn First & Second Aves, East Village; dinner $24-33, mains brunch $14-24; ⏱5:30-11pm, also 10am-3:30pm Sat & Sun; Ⓢ F to 2nd Ave)

Rai Rai Ken RAMEN $

20  MAP P84, C2

Rai Rai Ken's storefront may only be the size of its door, but it's pretty hard to miss since there's usually a small congregation of hungry locals lurking out the front. Inside, low-slung wooden stools are arranged around the noodle bar, where the cooks busily churn out piping-hot portions of tasty pork-infused broth. (☏212-477-7030; 218 E 10th St, btwn First & Second Aves, East Village; ramen $10-13; ⏰11:30am-11:45pm; ⑤L to 1st Ave; 6 to Astor Pl)

Esperanto BRAZILIAN $

21 MAP P84, F2

Esperanto's vibrant green facade and large patio call to mind the glory days of Alphabet City, before the neighborhood began to trend toward gray and glass condos and sleek cocktail bars. Here you can sit outside all night sipping caipirinhas or enjoying strips of brilliantly bloody steak with chimichurri sauce. It's also a great place to get *feijoada* (traditional Brazilian meat stew). (www.esperantony.com; 145 Ave C, at E 9th St, East Village; mains $18-24; ⏰10am-11pm Sun-Thu, to midnight Fri & Sat; ⑤L to 1st Ave)

Russ & Daughters Cafe EASTERN EUROPEAN $$

22 MAP P84, D7

Sit down and feast on bagels and lox in the comfort of an old-school diner. Aside from rich slices of smoked fish, you can nibble on potato latkes, warm up over a bowl of borscht or feast on eggs Benny. (☏212-475-4880 ext. 2;

Prune

International Flavors 🍽

Here lies the epitome of what is beautiful in New York's dining scene: mind-blowing variety – which can cover the full spectrum of continents and budgets – in just a single city block. In the Lower East Side and East Village you'll find every type of taste-bud tantalizer from hole-in-the-wall Italian trattorias, Sichuan hot pot spots, innovative sandwich shops, Ukrainian pierogi palaces, dozens of sushi and ramen joints, pizza parlors and falafel huts. E 6th St between First and Second Aves, sometimes known as 'Curry Row,' is no longer chock-a-block with cheap Indian restaurants, but still has a few holdouts.

www.russanddaughterscafe.com; 127 Orchard St, btwn Delancey & Rivington Sts, Lower East Side; mains $13-20; ⏰9am-10pm Mon-Fri, from 8am Sat & Sun; **S** F to Delancey St; J/M/Z to Essex St)

Clinton Street Baking Company   AMERICAN $$

23 🍴 MAP P84, E5

Mom-and-pop shop extraordinaire, Clinton Street Baking Company gets the blue ribbon in so many categories – best pancakes (blueberry!), best muffins, best po'boys (Southern-style sandwiches), best biscuits etc – that you're pretty much guaranteed a stellar meal no matter what time you stop by. In the evenings, you can opt for 'breakfast for dinner' (pancakes, eggs Benedict), fish tacos or the excellent buttermilk fried chicken. (☎646-602-6263; www.clintonstreet baking.com; 4 Clinton St, btwn Stanton & Houston Sts, Lower East Side; mains $12-20; ⏰8am-4pm & 5:30-11pm Mon-Sat, 9am-5pm Sun; **S** J/M/Z to Essex St; F to Delancey St; F to 2nd Ave)

Crif Dogs   HOT DOGS $

24 🍴 MAP P84, D3

Although it often gets overshadowed by the secret bar it houses – **PDT** (☎212-614-0386; www.pdtnyc.com; ⏰6pm-2am Sun-Thu, to 4am Fri & Sat), shhh – Crif Dogs is worth visiting in its own right if you're a hot dog connoisseur. Its basic dog is solid, but it's really about the toppings: everything from ketchup and relish to pineapple and Sriracha mayo can be loaded into your bun. (☎212-614-2728; www.crifdogs.com; 113 St Marks Pl, btwn Ave A & First Ave, East Village; hot dogs from $4; ⏰noon-2am Sun-Thu, to 4am Fri & Sat; **S** L to 1st Ave)

Mighty Quinn's   BARBECUE $

25 🍴 MAP P84, C3

Grab yourself a tray and join hordes of barbecue lovers at this buzzing, very popular meat eatery. Tender brisket, smoky spare ribs, juicy piles of pulled pork and ample portions of sides (coleslaw, sweet potato casserole, baked beans) add up to a decadent carnivorous feast. (☎212-677-3733; www.mightyquinnsbbq.com; 103 Second Ave, at 6th St, East Village; single serving of meat $8-10; ⏰11:30am-11pm Sun-Thu, to midnight Fri & Sat; Ⓢ6 to Astor Pl; F to 2nd Ave)

Drinking

Bar Goto
BAR

26 Ⓜ MAP P84, C6

Maverick mixologist Kenta Goto has cocktail connoisseurs spellbound at his eponymous hot spot. Expect meticulous, elegant drinks that revel in Koto's Japanese heritage (the sake-spiked Sakura Martini is utterly smashing), paired with authentic, Japanese comfort bites, such as *okonomiyaki* (savory pancakes). (☎212-475-4411; www.bargoto.com; 245 Eldridge St, btwn E Houston & Stanton Sts, Lower East Side; ⏰5pm-midnight Tue-Thu & Sun, to 2am Fri & Sat; Ⓢ F to 2nd Ave)

Rue B
BAR

27 Ⓜ MAP P84, E2

There's live jazz (and the odd rockabilly group) every night from 9pm to midnight at this tiny, amber-lit drinking den on a bar-dappled stretch of Ave B. A young, celebratory crowd packs the small space – so mind the tight corners, lest the trombonist end up in your lap. B&W photos of jazz greats and other NYC icons enhance the ambience. (☎212-358-1700; www.ruebnyc188.com; 188 Ave B, btwn E 11th & 12th Sts, East Village; ⏰5pm-4am; Ⓢ L to 1st Ave)

Berlin
CLUB

28 Ⓜ MAP P84, D5

Like a secret bunker hidden beneath the ever-gentrifying streets of the East Village, Berlin is a throwback to the neighborhood's more riotous days of wildness and dancing. Once you find the unmarked entrance, head downstairs to the grotto-like space with vaulted brick ceilings, a long bar and tiny dancefloor, with funk and rare grooves spilling all around. (☎646-827-3689; 25 Ave A, btwn First & Second Aves, East Village; ⏰8pm-4am; Ⓢ F to 2nd Ave)

Angel's Share
BAR

29 Ⓜ MAP P84, B3

Show up early and snag a seat at this hidden gem, behind a Japanese restaurant on the same floor. It's quiet and elegant, with seriously talented mixologists serving up creative cocktails, plus a top flight collection of whiskeys. You can't stay if you don't have a table or a seat at the bar, and they tend to go fast. (☎212-777-5415; 8 Stuyvesant St, 2nd fl, near Third Ave & E 9th St; ⏰6pm-1:30am Sun-Wed, to 2am Thu, to 2:30am Fri & Sat; Ⓢ 6 to Astor Pl)

Ten Bells
BAR

30 Ⓜ MAP P84, D8

This charmingly tucked-away tapas bar has a grotto-like design, with flickering candles, dark tin ceilings, brick walls and a U-shaped bar that's an ideal setting for a conversation with a new friend. (212-228-4450; www.tenbellsnyc.com; 247 Broome St, btwn Ludlow & Orchard Sts, Lower East Side; 5pm-2am Mon-Fri, from 3pm Sat & Sun; S F to Delancey St; J/M/Z to Essex St)

Jimmy's No 43
BAR

31 MAP P84, C3

Barrels and stag antlers line the walls up to the ceiling of this cozy basement beer hall as locals chug their drinks. Select from more than 50 imported favorites (a dozen on draft) to go with a round of delectable, locally sourced bar nibbles. (212-982-3006; www.jimmysno43.com; 43 E 7th St, btwn Second & Third Aves, East Village; 4pm-1am Mon & Tue, to 2pm Wed & Thu, to 4am Fri,

1pm-4am Sat, to 1am Sun; S R/W to 8th St-NYU; F to 2nd Ave; 6 to Astor Pl)

Wayland
BAR

32 MAP P84, F3

Whitewashed walls, weathered floorboards and salvaged lamps give this urban outpost a Mississippi flair, which goes well with the live music (bluegrass, jazz, folk) featured Monday to Wednesday nights. The drinks, though, are the real draw – try the 'I Hear Banjos—encore!,' made of apple-pie moonshine, rye whiskey and applewood-cinnamon smoke, which tastes like a campfire (but slightly less burning). (212-777-7022; www.thewaylandnyc.com; 700 E 9th St, cnr Ave C, East Village; 5pm-4am; S L to 1st Ave)

Mighty Quinn's (p92)

ROBERT K. CHIN - STOREFRONTS/ALAMY STOCK PHOTO ©

Barrio Chino
COCKTAIL BAR

33 🚇 MAP P84, D8

An eatery that spills easily into a party scene, with an airy Havana-meets-Beijing vibe and a focus on fine sipping tequilas. Or stick with fresh blood-orange or black-plum margaritas, guacamole and chicken tacos. (📞212-228-6710; 253 Broome St, btwn Ludlow & Orchard Sts, Lower East Side; ⏰11:30am-4:30pm & 5:30pm-1am; 🚇F, J/M/Z to Delancey-Essex Sts)

Phoenix
GAY & LESBIAN

34 🚇 MAP P84, D1

Nightly drink specials, pool tournaments and the cutest guys the East Village has to offer: just a few of the things you'll find at any given time at Phoenix. Check the website to see what you can drink for cheap on which night, as well as dates for special events like trivia nights and live music. (📞212-477-9979; www.phoenixbarnyc.com; 447 East 13th St, btwn First Ave & Ave A, East Village; ⏰3pm-4am; 🚇L to 1st Ave)

Immigrant
BAR

35 🚇 MAP P84, C2

Wholly unpretentious, these twin boxcar-sized bars could easily become your neighborhood local if you decide to stick around town. The staff are knowledgeable and kind, mingling with faithful regulars while dishing out tangy olives and topping up glasses with imported snifters.

One Block Over

Famed St Marks Place draws swarms of people shopping and carousing – though it's a bit of a circus most days. Hop a block over in either direction (or head east towards the Ave A end of the street) for some great retail and restaurant finds with half the crowds.

(📞646-308-1724; www.theimmigrantnyc.com; 341 E 9th St, btwn First & Second Aves, East Village; ⏰5pm-2am; 🚇L to 1st Ave; 6 to Astor Pl)

Crocodile Lounge
LOUNGE

36 🚇 MAP P84, C1

Hankering for Williamsburg but too lazy to cross the river? Dive into Crocodile Lounge, the outpost of Brooklyn success story Alligator Lounge. The lure of cheap drinks and signature free pizza with every drink (yes, really) makes this hideout a hit with East Village 20-somethings seeking budget-friendly fun. There's a Skee-Ball league (Tuesday), trivia (Wednesday and Sunday) and bingo (Thursday). (📞212-477-7747; www.crocodileloungenyc.com; 325 E 14th St, btwn First & Second Aves, East Village; ⏰3pm-4am; 🚇L to 1st Ave)

Lucy's
BAR

37 🚇 MAP P84, D3

Located just around the corner from St Marks Pl, Lucy's has all the makings of an iconic East Village

East Village & Lower East Side Drinking

haunt. The bar is named after the owner, who can occasionally be spotted wearing a babushka behind the bar, and is replete with dirt-cheap drinks, pool tables and arcade games. Most authentic of all: the bar is cash only. (📞212-673-3824; 135 Ave A, btwn St Marks Pl & E 9th St, East Village; ⏱7pm-4am; 🚇L to 1st Ave)

Entertainment

Metrograph

CINEMA

38 ⭐ MAP P84, D8

The newest movie mecca for downtown cinephiles, this two-screen theater with red velvet seats shows curated art-house flicks. Most you'll never find at any multiplex, though the odd mainstream pic like *Magic Mike* is occasionally screened. In addition to movie geeks browsing the bookstore, you'll find a stylish and glamorous set at the bar or in the upstairs restaurant. (📞212-660-0312; www.metrograph.com; 7 Ludlow St, btwn Canal & Hester Sts, Lower East Side; tickets $15; 🚇F to East Broadway; B/D to Grand St)

Performance Space New York

THEATER

39 ⭐ MAP P84, D2

Formerly PS 122, this cutting-edge theater reopened in January 2018 with an entirely new facade, state-of-the-art performance spaces, artist studios, a new lobby and roof deck. The bones of the former schoolhouse remain, as does its

experimental theater bona fides: Eric Bogosian, Meredith Monk, the late Spalding Gray and Elevator Repair Service have all performed here. (📞212-477-5829; https://performancespacenewyork.org; 150 First Ave, at E 9th St, East Village; 🚇L to 1st Ave; 6 to Astor Pl)

Rockwood Music Hall

LIVE MUSIC

40 ⭐ MAP P84, D6

Opened by indie rocker Ken Rockwood, this breadbox-sized concert space has three stages and a rapid-fire flow of bands and singer/songwriters. If cash is tight, try stage 1, which has free shows, with a maximum of one hour per band (die-hards can see five or more performances a night). Music kicks off at 3pm on weekends and 6pm on weeknights. (📞212-477-4155; www.rockwoodmusichall.com; 196 Allen St, btwn Houston & Stanton Sts, Lower East Side; ⏱5:30pm-2am Mon-Fri, from 3pm Sat & Sun; 🚇F to 2nd Ave)

New York Theatre Workshop

THEATER

41 ⭐ MAP P84, B4

For more than 30 years this innovative production house has been a treasure trove for those seeking cutting-edge, contemporary plays with purpose. It was the originator of two big Broadway hits, *Rent* and *Urinetown* – plus it's where the musical *Once* had its off-Broadway premiere – and offers a constant supply of high-quality drama.

Kiefer Sutherland performing at the Bowery Ballroom

(☎212-460-5475; www.nytw.org; 79 E 4th St, btwn Second & Third Aves, East Village; Ⓢ F to 2nd Ave)

Nuyorican Poets Café
LIVE PERFORMANCE

42 ⭐ MAP P84, F5

Still going strong after 40-plus years, the legendary Nuyorican is home to poetry slams, hip-hop performances, plays, and film and video events. It's a piece of East Village history, but also a vibrant and still-relevant nonprofit arts organization. Check the website for the events calendar and buy tickets online for the more popular weekend shows. (☎212-780-9386; www.nuyorican.org; 236 E 3rd St, btwn Aves B & C, East Village; tickets $8-25; Ⓢ F to 2nd Ave)

Mercury Lounge
LIVE MUSIC

43 ⭐ MAP P84, D5

The Mercury dependably pulls in a cool new or comeback band everyone downtown wants to see – such as Dengue Fever or the Slits. The sound is good, with an intimate seating area and dance space. (☎212-260-4700; www.mercuryloungenyc.com; 217 E Houston St, btwn Essex & Ludlow Sts, Lower East Side; cover charge $10-15; ⏱6pm-3am; Ⓢ F/V to Lower East Side-2nd Ave)

Bowery Ballroom
LIVE MUSIC

44 ⭐ MAP P84, C7

This terrific, medium-sized venue has the perfect sound and feel for well-known indie-rock acts such as The Shins, Stephen Malkmus and Patti Smith. (☎212-533-2111, 800-745-3000; www.boweryballroom. com; 6 Delancey St, at Bowery St, Lower East Side; ⑤J/Z to Bowery; B/D to Grand St)

Sing Sing Karaoke KARAOKE

45 ⭐ MAP P84, B3

Whether you're looking for a private room to show off for your friends or a bustling bar to find a new duet partner, Sing Sing Karaoke is a solid spot for karaoke fiends. The song selection is impressive, as are the specials at the bar. (☎212-387-7800; www. karaokesingsing.com; 9 St Marks Pl, btwn Second & Third Aves, East Village; private rooms per person $8, songs at the bar per person $2; ⊙5pm-4am Sun-Thu, until 5am Fri & Sat; ⑤W/R to 8th St-NYU; L to 3rd Ave; 6 to Astor Pl)

La MaMa ETC THEATER

46 ⭐ MAP P84, C4

A long-standing home for onstage experimentation (the ETC stands for Experimental Theater Club), La MaMa is now a three-theater complex with a cafe, an art gallery, and a separate studio building that features cutting-edge dramas, sketch comedy and readings of all kinds. There are $10 tickets available for each show. Book early to score a deal! (☎212-352-3101; www.lamama.org; 74a E 4th St, btwn Bowery & Second Ave, East Village; tickets from $20; ⑤F to 2nd Ave)

Shopping

Strand Book Store BOOKS

47 🅐 MAP P84, A1

Beloved and legendary, the iconic Strand embodies downtown NYC's intellectual bona fides – a bibliophile's Oz, where generations of book lovers carrying the store's trademark tote bags happily lose themselves for hours. In operation since 1927, the Strand sells new, used and rare titles, spreading an incredible 18 miles of books (over 2.5 million of them) among three labyrinthine floors. (☎212-473-1452; www.strandbooks. com; 828 Broadway, at E 12th St, East Village; ⊙9:30am-10:30pm Mon-Sat, from 11am Sun; ⑤L, N/Q/R/W, 4/5/6 to 14th St-Union Sq)

Tictail Market FASHION

48 🅐 MAP P84, D7

Tictail Market is located on a corner on the Lower East Side, but it specializes in clothing, accessories, trinkets and art from around the world. All products are sourced directly from the designers and artists so you can be sure you're supporting a small business with each purchase. The collection is eclectic, but tends to lean toward a cool, minimalist aesthetic. (☎917-388-1556; www. tictail.com; 90 Orchard St, at Broome St, Lower East Side; ⊙noon-9pm Mon-Sat, to 6pm Sun; ⑤B/D to Grand St; F to Delancey St; J/M/Z to Essex St)

Obscura Antiques

ANTIQUES

49 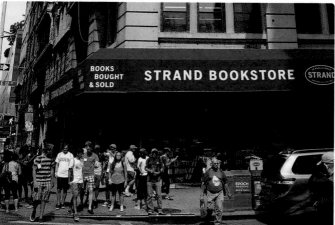 MAP P84, D1

This cabinet of curiosities pleases lovers of the macabre and inveterate antique hunters. Here you'll find taxidermied animal heads, tiny rodent skulls, butterfly displays in glass boxes, Victorian-era post-mortem photography, disturbing little (dental?) instruments, German landmine flags, old poison bottles and glass eyes. (📞212-505-9251; www.obscuraantiques.com; 207 Ave A, btwn E 12th & 13th Sts, East Village; ⏰noon-8pm Mon-Sat, to 7pm Sun; 🚇L to 1st Ave)

Russ & Daughters

FOOD

50 🔒 MAP P84, D5

In business since 1914, this landmark establishment serves up Eastern European Jewish delicacies, such as caviar, herring and lox, and, of course, smear by the pound. It's a great place to load up for a picnic or stock your fridge with breakfast goodies. (📞212-475-4800; www.russanddaughters.com; 179 E Houston St, btwn Orchard & Allen Sts, Lower East Side; ⏰8am-7pm Mon-Wed, to 7pm Thu, to 6pm Fri-Sun; 🚇F to 2nd Ave)

No Relation Vintage

VINTAGE

51 🔒 MAP P84, D1

Among the many vintage shops of the East Village, No Relation is a winner for its wide-ranging collections that run the gamut from designer denim and leather jackets to vintage flannels, funky sneakers, plaid shirts, irreverent branded T-shirts, varsity jackets,

Strand Book Store

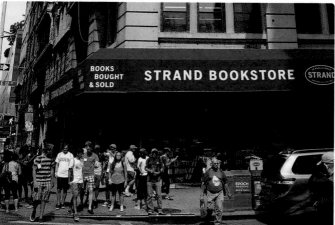

MATTHEW DICKER/SHUTTERSTOCK ©

clutches and more. Sharpen your elbows: hipster crowds flock here on weekends. (L Train Vintage; ☎212-228-5201; https://ltrainvintage.com; 204 First Ave, btwn E 12th & 13th Sts, East Village; ⏰noon-8pm Mon-Thu & Sun, to 9pm Fri & Sat; Ⓢ L to 1st Ave)

Edith Machinist

VINTAGE

52 MAP P84, D6

To properly strut about the Lower East Side, you've got to dress the part. Edith Machinist can help you get that rumpled but stylish look in a hurry – a bit of vintage glam via knee-high soft suede boots, 1930s silk dresses and beaded purses. (☎212-979-9992; www.edithmachinist.com; 104 Rivington St, btwn Ludlow & Essex Sts, Lower East Side; ⏰noon-7pm Tue-Thu, to 6pm Sun, Mon & Fri; Ⓢ F to Delancey St; J/M/Z to Essex St)

Reformation

CLOTHING

53 MAP P84, D6

This stylish boutique sells beautifully designed garments with minimal environmental impact. Aside from its green credentials, it sells unique tops, blouses, sweaters and dresses, with fair prices in comparison to other Lower East Side boutiques. (☎646-448-4925; www.thereformation.com; 156 Ludlow St, btwn Rivington & Stanton Sts, Lower East Side; ⏰noon-8pm Mon-Sat, to 7pm Sun; Ⓢ F to Delancey St or 2nd Ave; J/M/Z to Essex St)

A-1 Records

MUSIC

54 MAP P84, D3

One of the last of the many record stores that once graced the East Village, A-1 has been around for

Bluestockings

ROBERT K. CHIN - STOREFRONTS/ALAMY STOCK PHOTO ©

over two decades. The cramped aisles, filled with a large selection of jazz, funk and soul, draw vinyl fans and DJs from far and wide. (📞212-473-2870; www.a1recordshop.com; 439 E 6th St, btwn First Ave & Ave A, East Village; ⏰1-9pm; Ⓢ F/M to 2nd Ave)

Moo Shoes
SHOES

55 🔒 MAP P84, D8

This cruelty-free, earth-friendly boutique sells stylish microfiber (faux leather) shoes, handbags and wallets. Look for fashionable pumps from Olsenhaus, rugged men's Oxfords by Novacos and sleek Matt & Nat wallets. (📞212-254-6512; www.mooshoes.com; 78 Orchard St, btwn Broome & Grand Sts, Lower East Side; ⏰11:30am-7:30pm Mon-Sat, noon-6pm Sun; Ⓢ F to Delancey St; J/M/Z to Essex St)

By Robert James
FASHION & ACCESSORIES

56 🔒 MAP P84, D8

Rugged, beautifully tailored menswear is the mantra of Robert James, who sources and manufactures right in NYC (the design studio is just upstairs). The racks are lined with slim-fitting denim, handsome button-downs and classic-looking sports coats. James' black lab Lola sometimes roams the store. He also has a location in Williamsburg. (📞212-253-2121; www.byrobertjames.com; 74 Orchard St, btwn Broome & Grand Sts, Lower East Side; ⏰noon-8pm Mon-Sat, to 6pm Sun; Ⓢ F to Delancey St; J/M/Z to Essex St)

Kiehl's
COSMETICS

57 🔒 MAP P84, B1

Making and selling skincare products since it opened in NYC as an apothecary in 1851, this Kiehl's flagship store has doubled its size and expanded into an international chain, but its personal touch remains. (📞212-677-3171; 109 Third Ave, btwn 13th & 14th Sts, East Village; ⏰10am-9pm Mon-Sat, 11am-7pm Sun; Ⓢ L to 3rd Ave)

Bluestockings
BOOKS

58 🔒 MAP P84, D6

This independent bookstore is the place to expand your horizons on feminism, queer and trans issues, and African American studies, among other topics. It's also the site of an organic, fair-trade cafe with vegan treats, as well as speaking events. (📞212-777-6028; www.bluestockings.com; 172 Allen St, btwn Stanton & Rivington Sts, Lower East Side; ⏰11am-11pm; Ⓢ F/M to Lower East Side-2nd Ave)

Still House
HOMEWARES

59 🔒 MAP P84, D3

Step into this petite, peaceful boutique to browse sculptural glassware and pottery: handblown vases, geometric objects, ceramic bowls and cups, and other finery for the home. You'll also find minimalistic jewelry, delicately bound notebooks and small framed artworks for the wall. (📞212-539-0200; www.stillhousenyc.com; 117 E 7th St, btwn First Ave & Ave A, East Village; ⏰noon-8pm; Ⓢ 6 to Astor Pl)

Explore ✦

West Village, Chelsea & the Meatpacking District

The West Village's twisting streets offer intimate spaces for dining and drinking. Young professionals go to the Meatpacking District's trendy bars to see and be seen. Chelsea has art galleries and a vibrant LGBT scene. Tying them together is the High Line, a snake-like park, above.

Start your day with a stroll down the High Line (p104); start at W 30th St and head south. Stop for lunch and a quick browse at Chelsea Market (p112), then hit up the new Whitney Museum of American Art (p110). Wander the West Village's quaint, cobblestoned streets, lined with cafes and boutiques. For evening entertainment, take your pick from dozens of restaurants for dinner, then enjoy some live jazz at Smalls (p121) or Village Vanguard (p122), or whatever's on at Le Poisson Rouge (p123). Try the Comedy Cellar (p124) for some laughs or head back up to Chelsea for Sleep No More (p121). For late-night drinks try Bathtub Gin (p119).

Getting There & Around

Sixth, Seventh and Eighth Aves are graced with convenient subway stations for Chelsea and the Meatpacking District, but public transportation slims further west and south.

S Take the A/C/E or 1/2/3 lines to reach this colorful clump of neighborhoods – disembark at 14th St (on either line) or W 4th St-Washington Sq for the heart of the Village.

Neighborhood Map on p108

Top Sight 📷
The High Line

It's hard to believe that the High Line – a shining example of urban renewal – was once a dingy rail line that anchored an unsavory district of slaughterhouses. Today, this eye-catching attraction is one of New York's best-loved green spaces, drawing visitors who come to stroll, sit and picnic 30ft above the city, while enjoying fabulous views of Manhattan's ever-changing skyline.

◎ MAP P108, C4

☏ 212-500-6035

www.thehighline.org

🕑 7am-11pm Jun-Sep, to 10pm Apr, May, Oct & Nov, to 7pm Dec-Mar

🚌 M11 to Washington St; M11, M14 to 9th Ave; M23, M34 to 10th Ave, Ⓢ A/C/E, L to 8th Ave-14th St; 1, C/E to 23rd St

From Rails to Real Estate

In the early 1900s, the area around the Meatpacking District and Chelsea was the largest industrial section of Manhattan, where elevated rail tracks moved freight off the cluttered streets below. The rails eventually became obsolete, and in 1999 a plan was made to convert the scarring strands of metal into a public green space. On June 9, 2009, section one of the city's most beloved urban renewal project opened with much ado, and it's been one of New York's star attractions ever since.

Visiting the High Line

Section one runs from Gansevoort St to W 20th St; it's full of sitting space in various forms – from giant chaises longues to bleacher-like benching. Section two added another 10 blocks of green-ified tracks, with local native flora. The final section meanders from 30th up to 34th St, going up to and around the West Side Rail Yards; here the path widens, and you have open views of the Hudson, with the rusting, weed-filled railroad tracks running alongside the walkway (the designers wanted to evoke the same sense of overgrown wilderness in the heart of the metropolis that greeted visitors who stumbled upon the tracks prior to the park's creation). This section also feature a dedicated children's play area – a jungle gym made up of exposed beams covered in a soft play surface.

To reach the High Line, there are numerous stairways along the park (near Tenth Ave), including Gansevoort, 14th, 16th, 18th, 20th, 23rd, 26th, 28th, 30th and 34th Sts. There are also elevators at Gansevoort, 14th, 16th, 23rd, 30th and 34th Sts.

★ Top Tips

○ Beat the crowds by starting early at 30th or 34th St, wandering south and exiting at 14th St for a bite at Chelsea Market before exploring the West Village. If your tummy's grumbling, tackle the High Line in the reverse direction, gelato in hand.

○ The High Line also makes a convenient way to avoid walking through the convoluted streets of the Meatpacking District, especially if there's construction.

✖ Take a Break

A cache of eateries is stashed within the brick walls of Chelsea Market (p112) at the 14th St exit of the High Line. Head to the **Top of the Standard** (☏ 212-645-7600; www.standardhotels.com/high-line; 848 Washington St, btwn 13th & Little W 12th Sts, Meatpacking District; ⊘ 4pm-midnight Mon-Fri, from 2pm Sat & Sun; S A/C/E, L to 8th Ave-14th St) for a pricey cocktail with a million-dollar view.

Walking Tour 🥾

Chelsea Galleries

Chelsea is home to the highest concentration of art galleries in NYC. Most lie in the 20s, on the blocks between Tenth and Eleventh Aves, and openings are typically held on Thursday evenings. Most galleries are open Tuesday through Sunday, but double-check opening hours. Pick up Art Info's Gallery Guide (with map) for free at most galleries, or visit www.westchelseaarts.com.

Walk Facts

Start Pace Gallery;
[S] 1, C/E to 23rd St

End David Zwirner;
[S] 1, C/E to 23rd St

Length 1 mile;
three to four hours
depending on stops

❶ Pace Gallery

In a dramatically transformed garage, the **Pace Gallery** (☎212-255-4044; www.pacegallery.com; 510 W 25th St, btwn Tenth & Eleventh Aves; ⊙10am-6pm Tue-Sat; Ⓢ1, C/E to 23rd St) has worked with leading artists, including David Hockney.

❷ Cheim & Read

Sculptures abound at **Cheim & Read** (☎212-242-7727; www.cheim read.com; 547 W 25th St, btwn Tenth & Eleventh Aves; ⊙10am-6pm Tue-Sat; Ⓢ1, C/E to 23rd St); monthly rotations keep the exhibits fresh.

❸ Gagosian

Gagosian (☎212-741-1111; www. gagosian.com; 555 W 24th St, btwn Tenth & Eleventh Aves; ⊙10am-6pm Mon-Sat; Ⓢ1, C/E to 23rd St) is one of a constellation of showrooms spreading across the globe.

❹ Mary Boone Gallery

Make an appointment to visit **Mary Boone Gallery** (☎212-752-2929; www.maryboonegallery.com; 541 W 24th St, btwn Tenth & Eleventh Aves; ⊙10am-6pm Tue-Sat; Ⓢ1, CE to 23rd St), whose owner found fame in the '80s with Jean-Michel Basquiat and Julian Schnabel.

❺ Barbara Gladstone Gallery

The **Barbara Gladstone Gallery** (☎212-206-9300; www.gladstone gallery.com; 515 W 24th St, btwn Tenth & Eleventh Aves; ⊙10am-6pm Mon-Fri; Ⓢ1, C/E to 23rd St) consistently puts together the most talked-about and well-critiqued displays around.

❻ Refuel, Spanish-Style

Wielding Spanish tapas amid closet-sized surrounds, **Tía Pol** (☎212-675-8805; www.tiapol.com; 205 Tenth Ave, btwn 22nd & 23rd Sts; small plates $7-14; ⊙noon-11pm Tue-Sun, from 5:30pm Mon; Ⓢ1, C/E to 23rd St) is the real deal.

❼ Matthew Marks Gallery

Matthew Marks (☎212-243-0200; www.matthewmarks.com; 522 W 22nd St, btwn Tenth & Eleventh Aves; ⊙10am-6pm Tue-Sat; Ⓢ1, C/E to 23rd St) is famous for exhibiting big names such as Jasper Johns and Ellsworth Kelly.

❽ 192 Books

This small **bookshop** (☎212-255-4022; www.192books.com; 192 Tenth Ave, btwn W 21st & 22nd Sts; ⊙11am-7pm; Ⓢ1, C/E to 23rd St) makes a delightful reprieve from the big-gallery experience.

❾ Paula Cooper Gallery

An icon of the art world, **Paula Cooper** (☎212-255-1105; www. paulacoopergallery.com; 534 W 21st St, btwn Tenth & Eleventh Aves; ⊙10am-6pm Mon-Fri; Ⓢ1, C/E to 23rd St) continues to push boundaries and draw crowds.

❿ David Zwirner

Major player **David Zwirner** (☎212-517-8677; www.davidzwirner. com; 537 W 20th St, btwn Tenth & Eleventh Aves; ⊙10am-6pm Tue-Sat; Ⓢ1, C/E to 23rd St) has a five-story gallery with 30,000 sq ft of exhibition space.

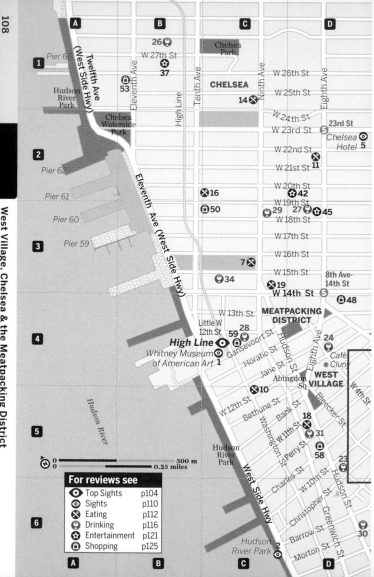

A

B

C

D

1

Pier 66

Twelfth Ave (West Side Hwy)

Hudson River Park

26 🏛

W 27th St

37 ★

53 🏛

Chelsea Park

Chelsea Waterside Park

High Line

Tenth Ave

CHELSEA

W 26th St

W 25th St

Ninth Ave

14 ❌

Eighth Ave

W 24th St

23rd St 🆂

W 23rd St

Chelsea Hotel 5 ◉

2

Pier 62

W 22nd St

W 21st St

11 🏛

Pier 61

Pier 60

Eleventh Ave (West Side Hwy)

16 ❌

W 20th St

42 ★

50 🏛

W 19th St

29 🍷 27 🍷 45 ★

W 18th St

3

Pier 59

W 17th St

W 16th St

7 ❌

W 15th St

8th Ave-14th St 🆂

34 🍷

19 ❌

W 14th St

48 🏛

MEATPACKING DISTRICT

W 13th St

24 ❌

Café Clum ●

4

Little W 12th St

59 🏛 28 🏛

Gansevoort St

Horatio St

Eighth Ave

WEST VILLAGE

W 4th St

High Line ◉

Whitney Museum ◉ of American Art 1

Jane St

Abingdon Sq

Hudson St

10 ❌

W 12th St

Bethune St

Bank St

Washington St

18 ❌

W 11th St

31 🏛

Bleecker St

Hudson River Park

Perry St

58 🏛

23 🏛

5

Hudson River

Charles St

West Side Hwy

W 10th St

Christopher St

Greenwich St

0 ——— 500 m
0 ——— 0.25 miles

For reviews see

◉ Top Sights   p104
◉ Sights   p110
❌ Eating   p112
🍷 Drinking   p116
★ Entertainment p121
🏛 Shopping   p125

6

Hudson River Park

2 ◉

Barrow St

Morton St

30 🏛

A

B

C

D

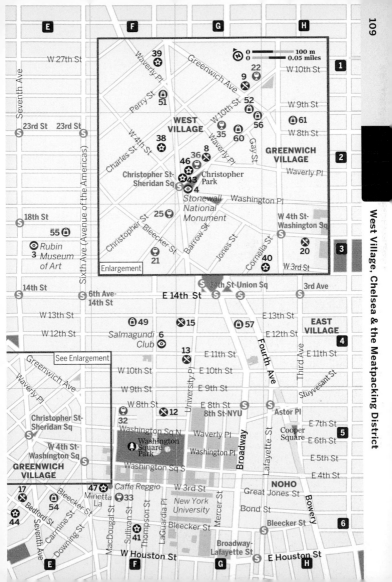

Sights

Whitney Museum of American Art

MUSEUM

1 ⊙ MAP P108, C4

After years of construction, the Whitney's new downtown location opened to much fanfare in 2015. Perched near the foot of the High Line (p104), this architecturally stunning building – designed by Renzo Piano – makes a suitable introduction to the museum's superb collection. Inside the spacious, light-filled galleries, you'll find works by all the great American artists, including Edward Hopper, Jasper Johns, Georgia O'Keeffe and Mark Rothko. (☑212-570-3600; www.whitney.org; 99 Gansevoort St, at Washington St, West Village; adult/child $25/free, pay-what-you-wish 7-10pm Fri; ☑10:30am-6pm Mon, Wed, Thu & Sun, to 10pm Fri & Sat; ⑤A/C/E, L to 8th Ave-14th St)

Hudson River Park

PARK

2 ⊙ MAP P108, C6

The High Line (p104) may be all the rage these days, but one block away from that famous elevated green space stretches a 5-mile-long ribbon of green that has dramatically transformed the city over the past decade. Covering 550 acres and running from Battery Park at Manhattan's southern tip to 59th St in Midtown, the Hudson River Park is Manhattan's wondrous backyard. The long riverside path is a great spot for cycling, running and strolling.

(www.hudsonriverpark.org; West Village; ⁂; 🚌M11 to Washington St; M11, M14 to 9th Ave; M23, M34 to 10th Ave, ⑤1 to Hudson Ave; A/C/E, L to 8th Ave-14th St; 1, C/E to 23rd St)

Rubin Museum of Art

GALLERY

3 ⊙ MAP P108, E3

The Rubin is the first museum in the Western world to dedicate itself to the art of the Himalayas and surrounding regions. Its impressive collections include embroidered textiles from China, metal sculptures from Tibet, Pakistani stone sculptures and intricate Bhutanese paintings, as well as ritual objects and dance masks from various Tibetan regions, spanning from the 2nd to the 19th centuries. (☑212-620-5000; www.rmanyc.org; 150 W 17th St, btwn Sixth & Seventh Aves, Chelsea; adult/child $15/free, 6-10pm Fri free; ☑11am-5pm Mon & Thu, to 9pm Wed, to 10pm Fri, to 6pm Sat & Sun; ⑤1 to 18th St)

Stonewall National Monument

NATIONAL PARK

4 ⊙ MAP P108, G2

In 2016 President Barack Obama declared Christopher Park, a small fenced-in square with benches and some greenery, a national park and on it the first national monument dedicated to LGBTQ history. The park is small, but it's well worth stopping here to reflect on the Stonewall uprising of 1969, when LGBTQ citizens fought back against discriminatory policing of their communities. Many cite these

Washington Square Park

Once a potter's field and a place of public executions, **Washington Square Park** (Map p108, F5; Fifth Ave at Washington Sq N, West Village; 🚹; ⓈA/C/E, B/D/F/M to W 4th St-Washington Sq; R/W to 8th St-NYU) is now the unofficial town square of Greenwich Village, and plays host to lounging NYU students, tuba-playing street performers, curious canines and their owners, speed-chess pros and bare-footed children who splash about in the fountain on warm days. The park has long provided a stage for political activity, from local protests against proposed changes to the shape and usage of the park to issues of national importance, such as the 1912 protests for better working conditions; these days rallies protesting the Trump administration's stance on immigrants are held regularly.

The iconic Stanford White Arch, colloquially known as the Washington Square Arch, dominates the park with its 72ft of beaming white Dover marble. Originally designed in wood to celebrate the centennial of George Washington's inauguration in 1889, the arch proved so popular that it was replaced with stone six years later.

events as the crucible of the modern LGBTQ rights movement in the US. (www.nps.gov/ston/index.htm; W 4th St, btwn Christopher & Grove Sts, West Village; ⏰9am–dusk; Ⓢ1 to Christopher St-Sheridan Sq; A/C/E, B/D/F/M to W 4th St-Washington Sq)

Chelsea Hotel   HISTORIC BUILDING

5 ◎ MAP P108, D2

This red-brick hotel, built in the 1880s and featuring ornate iron balconies and no fewer than seven plaques declaring its literary landmark status, has played a major role in pop-culture history. It's where the likes of Mark Twain, Thomas Wolfe, Dylan Thomas and Arthur Miller hung out; Jack Kerouac allegedly crafted *On the Road* during one marathon session here; and it's where Arthur C Clarke wrote *2001: A Space Odyssey*. (222 W 23rd St, btwn Seventh & Eighth Aves, Chelsea; Ⓢ1, C/E to 23rd St)

Salmagundi Club   GALLERY

6 ◎ MAP P108, F4

Far removed from the flashy Chelsea gallery scene, the Salmagundi Club features several gallery spaces, focusing on representational American art, set in a stunning historic brownstone on Fifth Ave below Union Sq. The club is one of the oldest art clubs in the US (founded in 1871) and still offers classes and exhibitions for its members. (📞212-255-7740; www.salmagundi.org; 47 Fifth Ave, btwn W 11th & 12th Sts, West Village; admission free; ⏰1-6pm Mon-Fri, to 5pm Sat & Sun; Ⓢ4/5/6, L, N/Q/R/W to 14th St-Union Sq)

West Village Cafes 🍴

The West Village is the most desirable residential neighborhood in Manhattan, so do as the locals do and make the most of this quaint district full of cute cafes, such as Parisian-vibed **Café Cluny** (Map p108, D4; 212-255-6900; www.cafecluny.com; 284 W 12th St, cnr W 12th & W 4th Sts, West Village; mains lunch $12-28, dinner $22-34; ⏱8am-10pm Mon, 8am-11pm Tue-Fri, 9am-11pm Sat, 9am-10pm Sun; ⓢA/C/E, L 8th Ave-14th St) or Italian-eclectic **Caffe Reggio** (Map p108, F6; 212-475-9557; www.cafferegio.com; 119 MacDougal St, near W 3rd St, West Village; sandwiches around $10; ⏱9am-3am Sun-Thu, to 4am Fri & Sat; ⓢA/C/E, B/D/F/M to W 4th St-Washington Sq). Grab a book and a latte and hunker down for a blissful afternoon of people-watching.

Eating

Chelsea Market MARKET $

7 ⊗ MAP P108, C3

In a shining example of redevelopment and preservation, the Chelsea Market has taken a factory formerly owned by cookie giant Nabisco (creator of Oreo) and turned it into an 800ft-long shopping concourse that caters to foodies. Taking the place of the old factory ovens that churned out massive numbers of biscuits are eclectic eateries that fill the renovated hallways of this food haven. (www.chelseamarket.com; 75 Ninth Ave, btwn 15th & 16th Sts, Chelsea; ⏱7am-9pm Mon-Sat, 8am-8pm Sun; ⓢA/C/E, L to 8th Ave-14th St)

Jeffrey's Grocery MODERN AMERICAN $$$

8 ⊗ MAP P108, G2

This West Village classic is a lively eating and drinking spot that hits all the right notes. Seafood is the focus: there's an oyster bar and beautifully executed selections, such as mussels with crème fraîche, tuna steak tartine and sharing platters. Meat dishes include hanger steak with roasted veggies in a *romesco* sauce. (646-398-7630; www.jeffreysgrocery.com; 172 Waverly Pl, at Christopher St, West Village; mains $23-30; ⏱8am-11pm Mon-Wed, to 1am Thu-Fri, 9:30am-1am Sat, to 11pm Sun; ⓢ1 to Christopher St-Sheridan Sq)

Rosemary's ITALIAN $$

9 ⊗ MAP P108, G1

One of the West Village's hottest restaurants, Rosemary's serves high-end Italian fare that more than lives up to the hype. In a vaguely farmhouse-like setting, diners tuck into generous portions of housemade pastas, rich salads, and cheese and *salumi* (cured meat) boards. Everything, from the simple walnut herb pesto to the succulent smoked lamb shoulder, is incredible. (212-647-1818; www.

rosemarysnyc.com; 18 Greenwich Ave, at W 10th St, West Village; mains $14-40; ⊙8am-4pm & 5-11pm Mon-Thu, until midnight Fri, from 10am Sat & Sun, until 11pm Sun; ⑤1 to Christopher St-Sheridan Sq)

Barbuto
MODERN ITALIAN $$

10 🗙 MAP P108, C5

Occupying a cavernous garage space with sweeping see-through doors that roll up and into the ceiling during the warmer months, Barbuto slaps together a delightful assortment of nouveau Italian dishes, such as duck breast with plum and crème fraîche, and calamari drizzled with squid ink and chili aioli. (☎212-924-9700; www.barbutonyc.com; 775 Washington St, at W 12th St, West Village; mains $22-28; ⊙noon-3:30pm & 5:30-11pm

Mon-Thu, until midnight Fri & Sat, until 10pm Sun; ⑤A/C/E, L to 8th Ave-14th St; 1 to Christopher St-Sheridan Sq)

Foragers Table
MODERN AMERICAN $$$

11 🗙 MAP P108, D2

Owners of this outstanding restaurant run a 28-acre farm in the Hudson Valley, from which much of their seasonal menu is sourced. It changes frequently, but recent temptations include Long Island duck breast with roasted acorn squash, apples, chanterelle mushrooms and figs, grilled skate with red quinoa, creamed kale and *cippolini* onion and deviled farm eggs with Dijon mustard. (☎212-243-8888; www.foragersmarket.com/restaurant; 300 W 22nd St, at Eighth Ave, Chelsea; mains $17-32;

Chelsea Market

⏱ 8am-4pm & 5:30-10pm Mon-Fri, 10am-2pm & 5:30-10pm Sat, to 9:30pm Sun; 🗾; **S**1, C/E to 23rd St)

Otto Enoteca Pizzeria   PIZZA $

12 🍴 MAP P108, F5

Just north of Washington Square Park, this is a refreshingly afford-able part of Mario Batali's empire, a pizza palace where thin pizzas are cooked on flat-iron grid-dles till they crackle perfectly. They come topped with items far beyond your standard pizza joint – asparagus, goat cheese, egg, fresh chilies, capers, the best fresh mozzarella – and sauce that has the perfect balance of smoky and sweet. (📞 212-995-9559; www.ottopizzeria.com; 1 Fifth Ave, entrance on E 8th St, West Village; pizzas $9-15;

⏱ 11:30am-midnight; 🗾; **S**A/C/E, B/D/F/M to W 4th St-Washington Sq)

Nix   VEGETARIAN $$

13 🍴 MAP P108, G4

At this understated Michelin-starred eatery, head chefs Nicolas Farias and John Fraser transform vegetables into high art in beauti-fully executed dishes that delight the senses. Start off with tandoor bread and creative dips like spiced eggplant with pine nuts before moving on to richly complex plates of cauliflower tempura with steamed buns, or spicy tofu with chanterelle mushrooms, kale and Szechuan pepper. (📞 212-498-9393; www.nixny.com; 72 University Pl, btwn 10th & 11th Sts, West Village; mains $20-28; ⏱ 11:30am-2:30pm & 5:30-11pm Mon-Fri, from 10:30am Sat

Otto Enoteca Pizzeria

ROBERT K. CHIN - STOREFRONTS/ALAMY ©

& Sun; S4/5/6, N/Q/R/W, L to 14th St-Union Sq)

Jun-Men   RAMEN $$

14 ✖ MAP P108, C1

This tiny, ultra-modern ramen joint whips up delectably flavored noodle bowls, in variants of pork shoulder, spicy miso or uni mushroom (with sea urchin). Don't skip the appetizers: the yellowtail ceviche and barbecue pork buns are outstanding. Service is speedy, and it's fun to watch the adroit prep team in action in the tiny kitchen at center stage. (☎646-852-6787; www.junmenramen.com; 249 Ninth Ave, btwn 25th & 26th Sts, Chelsea; ramen $16-19; ⏱11:30am-3pm & 5-10pm Mon-Thu, to 11pm Fri & Sat; S1, C/E to 23rd St)

Babu Ji   INDIAN $$

15 ✖ MAP P108, G4

A playful spirit marks this excellent Australian-run Indian restaurant, which recently relocated to Union Sq. You can assemble a meal from street food–style dishes such as *papadi chaat* (chickpeas, pomegranate and yogurt chutney) and potato croquettes stuffed with lobster, or feast on heartier dishes like tandoori lamb chops or scallop coconut curry. A $62 tasting menu is also on offer. (☎212-951-1082; www.babujinyc.com; 22 E 13th St, btwn University Pl & Fifth Ave, West Village; mains $16-26; ⏱5-10:30pm Sun-Thu, to 11:30pm Fri & Sat, also 10:30am-3pm Sat & Sun; S4/5/6, N/Q/R/W, L to 14th St-Union Sq)

Dining Options   🍴

While the West Village is known for its classy, cozy and intimate spots, the adjacent Meatpacking District's dining scene is a bit more ostentatious, complete with nightclub-like queues behind velvet ropes, bold decor and swarms of trend-obsessed patrons.

Chelsea strikes a balance between the two with a brash assortment of *très* gay eateries along the uber-popular Eighth Ave (a must for see-and-be-seen brunch), and more cafes lining Ninth Ave further west. In the warmer months expect windows and doors to fling open and plenty of alfresco seating to spill out onto the streets.

Cookshop   MODERN AMERICAN $$

16 ✖ MAP P108, C2

A brilliant brunching pit stop before (or after) tackling the High Line, Cookshop is a lively place that knows its niche and does it oh so well. Excellent service, eye-opening cocktails (good morning, bacon-infused BLT Mary!), a perfectly baked-bread basket and a selection of inventive egg mains make this a Chelsea favorite on a Sunday afternoon. (☎212-924-4440; www.cookshopny.com; 156 Tenth Ave, btwn W 19th & 20th Sts, Chelsea; mains brunch $15-22, lunch $17-21, dinner $22-48; ⏱8am-11pm Mon-Fri, from 10am Sat, 10am-10pm Sun; S1, C/E to 23rd St)

Sushi Nakazawa

SUSHI $$$

17 ❌ MAP P108, E6

The price is high, but the quality is nothing short of phenomenal at this sushi spot that opened to much acclaim in 2013. There are no cooked dishes and the meal is a 20-course fixed-price affair created by Chef Daisuke Nakazawa, who served under Jiro Ono, probably the world's finest sushi chef. (☏212-924-2212; www.sushinakazawa.com; 23 Commerce St, btwn Bedford St & Seventh Ave, West Village; prix-fixe menu $120-150; ⏰5-10:15pm; 🚇1 to Christopher St-Sheridan Sq)

Spotted Pig

PUB FOOD $$$

18 ❌ MAP P108, D5

This James Beard-award-winning gastropub is a favorite with restaurant industry types as well as celebrities. The kitchen serves an upscale blend of hearty Italian and British dishes, plus an ever popular cheeseburger with shoestring fries. Its two floors are bedecked with old-timey trinkets that give the whole place an air of relaxed elegance. (☏212-620-0393; www.thespottedpig.com; 314 W 11th St, at Greenwich St; mains lunch $17-36, dinner $25-39; ⏰noon-2am Mon-Fri, from 11am Sat & Sun; 🚇A/C/E, L to 8th Ave-14th St)

Gansevoort Market

MARKET $

19 ❌ MAP P108, C3

Inside a brick building in the heart of the Meatpacking District, this sprawling market is the latest and greatest food emporium to land in NYC. A raw, industrial space lit by skylights, it features several dozen gourmet vendors slinging tapas, arepas, tacos, pizzas, meat pies, ice cream, pastries and more. (www.gansmarket.com; 353 W 14th St, at Ninth Ave, Meatpacking District; mains $5-20; ⏰8am-8pm; 🚇A/C/E, L to 8th Ave-14th St)

Red Bamboo

VEGAN $

20 ❌ MAP P108, H3

Flaky, hot bites of popcorn shrimp, gooey chicken Parmesan, chocolate cake so rich you can barely finish – Red Bamboo offers all of that and more soul and Asian food options. The catch? Everything on its menu is vegan (some dishes do offer the option of real cheese). This is a must try for vegans, vegetarians or anyone looking to try something new. (☏212-260-7049; www.redbamboo-nyc.com; 140 W 4th St, btwn Sixth Ave & MacDougal St; mains $8-13; ⏰12:30-11pm Mon-Thu, to 11:30pm Fri, noon-11:30pm Sat, to 11pm Sun; 🚇A/C/E, B/D/F/M to W 4th St-Washington Sq)

Drinking

Buvette

WINE BAR

21 🍷 MAP P108, F3

The rustic-chic decor here (think delicate tin tiles and a swooshing marble counter) makes it the perfect place for a glass of wine – no matter the time of day. For the full experience at this self-proclaimed *gastrothèque,* grab a seat at one of

WENDY CONNETT/ALAMY STOCK PHOTO ©

Spotted Pig

the surrounding tables and nibble on small plates while enjoying old-world wines (mostly from France and Italy). (212-255-3590; www.ilovebuvette.com; 42 Grove St, btwn Bedford & Bleecker Sts, West Village; 7am-2am Mon-Fri, from 8am Sat & Sun; S 1 to Christopher St-Sheridan Sq; A/C/E, B/D/F/M to W 4th St-Washington Sq)

Happiest Hour   COCKTAIL BAR

22 🚇 MAP P108, G1

A super-cool, tiki-licious cocktail bar splashed with palm prints, '60s pop and playful mixed drinks that provide a chic take on the fruity beach cocktail. The crowd tends to be button-down after-work types and online daters. Beneath sits its serious sibling, **Slowly Shirley**, an art-deco-style

subterranean temple to beautifully crafted, thoroughly researched libations. (212-243-2827; www.happiesthournyc.com; 121 W 10th St, btwn Greenwich St & Sixth Ave, West Village; 5pm-late Mon-Fri, from 2pm Sat & Sun; S A/C/E, B/D/F/M to W 4th St-Washington Sq; 1 to Christopher St-Sheridan Sq)

Employees Only   BAR

23 🚇 MAP P108, D5

Duck behind the neon 'Psychic' sign to find this hidden hangout. Bartenders are ace mixologists, fizzing up crazy, addictive libations like the Ginger Smash and an upscale Bellini. Great for late-night drinking and eating, courtesy of the on-site restaurant that serves till 3:30am – housemade chicken soup is ladled out to stragglers.

The bar gets busier as the night wears on. (📞212-242-3021; www.employeesonlynyc.com; 510 Hudson St, btwn W 10th & Christopher Sts, West Village; ⏱6pm-4am; 🚇1 to Christopher St-Sheridan Sq)

Cubbyhole
LGBT

24 🚇 MAP P108, D4

This West Village dive bills itself as 'lesbian, gay and straight friendly since 1994.' While the crowd is mostly ladies, as its motto suggests it's a welcoming place for anyone looking for a cheap drink. It's got a great jukebox, friendly bartenders and plenty of regulars who prefer to hang and chat rather than hook up and leave. (📞212-243-9041; www.cubbyholebar.com; 281 W 12th St, at W 4th St, West Village; ⏱4pm-4am Mon-Fri, from 2pm Sat & Sun; 🚇A/C/E, L to 8th Ave-14th St)

Marie's Crisis
BAR

25 🚇 MAP P108, F3

Aging Broadway queens, wide-eyed out-of-towners , giggly tourists and various other fans of musical theater assemble around the piano here and take turns belting out campy show tunes, often joined by the entire crowd – and the occasional celebrity. It's old-school fun, no matter how jaded you might be when you go in. (📞212-243-9323; 59 Grove St, btwn Seventh Ave & Bleecker St, West Village; ⏱4pm-3am Mon-Thu, to 4am Fri & Sat, to midnight Sun; 🚇1 to Christopher St-Sheridan Sq; A/C/E, B/D/F/M to W 4th St-Washington Sq)

Eagle NYC
GAY

26 🚇 MAP P108, B1

A bi-level club full of hot men in leather, the Eagle is the choice for out-and-proud fetishists. Its two levels, plus roof deck, offer plenty of room for dancing and drinking, which are done with abandon. There are frequent theme nights, so make sure to check the website lest you arrive without the appropriate attire (which may be nothing). (📞646-473-1866; www.eaglenyc.com; 554 W 28th St, btwn Tenth & Eleventh Aves, Chelsea; ⏱10pm-4am Mon-Sat, from 5pm Sun; 🚇1, C/E to 23rd St)

Gym Sportsbar
GAY

27 🚇 MAP P108, D3

In the midst of Chelsea's famous gay nightlife scene, Gym Sportsbar offers a low-key vibe for LGBTQ patrons. There are friendly bartenders, cheap drinks, a pool table in the back, a smoking patio out front and TVs throughout the bar playing whatever sport is in season. Weekday happy hour offers two-for-one drinks. (📞212-337-2439; www.gymsportsbar.com; 167 8th Ave; drinks from $7; ⏱4pm-2am Mon-Fri, 2pm-2am Sat & Sun; 🚇A/C/E, L to 8th Ave-14th St)

Cielo
CLUB

28 🚇 MAP P108, C4

This long-running club boasts a largely attitude-free crowd and an excellent sound system. Join dance lovers on TOCA Tuesdays,

Go West, Young Man

Most of the West Village isn't served by any subway lines, and the L train goes only as far as Eighth Ave, so if you want to access the westernmost areas of Chelsea and the West Village by public transportation, try the M14 or the M8 bus. It's a shame, however, to use the bus or a taxi to get around the West Village – the charming cobblestone streets are perfect for a stroll.

when DJ Tony Touch spins classic hip-hop, soul and funk. Other nights feature various DJs from Europe, who mix entrancing, seductive sounds that pull everyone to their feet. (📞212-645-5700; www.cieloclub.com; 18 Little W 12th St, btwn Ninth Ave & Washington St, Meatpacking District; cover $15-25; Ⓢ A/C/E, L to 8th Ave-14th St)

Bathtub Gin   COCKTAIL BAR

29 🚌 MAP P108, C3

Amid New York City's obsession with speakeasy-styled hangouts, Bathtub Gin manages to poke its head above the crowd with its super-secret front door hidden on the wall of the Stone Street Coffee Shop (look for the woman in the bathtub). Once inside, chill seating, soft background beats and kindly staff make it a great place to sling back bespoke cocktails with friends. (📞646-559-1671; www.bathtubginnyc.com; 132 Ninth Ave, btwn W 18th & 19th Sts, Chelsea; ⏰5pm-2am Mon-Wed, to 4am Thu & Fri, 11:30am-3:30pm & 5pm-4am Sat, to 2am Sun; Ⓢ A/C/E, L to 8th Ave-14th St; 1, C/E to 23rd St; 1 to 18th St)

Henrietta Hudson   LESBIAN

30 🚌 MAP P108, D6

All sorts of young women, many from neighboring New Jersey and Long Island, storm this sleek lounge, where varying theme nights bring in spirited DJs, who stick to particular genres (hip-hop, house, rock). The owner, Brooklyn native Lisa Canistraci, is a favorite promoter in the world of lesbian nightlife, and is often on hand to mix it up with her fans. (📞212-924-3347; www.henriettahudson.com; 438 Hudson St; ⏰4pm-4am; Ⓢ1 to Houston St)

Aria   WINE BAR

31 🚌 MAP P108, D5

In the western reaches of the Village, Aria is an inviting music-filled space, with a mix of brick and tile walls and rustic wood tables. There's a good selection of wines by the glass, particularly organic labels, with prices starting around $8 a (small) glass. Recommended *cicchetti* (bite-sized plates, good for sharing) include Gorgonzola-stuffed dates, crab cakes and stewed calamari. (📞212-242-4233; www.ariawinebar.com; 117 Perry St, btwn Greenwich & Hudson Sts, West Village; ⏰11:30am-10pm Sun-Thu, 11am-11pm Fri & Sat; Ⓢ1 to Christopher St-Sheridan Sq)

Stumptown Coffee Roasters

COFFEE

32 MAP P108, F5

This renowned Portland roaster is helping to reinvent the NYC coffee scene with its exquisitely made brews. It has an elegant interior with coffered ceiling and walnut bar, though its few tables are often overtaken by the laptop-toting crowd. (☎855-711-3385; www. stumptowncoffee.com; 30 W 8th St, at MacDougal St, West Village; ⏰7am-8pm; ⑤A/C/E, B/D/F/M to W 4th St-Washington Sq)

124 Old Rabbit Club

BAR

33 MAP P108, F6

You'll wanna pat yourself on the back when you find this well-concealed bar (hint: look for the tiny word 'Rabbit' over the door). Once you're inside the narrow, cavern-like space with its low-key vibe, grab a seat at the dimly lit bar and reward yourself with a quenching stout or one of the dozens of imported beers. (☎212-254-0575; www.rabbitclubnyc.com; 124 MacDougal St, at Minetta Ln, West Village; ⏰6pm-2am Mon-Wed, to 4am Thu-Sat, to midnight Sun; ⑤A/C/E, B/D/F/M to W 4th St-Washington Sq; 1 to Houston St)

Blue Bottle

CAFE

34 MAP P108, C3

Blue Bottle may have originated in Oakland, but New Yorkers have happily embraced this high-quality third-wave roaster. Blue Bottle's small outpost across from the Chelsea Market uses scales and thermometers to make sure your pour over or espresso is perfect. Grab one of the few window seats, or head to one of the mezzanine tables above the baristas. (www. bluebottlecoffee.com; 450 W 15th St, btwn 9th & 10th Aves, Chelsea; ⏰7am-6pm Mon-Fri, from 8am Sat & Sun; ⑤A/C/E, L to 8th Ave-14th St)

Highlands

BAR

35 MAP P108, G2

This handsome Scottish-inspired drinkery is a fine place to while away an evening. Exposed brick, a fireplace and a mix of animal heads, pheasant wallpaper, oil paintings and Edinburgh tartans on the walls bring in more than a touch of the old country. Scottish beers and spirits, plus haggis, scotch eggs, shepherd's pie and other traditional bites round out the menu. (☎212-229-2670; www. highlands-nyc.com; 150 W 10th St, near Waverly Pl, West Village; ⏰5pm-1am Mon-Wed, to 2am Thu, to 3am Fri & Sat, 4pm-midnight Sun; ⑤1 to Christopher St-Sheridan Sq; A/C/E, B/D/F/M to W 4th St-Washington Sq)

Stonewall Inn

LGBT

36 MAP P108, G2

Site of the Stonewall riots in 1969, this bar, considered almost a pilgrimage site because of its historic significance, pulls in varied crowds for nightly parties catering to everyone under the LGBTIQ+ rainbow. It's far from trendy and more a welcoming, ordinary watering hole that otherwise might be overlooked. (📞212-488-2705; www.thestonewallinnnyc.com; 53 Christopher St; ⏰2pm-4am; §1 to Christopher St-Sheridan Sq)

Entertainment

Sleep No More   THEATER

37 ⭐ MAP P108, B1

One of the most immersive theater experiences ever conceived, *Sleep No More* is a loosely based retelling of *Macbeth* set inside a series of Chelsea warehouses that have been redesigned to look like the 1930s-era McKittrick Hotel and its hopping jazz bar. (📞866-811-4111; www.sleepnomorenyc.com; 530 W 27th St, btwn Tenth & Eleventh Aves, Chelsea; tickets from $105;

⏰7pm-midnight Mon-Sat; §1, C/E to 23rd St)

Smalls   JAZZ

38 ⭐ MAP P108, F2

Living up to its name, this cramped but appealing basement jazz den offers a grab-bag collection of jazz acts who take the stage nightly. Admission includes a come-and-go policy if you need to duck out for a bite. There is an afternoon jam session on Saturday and Sunday that's not to be missed. (📞646-476-4346; www.smallslive. com; 183 W 10th St, btwn W 4th St & Seventh Ave S, West Village; cover $20; ⏰7:05pm-3:30am Mon-Fri, from 4pm Sat & Sun; §1 to Christopher St-Sheridan Sq; A/C/E, B/D/F/M W 4th St-Washington Sq)

Stumptown Coffee Roasters

West Village, Chelsea & the Meatpacking District Entertainment

Queer New York

NYC – and the West Village area in particular – is out and proud. It was here that the Stonewall Riots took place, the modern gay rights movement bloomed and America's first Pride march hit the streets.

Before Stonewall
In the early 20th century a number of gay-owned businesses lined MacDougal St, Greenwich Village, among them the legendary Eve's Hangout at number 129, which was famous for two things: poetry readings and a sign on the door that read 'Men are admitted but not welcome.' The relative free-thinking of the era was replaced with a new conservatism in the following decades: tougher policing aimed to eradicate queer visibility in the public sphere, forcing the scene underground in the 1940s and '50s. Though crackdowns on gay venues had always occurred, they became increasingly common.

The Stonewall Revolution
On June 28, 1969, eight police officers raided the Stonewall Inn, a gay-friendly watering hole in Greenwich Village. Patrons did the unthinkable: they revolted. Fed up with harassment, they bombarded the officers with coins, bottles, bricks and chants of 'gay power' and 'we shall overcome.' Their collective anger and solidarity was a turning point, igniting intense and passionate debate about discrimination and forming the catalyst for the modern gay rights movement, not just in New York, but across the US and the world.

Marriage & the New Millennium
The fight for complete equality took two massive steps forward in 2011. A federal law banning LGBT military personnel from serving openly – the so-called 'Don't Ask, Don't Tell' policy – was repealed after years of intense lobbying. Also in 2011, persistence led to an even greater victory – the right to marry. The New York State Assembly passed the Marriage Equality Act, and it was signed into law on June 24, the very eve of New York City Gay Pride. State victory became a national one on June 26, 2015, when the US Supreme Court ruled that same-sex marriage is a legal right across the country, striking down the remaining marriage bans in 13 US states.

Village Vanguard

JAZZ

39 ⭐ MAP P108, F1

Possibly the city's most prestigious jazz club, the Vanguard has hosted literally every major star of the past 50 years. It started as a home to spoken-word performances and occasionally returns to its roots, but most of the time it's just big, bold jazz all night long. (☏212-255-4037; www.villagevanguard.com; 178 Seventh Ave S, at W 11th St, West Village; cover around $33; ⏰7:30pm-12:30am; Ⓢ A/C/E, L to 8th Ave-14th St; 1/2/3 to 14th St)

IFC Center

CINEMA

40 ⭐ MAP P108, H3

This art-house cinema in NYU-land has a solidly curated lineup of new indies, cult classics and foreign films. Catch shorts, documentaries, '80s revivals, director-focused series, weekend classics and frequent special series, such as cult favorites *(The Shining, Taxi Driver, Aliens)* at midnight. (☏212-924-7771; www.ifccenter.com; 323 Sixth Ave, at W 3rd St, West Village; tickets $15; 📶; Ⓢ A/C/E, B/D/F/M to W 4th St-Washington Sq)

Le Poisson Rouge

LIVE MUSIC

41 ⭐ MAP P108, F6

This high-concept art space hosts an eclectic lineup of live music, with the likes of Deerhunter, Marc Ribot and Yo La Tengo performing in past years. There's a lot of experimentation and cross-genre pollination between classical, folk music, opera and more. (☏212-505-3474; www.lepoissonrouge.com; 158 Bleecker St, btwn Sullivan & Thompson Sts, West Village; Ⓢ A/C/E, B/D/F/M to W 4th St-Washington Sq)

Atlantic Theater Company

THEATER

42 ⭐ MAP P108, D2

Founded by David Mamet and William H Macy in 1985, the Atlantic Theater is a pivotal anchor for the

Village Vanguard

off-Broadway community, hosting many Tony Award and Drama Desk winners over the last three decades. (📞212-691-5919; www.atlantictheater.org; 336 W 20th St, btwn Eighth & Ninth Aves, Chelsea; **S**1, C/E to 23rd St; 1 to 18th St)

Duplex
CABARET

43 ⭐ MAP P108, G2

Cabaret, karaoke and campy dance moves are par for the course at the legendary Duplex. Pictures of Joan Rivers line the walls, and the performers like to mimic her sassy form of self-deprecation while getting in a few jokes about audience members as well. It's a fun and unpretentious place, and certainly not for the bashful. (📞212-255-5438; www.theduplex.com; 61 Christopher St, at Seventh Ave S, West Village; cover $10-25; ⏰4pm-4am; **S**1 to Christopher St-Sheridan Sq; A/C/E, B/D/F/M to W 4th St-Washington Sq)

Cherry Lane Theater
THEATER

44 ⭐ MAP P108, E6

A theater with a distinctive charm hidden in the West Village, Cherry Lane has a long and distinguished history. Started by poet Edna St Vincent Millay, it has given a voice to numerous playwrights and actors over the years, remaining true to its mission of creating 'live' theater that's accessible to the public. Readings, plays and spoken-word performances rotate frequently. (📞212-989-2020; www.cherrylanetheater.org; 38 Commerce St, off Bedford St, West Village; **S**1 to Christopher St-Sheridan Sq)

Joyce Theater

Joyce Theater

DANCE

45 ⭐ MAP P108, D3

A favorite among dance junkies thanks to its excellent sight lines and offbeat offerings, this is an intimate venue, seating 472 in a renovated cinema. Its focus is on traditional modern companies, such as Martha Graham and Parsons Dance, as well as global stars, such as Dance Brazil, Ballet Hispanico and MalPaso Dance Company. (📞212-691-9740; www.joyce.org; 175 Eighth Ave, at W 19th St, Chelsea; S1 to 18th St; 1, C/E to 23rd St; A/C/E, L to 8th Ave-14th St)

55 Bar

LIVE MUSIC

46 ⭐ MAP P108, G2

Dating back to the Prohibition era, this friendly basement dive is great for low-key shows without high covers or dressing up. There are regular performances twice nightly by quality artists-in-residence, some blues bands and Miles Davis' super '80s guitarist Mike Stern. There's a two-drink minimum. (📞212-929-9883; www.55bar.com; 55 Christopher St, at Seventh Ave, West Village; cover $10; ⏰1pm-4am; S1 to Christopher St-Sheridan Sq)

Comedy Cellar

COMEDY

47 ⭐ MAP P108, F6

This long-established basement comedy club in Greenwich Village features mainstream material and a good list of regulars (Colin Quinn, Judah Friedlander, Wanda Sykes), plus occasional high-profile drop-ins like Dave Chappelle, Jerry Seinfeld and Amy Schumer. Its success continues: Comedy Cellar now boasts another location at the Village Underground around the corner on W 3rd St. (📞212-254-3480; www.comedycellar.com; 117 MacDougal St, btwn W 3rd St & Minetta Ln, West Village; cover $8-24; SA/C/E, B/D/F/M to W 4th St-Washington Sq)

Shopping

Screaming Mimi's

VINTAGE

48 🔒 MAP P108, D4

If you dig vintage threads, you may just scream, too. This funtastic shop carries an excellent selection of yesteryear pieces, organized – ingeniously – by decade, from the '50s to the '90s. (Ask to see the small, stashed-away collection of clothing from the 1920s through '40s.) (📞212-677-6464; www.screamingmimis.com; 240 W 14th St, btwn Seventh & Eighth Aves, Chelsea; ⏰noon-8pm Mon-Sat, 1-7pm Sun; SA/C/E, L to 8th Ave-14th St)

Beacon's Closet

VINTAGE

49 🔒 MAP P108, F4

You'll find a good selection of gently used clothing (which is of a decidedly downtown/Brooklyn hipster aesthetic) at only slightly higher prices than Beacon's sister store in Williamsburg. Thrift shops are thin on the ground in this area, which makes Beacon's even more of a draw. Come midweek or be prepared to brave the crowds. (📞917-261-4863; www.beaconscloset.

West Village Navigation

It's perfectly acceptable to arm yourself with a map (or rely on your smartphone) to get around the West Village's charming-but-challenging side streets. Even some locals have a tricky time finding their way! Just remember that 4th St makes a diagonal turn north – breaking away from usual east–west street grid – and you'll quickly become a Village pro.

com; 10 W 13th St, btwn Fifth & Sixth Aves, West Village; ⏰11am-8pm; Ⓢ L, N/Q/R/W, 4/5/6 to 14th St-Union Sq)

Story
GIFTS & SOUVENIRS

50 🔒 MAP P108, C3

This high-concept shop near the High Line functions like a gallery, showcasing new themes and products every month or two. The 2000-sq-ft space covers all the bases, from crafty jewelry and eye-catching accessories to lovely stationery, imagination-inspiring toys for kids, thick coffee-table books, environmentally-friendly soaps and whimsical souvenirs. (www.thisisstory.com; 144 Tenth Ave, btwn W 18th & 19th Sts, Chelsea; ⏰11am-8pm Mon-Wed, Fri & Sat, to 9pm Thu, to 7pm Sun; Ⓢ1, C/E to 23rd St; 1 to 18th St)

Idlewild Books
BOOKS

51 🔒 MAP P108, F1

Named after JFK airport's original moniker, this indie travel bookstore

gets feet seriously itchy. Books are divided by region and cover guidebooks as well as fiction, travelogues, history, cookbooks and other stimulating fare for delving into different corners of the world. The store also runs popular language classes in French, Italian, Spanish and German; see the website for details. (📞212-414-8888; www.idlewildbooks.com; 170 Seventh Ave S, at Perry St, West Village; ⏰noon-8pm Mon-Thu, to 6pm Fri-Sun; Ⓢ1 to Christopher St-Sheridan Sq; 1/2/3 to 14th St; A/C/E, L to 8th Ave-14th St)

Personnel of New York
FASHION & ACCESSORIES

52 🔒 MAP P108, G1

This small, delightful indie shop sells women's designer clothing from unique labels from the East and West Coasts and beyond. Look for easy-to-wear Sunja Link dresses, soft pullover sweaters by Ali Golden, statement-making jewelry by Marisa Mason, comfy canvas sneakers by Shoes Like Pottery and couture pieces by Rodebjer. (📞212-924-0604; www.personnelofnewyork.com; 9 Greenwich Ave, btwn Christopher & W 10th Sts, West Village; ⏰noon-7:30pm Mon-Sat, to 6pm Sun; Ⓢ A/C/E, B/D/F/M to W 4th St-Washington Sq; 1 to Christopher St-Sheridan Sq)

Printed Matter
BOOKS

53 🔒 MAP P108, B1

Printed Matter is a wondrous little shop dedicated to limited-edition artist monographs and strange little zines. Here you will find nothing carried by mainstream bookstores; instead, trim shelves hide call-to-arms manifestos, critical essays about comic books, flip books that reveal Jesus' face through barcodes and how-to guides written by prisoners. (📞212-925-0325; www.printedmatter.org; 231 Eleventh Ave, btwn 25th & 26th Sts, Chelsea; ⏰11am-7pm Sat & Mon-Wed, to 8pm Thu & Fri, to 6pm Sun; Ⓢ7 to 34th St-Hudson Yards; 1 to 28th St)

Murray's Cheese   FOOD & DRINKS

54 🅰 MAP P108, E6

Founded in 1914, this is one of New York's best cheese shops. Owner Rob Kaufelt is known for his talent for sniffing out devastatingly delicious varieties from around the world. You'll find (and be able to taste) all manner of *fromage*, be it stinky, sweet or nutty, from European nations and small farms in Vermont and upstate New York. (📞212-243-3289; www.murrayscheese.com; 254 Bleecker St, btwn Morton & Leroy Sts, West Village; ⏰8am-9pm Mon-Sat, 9am-8pm Sun; Ⓢ1 to Christopher St-Sheridan Sq; A/C/E, B/D/F/M to W 4th St-Washington Sq)

Housing Works Thrift Shop   VINTAGE

55 🅰 MAP P108, E3

With its swank window displays, this shop looks more boutique than thrift, but its selections of clothes, accessories, furniture, books and records are great value. It's the place to go to find

Beacon's Closet (p125)

discarded designer clothes for a bargain. All proceeds benefit the charity serving the city's HIV-positive and AIDS homeless communities. There are 13 other branches around town. (📞718-838-5050; www.housingworks.org; 143 W 17th St, btwn Sixth & Seventh Aves, Chelsea; ⏰10am-7pm Mon-Sat, 11am-5pm Sun; 🚇1 to 18th St)

Aedes de Venustas   COSMETICS

56 🏠 MAP P108, G2

Plush and inviting, Aedes de Venustas ('Temple of Beauty' in Latin) provides more than 40 brands of luxury European perfumes, including Hierbas de Ibiza, Mark Birley for Men, Costes, Odin and Shalini. It also stocks skincare products created by

Susanne Kaufmann and Acqua di Rose, and everyone's favorite scented candles from Diptyque (p191). (📞212-206-8674; www.aedes. com; 7 Greenwich Ave, at Christopher St, West Village; ⏰noon-8pm Mon-Sat, 1-7pm Sun; 🚇A/C/E, B/D/F/M to W 4th St-Washington Sq; 1 to Christopher St-Sheridan Sq)

Forbidden Planet   BOOKS

57 🏠 MAP P108, G4

Indulge your inner sci-fi and fantasy nerd with heaps of comics, manga, graphic novels, posters and toys. The products represent everything from *Star Wars* and *Doctor Who* to the latest indie sensations. Stop in, or check the website for upcoming book signings and other events. (📞212-473-1576;

Murray's Cheese (p127)

PETER HORREE/ALAMY STOCK PHOTO ©

www.fpnyc.com; 832 Broadway, btwn E 12th & 13th Sts, West Village; ⏰9am-10pm Mon-Tue, 8am-midnight Wed, from 9am Thu-Sat, 10am-10pm Mon; Ⓢ L, N/Q/R/W, 4/5/6 to 14th St-Union Sq)

Monocle FASHION & ACCESSORIES

58 🔒 MAP P108, D5

Tyler Brûlé, the man behind one of the great magazines of the 21st century, founded this tiny bento-box-sized shop in 2010, featuring stylish, well-made products for both the urbanite and the global traveler. Stock includes leather-bound journals, elegant stationary, Japanese body soaps, passport holders and swimming trunks. (☏212-229-1120; www.monocle.com/shop; 535 Hudson St, at Charles St, West Village; ⏰11am-7pm Mon-Sat, noon-6pm Sun; Ⓢ1 to Christopher St-Sheridan Sq)

Trina Turk CLOTHING

59 🔒 MAP P108, C4

Anyone with a yen for '70s-inspired prints should take themselves to the Trina Turk boutique. The wife and husband team behind the unisex brand have cultivated a range that harkens back to the vibrant heyday of California cool with shift dresses, floral blazers, statement pants, and swimsuits that range from board shorts to ultra-skimpy briefs. (☏212-206-7383; www.trinaturk.com; 67 Gansevoort St, btwn Greenwich

& Washington Sts, West Village; ⏰11am-7pm Mon-Sat, noon-6pm Sun; Ⓢ A/C/E, L to 8th Ave-14th St)

Greenwich Letterpress GIFTS & SOUVENIRS

60 🔒 MAP P108, G2

Founded by two sisters, this cute card shop specializes in wedding announcements and other specially made letterpress endeavors, so skip the stock postcards of the Empire State Building and send your loved ones a bespoke greeting card from this stalwart stationer. (☏212-989-7464; www.greenwichletterpress.com; 15 Christopher St, at Gay St, West Village; ⏰noon-6pm Sat-Mon, 11am-7pm Tue-Fri; Ⓢ1 to Christopher St-Sheridan Sq; A/C/E, B/D/F/M to W 4th St; 1/2/3 to 14th St)

CO Bigelow Chemists COSMETICS

61 🔒 MAP P108, H2

The 'oldest apothecary in America' is a favorite among New Yorkers and a convenient spot to grab upscale lotions and face masks, organic soaps and bath bombs, and basic toiletries. It's a fun place to test high-end products before you grab a tube of toothpaste. (☏212-533-2700; 414 Sixth Ave, btwn 8th & 9th Sts, West Village; ⏰7:30am-9pm Mon-Fri, 8:30am-7pm Sat, 8:30am-5:30pm Sun; Ⓢ1 to Christopher St-Sheridan Sq; A/C/E, B/D/F/M to W 4th St-Washington Sq)

Explore ◉

Union Square, Flatiron District & Gramercy

The bustling heart of this area is Union Square, with a mix of skateboarders, chess champs and New Yorkers of all stripes meeting for lunch. The triangular Flatiron Building and the verdant respite of Madison Square Park are to the northwest. Gramercy Park, a romantic private oasis, offers a subdued residential area to roam.

Fuel up with a huge omelette at Big Daddy's (p138), then spend the morning browsing the Greenmarket (p143), the best of its kind in NYC. Duck into DSW (p145) for a bit of shopping, or just grab a seat in the park and people-watch. Walk up Broadway, ducking into shops like ABC Carpet & Home (p143) and Fishs Eddy (p144). When you get to 23rd St, take some time to admire the Flatiron Building (p134), then consider a late-afternoon beer at Birreria (p139). Book a table at Clocktower (p137), Craft (p135) or Gramercy Tavern (p135) for a splurge-worthy meal; for something more wallet-friendly, head to Boqueria Flatiron (p137). Catch some live music at Irving Plaza (p143) or knock back a drink at the old-timey Old Town Bar (p139).

Getting There & Around

S A slew of subway lines converge below Union Square: the 4/5/6 lines to the Upper East, the L to 8th Ave or Williamsburg, and the N/Q/R lines to Queens and Brooklyn. Take the Q for an express link to Herald Sq and Times Sq.

🚌 The M14A and M14D provide cross-town services along 14th St, while the M23 runs cross-town along 23rd St.

Neighborhood Map on p132

Flatiron Building (p134) TONY SHI PHOTOGRAPHY/GETTY IMAGES©

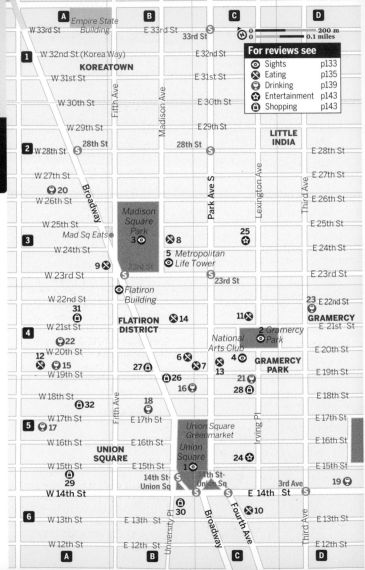

A Empire State Building

W 33rd St
E 33rd St
33rd St **S**

1 W 32nd St (Korea Way)
KOREATOWN
E 32nd St

W 31st St
E 31st St

W 30th St
E 30th St

W 29th St
E 29th St

Fifth Ave

Madison Ave

W 28th St
28th St **S**
28th St **S**
LITTLE INDIA
E 28th St

2 W 28th St **S**

W 27th St
E 27th St

W 26th St
20
E 26th St

Broadway

Park Ave S

Lexington Ave

Third Ave

W 25th St
E 25th St

Mad Sq Eats
Madison Square Park **3**
8
25
E 24th St

3 W 24th St

9
5 Metropolitan Life Tower
E 23rd St

W 23rd St
23rd St **S**
23rd St **S**

Flatiron Building

W 22nd St
23 E 22nd St

31
11
GRAMERCY

4 W 21st St
FLATIRON DISTRICT
14
E 21st St

2 Gramercy Park

22
National Arts Club
4
GRAMERCY PARK
E 20th St

12 W 20th St
6
13

15 W 19th St
27
7
21
E 19th St

26
16
28
E 18th St

32 W 18th St

18
E 17th St

5 W 17th St
17

Fifth Ave

University Pl

Irving Pl

Union Square Greenmarket

W 16th St
E 16th St

UNION SQUARE
Union Square
24
E 15th St

W 15th St
E 15th St

29
14th St-Union Sq
1
14th St-Union Sq **S**
3rd Ave
19

30
E 14th St **S**

6 W 13th St
E 13th St
10
E 13th St

W 12th St
E 12th St
E 12th St

For reviews see

⊙ Sights	p133
✕ Eating	p135
⊖ Drinking	p139
✪ Entertainment	p143
🔒 Shopping	p143

0 — 200 m
0 — 0.1 miles

Sights

Union Square

SQUARE

1 ◉ MAP P132, B5

Union Square is like the Noah's Ark of New York, rescuing at least two of every kind from the curling seas of concrete. In fact, one would be hard pressed to find a more eclectic cross-section of locals gathered in one public place: suited businessfolk gulping fresh air during their lunch breaks, dreadlocked loiterers tapping beats on their tabla, skateboarders flipping tricks on the south-eastern stairs, rowdy college kids guzzling student-priced eats, and throngs of protesting masses chanting fervently for various causes. (www.unionsquarenyc.org; 17th St, btwn Broadway & Park Ave S, Union Square; Ⓢ 4/5/6, N/Q/R, L to 14th St-Union Sq)

Gramercy Park

PARK

2 ◉ MAP P132, C4

Romantic Gramercy Park was created by Samuel Ruggles in 1831 after he drained the area's swamp and laid out streets in an English style. You can't enter the private park (the only one in Manhattan), but peer through the gate and imagine tough guy James Cagney enjoying it – the Hollywood actor once resided at 34 Gramercy Park E. At 15 Gramercy Park S stands the National Arts Club (p133), whose members include Martin Scorsese, Uma Thurman and

Ethan Hawke. (E 20th St, btwn Park & Third Aves, Gramercy; Ⓢ N/R, 6 to 23rd St)

Madison Square Park

PARK

3 ◉ MAP P132, B3

This park defined the northern reaches of Manhattan until the island's population exploded after the Civil War. These days it's a much-welcome oasis from Manhattan's relentless pace, with a popular children's playground, dog-run area and the **Shake Shack** (⏎ 646-889-6600; www.shakeshack.com; cnr E 23rd St & Madison Ave; burgers $4.20-9.50; ⏱ 7:30am-11pm Mon-Fri, from 8:30am Sat & Sun) burger joint. It's also one of the city's most cultured parks, with specially commissioned art installations and (in the warmer months) activities ranging from literary discussions to live-music gigs. See the website for more information. (⏎ 212-520-7600; www.madisonsquarepark.org; E 23rd to 26th Sts, btwn Fifth & Madison Aves, Flatiron District; ⏱ 6am-11pm; ⏯; Ⓢ R/W, F/M, 6 to 23rd St)

National Arts Club

CULTURAL CENTER

4 ◉ MAP P132, C4

Founded in 1898 to promote public interest in the arts, the National Arts Club holds art exhibitions, usually open to the public from 10am to 5pm Monday to Friday (check the website for upcoming shows). Calvert Vaux – one

The Flatiron Building

Designed by Daniel Burnham and built in 1920, the 20-story **Flatiron Building** (See map p132, B4; Broadway, cnr Fifth Ave & 23rd St; N/R, F/M, 6 to 23rd St) has a uniquely narrow triangular footprint that resembles the prow of a massive ship. It also features a traditional beaux-arts limestone and terra-cotta facade, built over a steel frame, that gets more complex and beautiful the longer you stare at it. Best viewed from the traffic island north of 23rd St between Broadway and Fifth Ave, this unique structure dominated the plaza back in the dawning skyscraper era of the early 1900s. The construction coincided with the proliferation of mass-produced picture postcards – the partnership was kismet. Even before its completion, images of the soon-to-be tallest tower circulated the globe, creating much wonder and excitement.

Publisher Frank Munsey was one of the building's first tenants. From his 18th-floor offices he published *Munsey's Magazine*, featuring the work of writer O Henry (known for his story 'The Gift of the Magi'), the paintings of John Sloan and photographs of Alfred Stieglitz, which best immortalized the Flatiron back in the day. Actress Katharine Hepburn once quipped that she'd like to be admired as much as the grand old building.

Future plans to transform the Flatiron into a five-star hotel are on hold until the final business tenants willingly vacate. In the meantime, the ground floor of the building's 'prow' has been transformed into a glassed-in art space. Past installations have included a life-size 3D-cutout replica of Edward Hopper's 1942 painting *Nighthawks,* its angular diner remarkably similar to the Flatiron's distinctive shape.

of the creators of Central Park – designed the building itself, its picture-lined front parlor adorned with a beautiful, vaulted stained-glass ceiling. The place was once home to Samuel J Tilden, a former New York governor, and failed presidential candidate in 1876. (212-475-3424; www.nationalartsclub.org; 15 Gramercy Park S, Gramercy; drawing classes $15-25; N/R, 6 to 23rd St)

Metropolitan Life Tower
HISTORIC BUILDING

5 MAP P132, B3

Completed in 1909, this 700ft-high clock tower soaring above Madison Square Park's southeastern corner is the work of Napoleon LeBrun, a Philadelphia-born architect of French stock. Italophiles may feel a certain déjà vu gazing at the tower. After all,

LeBrun's inspiration was Venice's world-famous *campanile* (bell tower) in Piazza San Marco. Ironically, LeBrun's New World version is now older than its muse: the original Venetian tower collapsed in 1902, with its replacement not completed until 1912. Despite being upstaged by taller Manhattan skyscrapers these days, the 41-level building remains one of the largest four-dial timepieces in the world, each of its four clock faces measuring a big-is-better 26.5ft in diameter. (1 Madison Ave, btwn E 23rd & E 24th Sts, Flatiron District; 🚇N/R, F/M, 6 to 23rd St)

Eating

Gramercy Tavern   MODERN AMERICAN $$$

6 🍴 MAP P132, B4

Seasonal, local ingredients drive this perennial favorite, a vibrant, country-chic institution aglow with copper sconces, murals and dramatic floral arrangements. Choose from two spaces: the walk-in-only tavern and its à la carte menu, or the swankier dining room and its fancier prix-fixe and degustation feasts. Tavern highlights include a showstopping duck meatloaf with mushrooms, chestnuts and brussels sprouts. (📞212-477-0777; www.gramercytavern.com; 42 E 20th St, btwn Broadway & Park Ave S, Flatiron District; tavern mains $29-36, dining room 3-course menu $125, tasting menus $149-179; ⏱tavern noon-11pm Sun-Thu, to midnight Fri & Sat, dining room noon-2pm & 5:30-10pm Mon-Thu,

to 11pm Fri, noon-1:30pm & 5:30-11pm Sat, 5:30-10pm Sun; 🛜🍸; 🚇R/W, 6 to 23rd St)

Craft   MODERN AMERICAN $$$

7 🍴 MAP P132, C4

Humming, high-end Craft flies the flag for small, family-owned farms and food producers, their bounty transformed into pure, polished dishes. Whether nibbling on flawlessly charred braised octopus, pillowy scallops or pumpkin mezzaluna pasta with sage, brown butter and Parmesan, expect every ingredient to sing with flavor. Book ahead Wednesday to Saturday or head in by 6pm or after 9:30pm. (📞212-780-0880; www.craftrestaurant.com; 43 E 19th St, btwn Broadway & Park Ave S, Union Square; lunch $29-36, dinner mains $24-55; ⏱noon-2:30pm & 5:30-10pm Mon-Thu, to 11pm Fri, 5:30-11pm Sat, to 9pm Sun; 🛜; 🚇4/5/6, N/Q/R/W, L to 14th St-Union Sq)

Eleven Madison Park   MODERN AMERICAN $$$

8 🍴 MAP P132, B3

Fine-dining Eleven Madison Park came in at number one in the 2017 San Pellegrino World's 50 Best Restaurants list. Frankly, we're not surprised: this revamped poster child of modern, sustainable American cooking is also one of only six NYC restaurants sporting three Michelin stars. (📞212-889-0905; www.elevenmadisonpark.com; 11 Madison Ave, btwn 24th & 25th Sts, Flatiron District; tasting menu $295;

Mad About Eating 🍽

Each spring and fall, foodies flock to tiny General Worth Sq – wedged between Fifth Ave and Broadway, opposite Madison Square Park – for **Mad Sq Eats** (Map p132, B3; www.madisonsquarepark.org/mad-sq-food/mad-sq-eats; General Worth Sq, Flatiron District; ⏱spring & fall 11am-9pm; S R/W, F/M, 6 to 23rd St), a month-long culinary pop-up market. Its 30 or so vendors include some of the city's hottest eateries, cooking up anything from proper pizza to brisket tacos using top local produce.

⏱5:30-10pm Mon-Wed, to 10:30pm Thu-Sun, also noon-1pm Fri-Sun; S R/W, 6 to 23rd St)

Eataly   FOOD HALL $$

9 ❌ MAP P132, A3

Mario Batali's sleek, sprawling temple to Italian gastronomy is a veritable wonderland. Feast on everything from vibrant *crudo* (raw fish) and *fritto misto* (tempura-style vegetables) to steamy pasta and pizza at the emporium's string of sit-down eateries. Alternatively, guzzle espresso at the bar and scour the countless counters and shelves for a DIY picnic hamper *nonna* would approve of. (📞212-229-2560; www.eataly.com; 200 Fifth Ave, at W

23rd St, Flatiron District; ⏱7am-11pm; 📷; S R/W, F/M, 6 to 23rd St)

Dos Toros Taqueria   MEXICAN $

10 ❌ MAP P132, C6

Skip the national Mexican-food chains in favor of this citywide favorite that promises high-quality meats tucked safely in a sea of thick guacamole and refried beans. Lines can be long (so you know it's good) but efficient staffers whip up your Tex-Mex treat in minutes. (📞212-677-7300; www.dostoros.com; 137 Fourth Ave, btwn 13th & 14th Sts, Union Square; burritos from $7.50, quesadillas from $6.20; ⏱11:30am-10:30pm Mon & Sun, to 11pm Tue-Sat; S 4/5/6, N/Q/R, L to 14th St-Union Sq)

Maialino   ITALIAN $$$

11 ❌ MAP P132, C4

Fans reserve tables up to four weeks in advance at this Danny Meyer classic, but the best seats in the house are at the walk-in bar, manned by sociable, knowledge-able staffers. Wherever you're plonked, take your taste buds on a Roman holiday. Maialino's lip-smacking, rustic Italian fare is created using produce from the nearby Union Square Green-market. (📞212-777-2410; www.maialinonyc.com; Gramercy Park Hotel, 2 Lexington Ave, at 21st St; mains lunch $24-34, dinner $27-44; ⏱7:30-10am, noon-2pm & 5:30-10pm Mon-Wed, to 10:30pm Thu, 10am-2pm & 5:30-10:30pm Fri, to 10pm Sat; S 6, R/W to 23rd St)

Boqueria Flatiron

TAPAS $$

12  MAP P132, A4

A holy union between Spanish-style tapas and market-fresh fare, Boqueria woos the after-work crowd with a brilliant lineup of small plates and larger *raciones*. Lick lips and fingers over the likes of garlicky shrimp with brandy and *guindilla* pepper, or bacon-wrapped dates stuffed with almonds and Valdeón blue cheese. A smooth selection of Spanish wines tops it all off. *iBuen provecho!* (📞212-255-4160; www.boquerianyc.com; 53 W 19th St, btwn Fifth & Sixth Aves, Flatiron District; tapas $6-18; ⏰11-10:30pm Sun-Thu, to 11:30pm Fri & Sat; 📶; 🚇1 to 18th St, F/M, R/W to 23rd St)

Clocktower

MODERN BRITISH $$$

Brits do it best at Jason Atherton's clubby, new A-lister, hidden away inside the landmark Metropolitan Life Tower (see 5 ◉ Map p132, B3). This is the latest venture for the Michelin-starred British chef, its wood-and-stucco dining rooms setting a handsome scene for high-end comfort grub like a rack of Colorado lamb with crispy quinoa and a locally sourced duck with a sweet peach salad. (📞212-413-4300; http://theclocktowernyc.com; 5 Madison Ave, btwn 23rd & 24th Sts, Gramercy; dinner mains $25-65; ⏰6:30-10am, 11:30am-3pm & 5:30-10pm Mon & Tue, to 11pm Wed-Fri, dinner 5-11pm Sat, to 10pm Sun; 📶; 🚇F/M, R/W, 6 to 23rd St)

Eatly

Big Daddy's

DINER $

13 MAP P132, C4

Giant, fluffy omelettes, hearty burgers and heaps of tater tots (regular or sweet potato) have made Big Daddy's a top choice for both breakfast and late-night treats. The interior is all Americana kitsch, but unlike some theme restaurants the food doesn't break the bank and actually satisfies. Don't think about leaving without trying one of its gargantuan shakes. (212-477-1500; www.bigdaddysnyc.com; 239 Park Ave S, btwn E 19th & E 20th Sts, Gramercy; mains $13-16; 8am-midnight Mon-Thu, to 5am Fri & Sat, to 11pm Sun; S 6 to 23rd St; 4/5/6, L, N/Q/R/W to 14th St-Union Sq)

Cosme

MEXICAN $$$

14 MAP P132, B4

Mexican gets haute at this slinky, charcoal-hued restaurant, home to chef Enrique Olvera and his innovative takes on south-of-the-border flavors. Subvert culinary stereotypes with the likes of delicate, invigorating scallops with avocado and jicama, a fresh bean salad with a charred cucumber vinaigrette, herb guacamole or Cosme's cult-status duck carnitas. Book ahead or try your luck at the walk-in bar. (212-913-9659; http://cosmenyc.com; 35 E 21st St, btwn Broadway & Park Ave S, Flatiron District; dinner dishes $19-29; noon-2:30pm & 5:30-11pm Mon-Thu, to midnight Fri, 11:30-2:30

Big Daddy's

PATTI MCCONVILLE/ALAMY STOCK PHOTO ©

& 5:30-11pm Sat, to 11pm Sun; 📶;
SR/W, 6 to 23rd St)

Drinking

Flatiron Lounge
COCKTAIL BAR

15 🍷 MAP P132, A4

Head through a dramatic archway
and into a dark, swinging, art
deco–inspired fantasy of lipstick-
red booths, racy jazz tunes and
sassy grown-ups downing seasonal drinks. Cocktails run $14 a
pop, but happy-hour cocktails are
only $10 (4pm to 6pm weekdays).
(📞212-727-7741; www.flatironlounge.
com; 37 W 19th St, btwn Fifth & Sixth
Aves, Flatiron District; 🕐4pm-2am
Mon-Wed, to 3am Thu, to 4am Fri,
5pm-4am Sat; 📶; **S**F/M, R/W, 6 to
23rd St)

Old Town Bar & Restaurant
BAR

16 🍺 MAP P132, B5

It still looks like 1892 in here, with
the mahogany bar, original tile
floors and tin ceilings – the Old
Town is an old-world drinking-
man's classic (and -woman's:
Madonna lit up at the bar here –
when lighting up in bars was still
legal – in her 'Bad Girl' video).
There are cocktails around,
but most come for beers and a
burger (from $11.50). (📞212-
529-6732; www.oldtownbar.com; 45
E 18th St, btwn Broadway & Park Ave
S, Union Square; 🕐11:30am-11:30pm
Mon-Fri, noon-11:30pm Sat, to 10pm
Sun; **S**4/5/6, N/Q/R/W, L to 14th
St-Union Sq)

Birreria
BEER HALL

The crown jewel of Italian food
emporium Eataly (p136) is this
rooftop beer garden (see 9 🍴
Map p132, A3) tucked betwixt the
Flatiron's corporate towers. An
encyclopedic beer menu offers
drinkers some of the best suds
on the planet. If you're hungry,
the signature beer-braised pork
shoulder will pair nicely, or check
out the seasonally changing menu
of the on-site pop-up restaurant
(mains $17 to $37). The sneaky
access elevator is near the
checkouts on the 23rd St side of
the store. (📞212-937-8910; www.
eataly.com; 200 Fifth Ave, at W 23rd
St, Flatiron District; 🕐11:30am-11pm;
SF/M, R/W, 6 to 23rd St)

Raines Law Room
COCKTAIL BAR

17 🍷 MAP P132, A5

A sea of velvet drapes and over-
stuffed leather lounge chairs, the
perfect amount of exposed brick,
expertly crafted cocktails using
meticulously aged spirits – these
folks are as serious as a mort-
gage payment when it comes to
amplified atmosphere. Reservations (recommended) are only
accepted Sunday to Tuesday.
Whatever the night, style up for
a taste of a far more sumptuous
era. (www.raineslawroom.com; 48 W
17th St, btwn Fifth & Sixth Aves, Flatiron District; 🕐5pm-2am Mon-Wed, to
3am Thu-Sat, 7pm-1am Sun; **S**F/M to
14th St, L to 6th Ave, 1 to 18th St)

Union Square Art

A walk around Union Square will reveal a string of whimsical, temporary sculptures. Of the permanent offerings is an imposing equestrian statue of George Washington (one of the first public pieces of art in New York City) and a statue of peacemaker Mahatma Gandhi.

Trumping both on the southeastern side of the square is a massive art installation that either earns confused stares or simply gets overlooked by passersby. A symbolic representation of the passage of time, *Metronome* has two parts – a digital clock with a puzzling display of numbers, and a wandlike apparatus with smoke puffing out of concentric rings.

We'll let you ponder the latter while we give you the skinny on what exactly the winking orange digits denote: the 14 numbers must be split into two groups of seven – the seven from the left tell the current time (hour, minute, second, tenth-of-a-second) and the seven from the right are meant to be read in reverse order; they represent the remaining amount of time in the day.

Lillie's Victorian Establishment

BAR

18 🚇 MAP P132, B5

This is one of those places where the name says it all. Step in and be taken to the era of petticoats and watch fobs with high, stamped-tin ceilings, red-velvet love seats and walls covered in vintage photographs in extravagant gilded frames. The food and cocktail list is decidedly modern, but the ambience is enough to fulfill the fantasy. (📞212-337-1970; www.lilliesnyc.com; 13 E 17th St, btwn Broadway & Fifth Ave, Union Square; ⏰11am-4am; 🚇4/5/6, L, N/Q/R/W to 14th St-Union Sq)

Beauty Bar

BAR

19 🚇 MAP P132, D6

A kitschy favorite since the mid-'90s, this homage to old-fashioned beauty parlors pulls in a cool local crowd with its retro soundtrack, nostalgic vibe and $10 manicures (with a free Blue Rinse margarita thrown in) from 6pm to 11pm on weekdays, and 3pm to 11pm on weekends. Nightly events range from comedy to burlesque. (📞212-539-1389; www.thebeautybar.com/home-new-york; 231 E 14th St, btwn Second & Third Aves, Union Square; ⏰5pm-4am Mon-Fri, from 2pm Sat & Sun; 🚇L to 3rd Ave)

Flatiron Room
COCKTAIL BAR

20 MAP P132, A2

Vintage wallpaper, a glittering chandelier and hand-painted coffered ceilings make for a suitably elegant scene at this grown-up drinking den, its artfully lit cabinets graced with rare whiskeys. Fine cocktails pair nicely with high-end sharing plates, from citrus-marinated olive tapenade to flatbread with *guanciale* (cured pork jowl) and fig. Most nights also feature live music, including bluegrass and jazz. Reservations are highly recommended. (212-725-3860; www.theflatironroom.com; 37 W 26th St, btwn Sixth Ave & Broadway, Flatiron District; 4pm-2am Mon-Fri, 5pm-2am Sat, to midnight Sun; S R/W to 28th St, F/M to 23rd St)

Irving Farm Roasters
CAFE

21 MAP P132, C5

From keyboard-tapping scribes to gossiping friends and academics, this bustling cafe is never short of a crowd. Hand-picked beans are lovingly roasted on a farm in the Hudson Valley (about 90 miles from NYC), and served alongside tasty edibles like Balthazar-baked croissants, granola, egg dishes, bagels and pressed sandwiches. The large crowds make it a better spot to grab and go or chat with friends rather than sit and read or get work done. (212-995-5252; www.irvingfarm.com; 71 Irving Pl, btwn 18th & 19th Sts, Gramercy; 7am-8pm Mon-Fri, from 8am Sat & Sun; S 4/5/6, N/Q/R/W, L to 14th St-Union Sq)

Union Square

Union Square, Flatiron District & Gramercy Drinking

Boxers NYC

GAY

22 MAP P132, A4

The beers and potential new buds are plentiful at this gay sports bar in the heart of the Flatiron District. There's football on TV, buffalo wings at the bar, and topless wait staff keeping the pool cues polished. And in case you think Boxers is all brawn, think again: Tuesday's popular Trivia Night gives brains a good, hard workout. While there's a second Boxers branch in Hell's Kitchen, nothing beats the original. (212-255-5082; www.boxersnyc.com; 37 W 20th St, btwn Fifth & Sixth Aves, Flatiron District; 4pm-2am Mon-Thu, to 4am Fri, 1pm-4am Sat, 1pm-2am Sun; SF/M, R/W, 6 to 23rd St)

Rolf's Bar & German Restaurant

BAR

23 MAP P132, D4

During the six weeks before Christmas, Rolf's transforms itself from average German bar into a whimsical tribute to the yuletide season that falls somewhere between Santa's workshop and an Addams Family holiday party, with bulbous ornaments and hundreds of dolls that stare at you blankly while you swig your pint. Sometimes the timing is extended, and other seasons are celebrated too. Check the infrequently updated website for a little more info. (212-477-4750; www.rolfsnyc.com; 281 Third Ave, at 22nd St, Gramercy; noon-4am; S6 to 23rd St)

Bad Brains performing at Irving Plaza

Entertainment

Irving Plaza
LIVE MUSIC

24 ⭐ MAP P132, C5

Rocking since 1978, Irving Plaza has seen them all: the Ramones, Bob Dylan, U2, Pearl Jam, you name it. These days it's a great in-between stage for quirkier rock and pop acts, from indie chicks Sleater-Kinney to hard rockers Disturbed. There's a cozy floor around the stage, and good views from the mezzanine. (☏212-777-6817; www.irvingplaza.com; 17 Irving Pl, at 15th St, Union Square; ⓢ4/5/6, N/Q/R, L to 14th St-Union Sq)

Peoples Improv Theater
COMEDY

25 ⭐ MAP P132, C3

Aglow in red neon, this bustling comedy club serves up top-notch laughs at dirt-cheap prices. The string of nightly acts ranges from stand-up to sketch and musical comedy, playing in either the main stage theater or the basement lounge. PIT also runs courses, including three-hour, drop-in improv workshops at its Midtown venue, **Simple Studios** (☏212-273-9696; http://simplestudiosnyc.com; 134 W 29th St, btwn Sixth & Seventh Aves, Midtown West; ⊙9am-11pm Mon-Fri, to 10pm Sat & Sun; ⓢ1, N/R to 28th St). See the website for all classes and schedules. (PIT; ☏212-563-7488; www.thepit-nyc.com; 123 E 24th St, btwn Lexington & Park Aves, Gramercy; �; ⓢF/M, N/R, 6 to 23rd St)

Union Square Greenmarket

Four days a week, you'll find the **Union Square Greenmarket** (Map p132, B5; www.grownyc.org; Union Square, 17th St btwn Broadway & Park Ave S, Union Square; ⊙8am-6pm Mon, Wed, Fri & Sat; ⓢ4/5/6, N/Q/R, L to 14th St-Union Sq) sprawling along the square's northern end – it's the most popular of the 53 greenmarkets throughout the five boroughs. Whet your appetite trawling the stalls, with anything and everything from upstate fruit and vegetables to artisanal breads, cheeses and cider.

Shopping

ABC Carpet & Home
HOMEWARES

26 🔒 MAP P132, B4

A mecca for home designers and decorators brainstorming ideas, this beautifully curated, seven-level temple to good taste heaves with all sorts of furnishings, small and large. Shop for easy-to-pack knickknacks, textiles and jewelry, as well as statement furniture, designer lighting, ceramics and antique carpets. Come Christmas season the shop is a joy to behold. (☏212-473-3000; www.abchome.com; 888 Broadway, at E 19th St; ⊙10am-7pm Mon-Wed, Fri & Sat, to 8pm Thu, 11am-6:30pm Sun; ⓢ4/5/6, N/Q/R/W, L to 14th St-Union Sq)

Fishs Eddy HOMEWARES

27 🔒 MAP P132, B4

High-quality and irreverent design has made Fishs Eddy a staple in the homes of hip New Yorkers for years. Its store is a veritable landslide of cups, saucers, butter dishes, carafes and anything else that belongs in a cupboard. Styles range from tasteful color blocking to delightfully outrageous patterns. (📞212-420-9020; www.fishseddy.com; 889 Broadway, at E 19th St, Union Square; ⏰9am-9pm Mon-Thu, to 10pm Fri & Sat, 10am-8pm Sun; ⑤R/W, 6 to 23rd St)

Bedford Cheese Shop FOOD

28 🔒 MAP P132, C5

Whether you're after local, raw cow's-milk cheese washed in absinthe or garlic-infused goat's-milk cheese from Australia, chances are you'll find it among the 200-strong selection at this outpost of Brooklyn's most celebrated cheese vendor. Pair the cheesy goodness with artisanal charcuterie, deli treats and ready-to-eat sandwiches ($8 to $11), as well as a proud array of Made-in-Brooklyn edibles. (📞718-599-7588; www.bedfordcheeseshop.com; 67 Irving Pl, btwn E 18th & 19th Sts, Gramercy; ⏰8am-9pm Mon-Sat, to 8pm Sun; ⑤4/5/6, N/Q/R/W, L to 14th St-Union Sq)

Rent the Runway CLOTHING

29 🔒 MAP P132, A6

At the flagship store of this popular fashion rental service anyone can pop in for an

Rent the Runway

ASTRID STAWIARZ/CONTRIBUTOR/GETTY IMAGES ©

affordable fashion consultation ($30) for both planned and last-minute events. It's full of looks by high-end designers (Narciso Rodriguez, Badgley Mischka, Nicole Miller) available to rent. Perfect for those who pack light, but want to make a splash. (www.r014therunway.com; 30 W 15th St, btwn Fifth & Sixth Aves; ⏰9am-9pm Mon-Fri, to 8pm Sat, to 7pm Sun; §L, F/M to 14th St-6th Ave; 4/5/6, L, N/Q/R/W to 14th St-Union Sq)

DSW
SHOES

30 ⓐ MAP P132, B6

If your idea of paradise involves a great selection of cut-price kicks, make a beeline for this sprawling unisex chain. Shoes range from formal to athletic, with no shortage of popular and higher-end labels. Unobstructed views of Union Square Park are a bonus. The sales racks are legendary for their through-the-floor deals. (📞212-674-2146; www.dsw.com; 40 E 14th St, btwn University Pl & Broadway, Union Square; ⏰9am-9:30pm Mon-Sat, from 10am Sun; §4/5/6, N/Q/R/W, L to 14th St-Union Sq)

Abracadabra
FASHION & ACCESSORIES

31 ⓐ MAP P132, A4

It's not just a Steve Miller Band song, it's also an emporium of horror, costumes and magic. The shelves are packed with wigs, makeup, accessories and more. Those who like this sort of thing

Pedestrian Express (ⓘ)

Human traffic can be overwhelming in Union Square, especially along 14th St. If you're in a rush, or trying to hoof it on foot, switch over to 13th St and you'll cover a lot more ground in much less time.

will be hard-pressed to leave without racking up some credit-card bills. (📞212-627-5194; www.abracadabrasuperstore.com; 19 W 21st St, btwn Fifth & Sixth Aves, Flatiron District; ⏰11am-7pm Mon-Sat, noon-5pm Sun; §R/W, F/M to 23rd St)

Books of Wonder
BOOKS

32 ⓐ MAP P132, A5

Devoted to children's and young-adult titles, this wonderful bookstore is a great place to take little ones on a rainy day, especially when a kids' author is giving a reading or a storyteller is on hand. There's an impressive range of NYC-themed picture books, plus a section dedicated to rare and vintage children's books and limited-edition children's-book artwork. (📞212-989-3270; www.booksofwonder.com; 18 W 18th St, btwn Fifth & Sixth Aves, Flatiron District; ⏰10am-7pm Mon-Sat, 11am-6pm Sun; 🚼; §F/M to 14th St, L to 6th Ave)

Explore ◈

Midtown

The hub of the city, Midtown sees more than 300,000 people a day jostle their way through its busy streets. It's home to icons including Times Square, Broadway theaters, Grand Central Terminal and the Empire State Building. Cultural knockouts include MoMA and the New York Public Library, with the eatery-packed streets of Hell's Kitchen nearby.

Grab a fresh bagel for breakfast at Ess-a-Bagel (p162), then get a bird's-eye view of New York by heading to either the Empire State Building (p150) or Top of the Rock (p156) observatories. Once back on the ground, get your fill of culture at the Museum of Modern Art (p152). For fine dining without breaking the bank, try booking (well in advance) the prix-fixe lunch at Le Bernardin (p160) – or else cheap out at Totto Ramen (p161) or Burger Joint (p162). Navigate the crush of humanity in Times Square (p148) to line up at the TKTS Booth (p170) for some discounted tickets for a Broadway or Off-Broadway show later on. Continue your stroll around Midtown to gawp at the skyscrapers all around, or else zip over to Roosevelt Island for spectacular skyline views. Head over to Koreatown (p164) for a pre-theater BBQ dinner, then catch your show. Other entertainment options include jazz at Birdland (p170), comedy at Caroline's (p171) or classical music at Carnegie Hall (p169).

Getting There & Around

S The A/C/E and 1/2/3 lines run north–south through Midtown West and the 4/5/6 through Midtown East. The central B/D/F/M lines run up Sixth Ave, while N/Q/R/W lines follow Broadway. The 7, E and M lines offer some crosstown service.

Neighborhood Map on p154

New York Public Library (p157) JIAWANGKUN/SHUTTERSTOCK ©

Top Sight 📷
Times Square

Love it or hate it, the intersection of Broadway and Seventh Ave – better known as Times Square – is New York City's heart. It's a restless, hypnotic torrent of glittering lights, giant billboards and raw urban energy that doesn't seem to have an off switch: it's nearly as busy in the wee hours as it is in the afternoon.

◎ MAP P154, D4

www.timessquarenyc.org

Broadway, at Seventh Ave

S N/Q/R/W, S, 1/2/3, 7 to Times Sq-42nd St

The Bustling Heart of NYC

This is the New York of collective fantasies – the place where Al Jolson 'makes it' in the 1927 film *The Jazz Singer* and where Alicia Keys and Jay-Z waxed lyrically about the concrete jungle.

But for several decades, the dream here was a sordid one. The economic crash of the early 1970s led to a mass exodus of corporations from Times Square. Billboard niches went dark, stores shut and once grand hotels were converted into SRO (single-room occupancy) dives. While the adjoining Theater District survived, its respectable playhouses shared the streets with porn cinemas and strip clubs. That all changed with tough-talking former mayor Rudolph Giuliani, who, in the 1990s, boosted police numbers and lured in a wave of 'respectable' retail chains, restaurants and attractions. By the new millennium, Times Square had gone from X-rated to G-rated, drawing almost 40 million visitors annually.

Today's Times Square

Nearly as bright at 2am as it is at noon, and always jammed with people, Times Square proves that New York truly is the city that never sleeps. The massive billboards stretch half a skyscraper tall, and LED signs are lit for shows and performances. A mishmash of characters on the square – from the cute (Elmo); the noble (the Statue of Liberty); the popular (superheroes); to the just plain bizarre (Naked Cowboy) – mix with the jumble of humanity from every corner of the globe. Walk around and in minutes you'll hear more languages being spoken than you even knew existed. It's the world's most famous spot to celebrate New Year's Eve, to boot. If you have only five minutes to spend in all of New York City, you'll want to spend them here.

★ Top Tips

For a birds-eye view of Times Square (and a perfectly framed photo), visit the Broadway Lounge on the 8th floor of the Marriott Marquis.

✕ Take a Break

For a panoramic vista, order a drink at the Renaissance Hotel's **R Lounge** (☎ 212-261-5200; www.rlounge times square.com; Two Times Sq, 714 Seventh Ave, at W 48th St; ⊙ 5-11pm Mon, to 11:30pm Tue-Thu, to midnight Fri, 7:30am-midnight Sat, to 11pm Sun; ⑤ N/R/W to 49th St), which offers floor-to-ceiling glass windows. Or walk a bit further to **Margon** (☎ 212-354-5013; 136 W 46th St, btwn Sixth & Seventh Aves; sandwiches $11-12, mains from $11; ⊙ 6am-5pm Mon-Fri, from 7am Sat; ⑤ B/D/F/M to 47th-50th Sts-Rockefeller Center), a sumptuous greasy spoon with Cuban cheap eats. (Don't let the line scare you: it moves quickly.)

Top Sight 📷
Empire State Building

The Chrysler Building may be prettier, and One World Trade Center may be taller, but the Queen Bee of the New York skyline remains the Empire State Building. NYC's tallest star has enjoyed close-ups in around 100 films, from King Kong to Independence Day. Heading up to the top is as quintessential as pastrami, rye and pickles at a delicatessen.

◎ **MAP P154, E5**

www.esbnyc.com

350 Fifth Ave, at W 34th St

86th-fl deck adult/child $34/27, incl 102nd-fl deck $54/47

🕑 8am-2am, last elevators up 1:15am

S 4, 6 to 33rd; Blue and Orange PATH to 33rd St; B/D/F/M, N/Q/R/W to 34th St-Herald Sq

By the Numbers

The statistics are astounding: 10 million bricks, 60,000 tons of steel, 6400 windows and 328,000 sq ft of marble. Built on the original site of the Waldorf-Astoria, construction took a record-setting 410 days, using seven million hours of labor and costing a mere $41 million. It might sound like a lot, but it fell well below its $50 million budget (just as well, given it went up during the Great Depression). Coming in at 102 stories and 1472ft from top to bottom, the limestone phallus opened for business on May 1, 1931. Generations later, Deborah Kerr's words to Cary Grant in *An Affair to Remember* still ring true: 'It's the nearest thing to heaven we have in New York.'

Observation Decks

Unless you're Ann Darrow (the unfortunate woman caught in King Kong's grip), heading to the top of the Empire State Building should leave you beaming. There are two observation decks. The open-air 86th-floor deck offers an alfresco experience, with coin-operated telescopes for close-up glimpses of the metropolis in action. Further up, the enclosed 102nd-floor deck is New York's second-highest observation deck, trumped only by the observation deck at One World Trade Center. Needless to say, the views over the city's five boroughs (and five neighboring states, weather permitting) are quite simply exquisite. The views from both decks are especially spectacular at sunset, when the city dons its nighttime cloak in dusk's afterglow. Alas, the passage to heaven will involve a trip through purgatory: the queues to the top are notorious.

★ Top Tips

o Getting here very early or very late helps avoid delays, as will buying tickets on-line in advance (the extra $2 convenience fee is well worth it).

o On the 86th floor between 9pm and 1am from Thursday to Saturday, the twinkling sea of lights below is accompanied by a live saxophone soundtrack (yes, requests are taken).

✕ Take a Break

You're just a short walk from the lively buzz of Koreatown, with abundant eating options along 32nd St, including peaceful Hangawi (p163). Or stroll northward and lunch at the **Bryant Park Grill** (✆ 212-840-6500; www.arkrestaurants.com/bryant_park; Bryant Park, 25 W 40th St, btwn Fifth & Sixth Aves; mains $19-47; ⏱11:30am-3:30pm & 5-11pm; Ⓢ B/D/F/M to 42nd St-Bryant Park; 7 to 5th Ave).

Top Sight 📷
Museum of Modern Art

*MoMA boasts more A-listers than an Oscars
after-party: Van Gogh, Matisse, Picasso, Warhol,
Rothko, Pollock and Bourgeois. Since its founding in 1929, the museum has amassed almost
200,000 artworks, documenting the creativity
of the late 19th century through to today. For art
buffs, it's Valhalla. For the uninitiated, it's a crash
course in all that is addictive about art.*

◎ MAP P154, E2

www.moma.org

11 W 53rd St, btwn Fifth &
Sixth Aves

adult/child 16yr & under
$25/free, 4-9pm Fri free

⊘ 10:30am-5:30pm Sat-
Thu, to 9pm Fri

Ⓢ E/M to 5th Ave-53rd St;
F to 57th St; E/B/D to 7th
Ave-57th St

Collection Highlights

MoMA's permanent collection spans four levels. Prints, illustrated books and the unmissable Contemporary Galleries are usually on level two; architecture, design, drawings and photography are on level three; and painting and sculpture are on levels four and five. Must-sees include Van Gogh's *Starry Night*, Cézanne's *The Bather*, Picasso's *Les Demoiselles d'Avignon* and Henri Rousseau's *The Sleeping Gypsy*, not to mention iconic American works like Warhol's *Campbell's Soup Cans* and *Gold Marilyn Monroe*, Lichtenstein's equally poptastic *Girl with Ball* and Hopper's haunting *House by the Railroad*.

Abby Aldrich Rockefeller Sculpture Garden

The museum's acclaimed 2004 reconstruction saw the restoration of the Sculpture Garden to the original, larger vision of Philip Johnson's 1953 design. Johnson described the space as a 'sort of outdoor room,' and on warm, sunny days, it's hard not to think of it as a soothing alfresco lounge – one with works from artists like Matisse, Miró and Picasso. The Sculpture Garden is open free of charge from 9:30am to 10:15am daily, except in inclement weather and during maintenance.

Film Screenings

MoMA screens an incredibly well-rounded selection of celluloid gems from its collection of over 22,000 films, including the works of the Maysles Brothers and every Pixar animation film ever produced. Expect anything from Academy Award–nominated documentary shorts and Hollywood classics to experimental works and international retrospectives. Your museum ticket gets you in for free.

★ Top Tips

o Mondays and Tuesdays are the least-crowded days to visit, except on public holidays. Friday evenings and weekends can be incredibly crowded.

o Download the museum's free smartphone app from the website before you go.

o Many of the star pieces are on the top two levels, so tackle the museum from the top down.

✕ Take a Break

Cafe 2 (📞 212-333-1299; www.moma cafes.com; sandwiches & salads $8-14, mains $12-18; ⏱ 11am-5pm, to 7:30pm Fri; 📶) has Italian-inspired fare with a casual vibe.
Terrace Five (📞 212-333-1288; mains $12-19; ⏱ 11am-5pm Sat-Thu, to 7:30pm Fri; 📶) has table service and an outdoor terrace overlooking the Sculpture Garden.

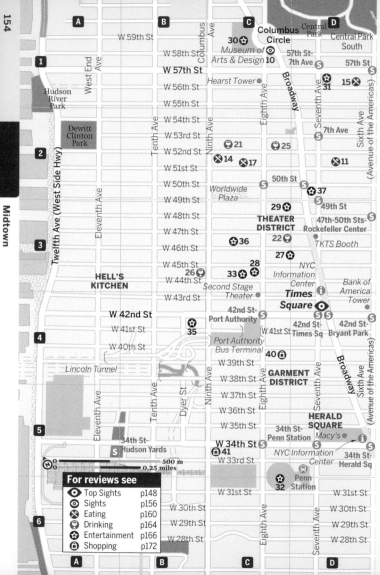

Midtown

W 59th St
W 58th St
Columbus Circle
Central Park
Central Park South

A
B
C
D

West End Ave

Hudson River Park

Dewitt Clinton Park

Twelfth Ave (West Side Hwy)

Eleventh Ave

Tenth Ave

Ninth Ave

Eighth Ave

Broadway

Seventh Ave

Sixth Ave (Avenue of the Americas)

Columbus Ave

Columbus Circle

Museum of Arts & Design 10

Hearst Tower

Central Park

Central Park South

57th St-7th Ave

57th St

30

31   15

7th Ave

W 57th St
W 56th St
W 55th St
W 54th St
W 53rd St
W 52nd St
W 51st St
W 50th St
W 49th St
W 48th St
W 47th St
W 46th St
W 45th St
W 44th St
W 43rd St

21   25
14   17   11
Worldwide Plaza

50th St
37
49th St
29
THEATER DISTRICT
47th-50th Sts-Rockefeller Center
TKTS Booth
22
36
27
NYC Information Center
Bank of America Tower
26   28   33
Second Stage Theater
Times Square
42nd St-Times Sq
42nd St-Bryant Park

HELL'S KITCHEN

W 42nd St
W 41st St
W 40th St

35
42nd St-Port Authority
Port Authority Bus Terminal
40

Lincoln Tunnel

W 39th St
W 38th St
W 37th St
W 36th St
W 35th St
W 34th St
W 33rd St
W 31st St
W 30th St
W 29th St
W 28th St

GARMENT DISTRICT

HERALD SQUARE
Macy's
34th St-Penn Station
NYC Information Center
34th St-Herald Sq

Dyer St

34th St-Hudson Yards

41   32

Penn Station

500 m
0.25 miles

For reviews see

◉	Top Sights	p148
◎	Sights	p156
✖	Eating	p160
◯	Drinking	p164
✪	Entertainment	p166
🔒	Shopping	p172

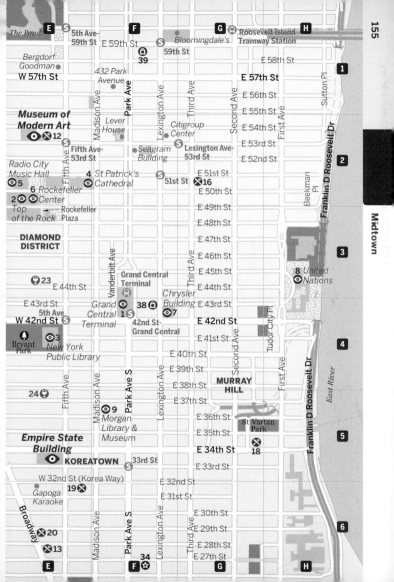

Midtown

The Pond

E 5th Ave-59th St

S

E 59th St

Bloomingdale's

Roosevelt Island Tramway Station

59th St

S

39

Bergdorf Goodman

E 58th St

432 Park Avenue

W 57th St

E 57th St

Park Ave

Madison Ave

Lexington Ave

Third Ave

Second Ave

First Ave

Sutton Pl

E 56th St

E 55th St

1

Museum of Modern Art

12

Lever House

E 54th St

E 53rd St

Citigroup Center

Fifth Ave-53rd St

S

Seagram Building

S

Lexington Ave-53rd St

E 52nd St

2

Radio City Music Hall

5

4

St Patrick's Cathedral

E 51st St

51st St

16

Beekman Pl

6 Rockefeller Center

E 50th St

E 49th St

2

Top of the Rock

Rockefeller Plaza

E 48th St

E 47th St

3

DIAMOND DISTRICT

Vanderbilt Ave

E 46th St

E 45th St

8 United Nations

23

E 44th St

Grand Central Terminal

Third Ave

E 44th St

E 43rd St

Grand Central Terminal

38

Chrysler Building

E 43rd St

7

Franklin D Roosevelt Dr

E 43rd St

W 42nd St

5th Ave

S

1

42nd St-Grand Central

E 42nd St

E 41st St

Tudor City Pl

4

Bryant Park

3

New York Public Library

E 40th St

E 39th St

Second Ave

First Ave

East River

MURRAY HILL

E 38th St

E 37th St

24

Madison Ave

Park Ave S

Lexington Ave

9

Morgan Library & Museum

E 36th St

St Vartan Park

E 35th St

5

Empire State Building

KOREATOWN

33rd St

S

E 34th St

18

E 33rd St

W 32nd St (Korea Way)

E 32nd St

19

Gapoga Karaoke

E 31st St

E 30th St

6

20

Park Ave S

Lexington Ave

Third Ave

E 29th St

13

E 28th St

34

E 27th St

Broadway

E

F

G

H

Sights

Grand Central Terminal

HISTORIC BUILDING

1  MAP P154, F4

Completed in 1913, Grand Central Terminal – more commonly, if technically incorrectly, called Grand Central Station – is one of New York's beaux-arts beauties. Adorned with Tennessee-marble floors and Italian-marble ticket counters, its glorious main concourse is capped by a **vaulted ceiling** depicting the constellations, designed by French painter Paul César Helleu. When commuters complained that the sky is backwards – painted as if looking down from above, not up – it was asserted as intentional (possibly to avoid having to admit an error). (www.grandcentralterminal.com; 89 E 42nd St, at Park Ave; ⏰5:30am-2am; ⑤S, 4/5/6, 7 to Grand Central-42nd St)

Top of the Rock

VIEWPOINT

2 MAP P154, E2

Designed in homage to ocean liners and opened in 1933, this 70th-floor open-air observation deck sits atop the **GE Building**, the tallest skyscraper at the Rockefeller Center. Top of the Rock beats the Empire State Building (p150) on several levels: it's less crowded, has wider observation decks (both outdoor and indoor) and offers a view of the Empire State Building itself. (📞212-698-2000, toll free 877-692-7625; www.topoftherocknyc.com; 30 Rockefeller Plaza, entrance on W

Grand Central Terminal

50th St, btwn Fifth & Sixth Aves; adult/child $37/31, sunrise/sunset combo $54/43; ⏱8am-midnight, last elevator at 11pm; S B/D/F/M to 47th-50th Sts-Rockefeller Center)

New York Public Library

HISTORIC BUILDING

3 ◎ MAP P154, E4

Loyally guarded by 'Patience' and 'Fortitude' (the marble lions overlooking Fifth Ave), this beaux-arts show-off is one of NYC's best free attractions. When dedicated in 1911, New York's flagship library ranked as the largest marble structure ever built in the US, and to this day its recently restored **Rose Main Reading Room** steals the breath away with its lavish coffered ceiling. It's only one of several glories inside, among them the **DeWitt Wallace Periodical Room**. (Stephen A Schwarzman Building; ☎212-340-0863; www.nypl.org; Fifth Ave, at W 42nd St; admission free; ⏱8am-8pm Mon & Thu, 8am-9pm Tue & Wed, 8am-6pm Fri, 10am-6pm Sat, 10am-5pm Sun, guided tours 11am & 2pm Mon-Sat, 2pm Sun; S B/D/F/M to 42nd St-Bryant Park, 7 to 5th Ave)

St Patrick's Cathedral

CATHEDRAL

4 ◎ MAP P154, E2

Still shining after a $200 million restoration in 2015, America's largest Catholic cathedral graces Fifth Ave with Gothic Revival splendor. Built at a cost of nearly $2 million during the Civil War, the building did not originally

Bryant Park

European coffee kiosks, alfresco chess games, summer film screenings and winter ice-skating: nestled behind the beaux-arts New York Public Library building, **Bryant Park** (Map p154, E4; ☎212-768-4242; www.bryant park.org; 42nd St, btwn Fifth & Sixth Aves; ⏱7am-midnight Mon-Fri, to 11pm Sat & Sun Jun-Sep, shorter hrs rest of yr; S B/D/F/M to 42nd St-Bryant Park; 7 to 5th Ave) offers a smorgasbord of quirky activities daily – great for a little time-out from Midtown madness.

include the two front spires; those were added in 1888. Step inside to appreciate the Louis Tiffany–designed **altar** and Charles Connick's stunning **Rose Window**, the latter gleaming above a 7000-pipe church organ. Walk-in **guided tours** are available several days a week; check the website for details. (☎212-753-2261; www.saint patrickscathedral.org; Fifth Ave, btwn E 50th & 51st Sts; ⏱6:30am-8:45pm; S B/D/F/M to 47th-50th Sts-Rockefeller Center, E/M to 5th Ave-53rd St)

Radio City Music Hall

HISTORIC BUILDING

5 ◎ MAP P154, E2

This spectacular Moderne movie palace was the brainchild of vaudeville producer Samuel Lionel

'Roxy' Rothafel. Never one for understatement, Roxy launched his venue on December 23, 1932 with an over-the-top extravaganza that included camp dance troupe the Roxyettes (mercifully renamed the Rockettes). **Guided tours** (75 minutes) of the sumptuous interiors include the glorious auditorium, Witold Gordon's classically inspired mural *History of Cosmetics* in the Women's Downstairs Lounge, and the *très* exclusive VIP Roxy Suite. (www.radiocity.com; 1260 Sixth Ave, at W 51st St; tours adult/child $27/20; ⏱tours 9:30am-5pm; 👪; 🚇B/D/F/M to 47th-50th Sts-Rockefeller Center)

Rockefeller Center

HISTORIC BUILDING

6 ◉ MAP P154, E2

This 22-acre 'city within a city' debuted at the height of the Great Depression, with developer John D Rockefeller Jr footing the $100 million price tag. Taking nine years to build, it was America's first multiuse retail, entertainment and office space – a sprawl of 19 buildings (14 of which are the original Moderne structures). The center was declared a National Landmark in 1987. Highlights include **NBC Studio Tours** (📞212-664-3700; www.thetouratnbcstudios.com; 30

Skyscrapers in Midtown

Midtown's skyline is more than just the Empire State and Chrysler Buildings, with enough modernist and postmodernist beauties to satisfy the wildest of high-rise dreams. Here are six of Midtown's finest.

Seagram Building (Map p154, F2; 100 E 53rd St, at Park Ave, Midtown East; 🚇6 to 51st St; E, M to Fifth Ave-53rd St) 1956–58; 514ft

Lever House (Map p154, F2; 390 Park Ave, btwn 53rd & 54th Sts, Midtown East; 🚇E, M to 5th Ave-53rd St) 1950–52; 306ft

Citigroup Center (Map p154, F2; 139 E 53rd St, at Lexington Ave, Midtown East; 🚇6 to 51st St; E, M to Lexington Ave-53rd St) 1974–77; 915ft

Hearst Tower (Map p154, C1; 949 Eighth Ave, btwn 56th & 57th Sts, Midtown West; 🚇A/C, B/D, 1 to 59th St-Columbus Circle) 2003–06; 597ft

Bank of America Tower (One Bryant Park; Map p154, D4; Sixth Ave, btwn W 42nd & 43rd Sts; 🚇B/D/F/M to 42nd St-Bryant Park) 2004–09; 1200ft

432 Park Avenue (Map p154, F1; 432 Park Ave, btwn 56th & 57th Sts, Midtown East; 🚇N/Q/R to Lexington Ave-59th St) 2011–15; 1396ft

Rockefeller Plaza, entrance at 1250 Sixth Ave; tours adult/child $33/29, children under 6yr not admitted; ⏱8:20am-2pm Mon-Fri, to 5pm Sat & Sun) and the Top of the Rock (p156) observation deck. (☏212-332-6868; www.rockefellercenter. com; Fifth to Sixth Aves, btwn W 48th & 51st Sts; Ⓢ B/D/F/M to 47th-50th Sts-Rockefeller Center)

Chrysler Building
HISTORIC BUILDING

7 ◉ MAP P154, F4

Designed by William Van Alen in 1930, the 77-floor Chrysler Building is prime-time architecture: a fusion of Moderne and Gothic aesthetics, adorned with steel eagles and topped by a spire that screams *Bride of Frankenstein*. The building was constructed as the headquarters for Walter P Chrysler and his automobile empire; unable to compete on the production line with bigger rivals Ford and General Motors, Chrysler trumped them on the skyline, and with one of Gotham's most beautiful lobbies. (405 Lexington Ave, at E 42nd St; ⏱lobby 8am-6pm Mon-Fri; Ⓢ S, 4/5/6, 7 to Grand Central-42nd St)

United Nations
HISTORIC BUILDING

8 ◉ MAP P154, H3

Welcome to the headquarters of the UN, a worldwide organization overseeing international law, international security and human rights. While the Le Corbusier–designed Secretariat building is off-limits, one-hour guided tours do cover the restored General Assembly Hall, Security Council Chamber, Trusteeship Council Chamber and Economic and Social Council (ECOSOC) Chamber, as well as exhibitions about the UN's work and artworks given by member states. Weekday tours must be booked online and photo ID is required to enter the site. (☏212-963-4475; http://visit. un.org; visitors gate First Ave at 46th St, Midtown East; guided tour adult/ child $20/13, children under 5yr not admitted, grounds access Sat & Sun free; ⏱tours 9am-4:45pm Mon-Fri, visitor center also open 10am-4:45pm Sat & Sun; Ⓢ S, 4/5/6, 7 to Grand Central-42nd St)

Morgan Library & Museum
MUSEUM

9 ◉ MAP P154, F5

Incorporating the mansion once owned by steel magnate JP Morgan, this sumptuous cultural center houses a phenomenal array of manuscripts, tapestries and books (with no fewer than three Gutenberg Bibles). Adorned with Italian and Dutch Renaissance artworks, Morgan's personal study is only trumped by his personal library (East Room), an extraordinary, vaulted space adorned with walnut bookcases, a 16th-century Dutch tapestry and zodiac-themed ceiling. The center's rotating exhibitions are often superb, as are its regular cultural events. (☏212-685-0008; www.themorgan.org; 225

Madison, at E 36th St, Midtown East; adult/child $20/free; ☺10:30am-5pm Tue-Thu, to 9pm Fri, 10am-6pm Sat, 11am-6pm Sun; Ⓢ6 to 33rd St)

Museum of Arts & Design
MUSEUM

10 ◉ MAP P154, C1

MAD offers four floors of superlative design and handicrafts, from blown glass and carved wood to elaborate metal jewelry. Its temporary exhibitions are top-notch and innovative: one past show explored the art of scent. Usually on the first Sunday of the month, professional artists lead family-friendly explorations of the galleries, followed by hands-on workshops inspired by the current exhibitions. The museum

gift shop sells some fantastic contemporary jewelry, while the 9th-floor restaurant/bar Robert (p164) is perfect for panoramic cocktails. (MAD; ☎212-299-7777; www.madmuseum.org; 2 Columbus Circle, btwn Eighth Ave & Broadway; adult/18yr & under $16/free, by donation 6-9pm Thu; ☺10am-6pm Tue-Sun, to 9pm Thu; 🚻; Ⓢ A/C, B/D, 1 to 59th St-Columbus Circle)

Eating

Le Bernardin
SEAFOOD $$$

11 ✖ MAP P154, D2

The interiors may have been subtly sexed-up for a 'younger clientele' (the stunning storm-themed triptych is by Brooklyn artist Ran Ortner), but triple-Michelin-starred Le Bernardin remains a luxe,

View of the Chrysler Building (p159)

SONGQUAN DENG/SHUTTERSTOCK ©

fine-dining holy grail. At the helm is French-born celebrity chef Éric Ripert, whose deceptively simple-looking seafood often borders on the transcendental. Life is short, and you only live (er, eat!) once. (📞212-554-1515; www.le-bernardin.com; 155 W 51st St, btwn Sixth & Seventh Aves; prix-fixe lunch/dinner $88/157, tasting menus $185-225; 🕐noon-2:30pm & 5:15-10:30pm Mon-Thu, to 11pm Fri, 5:15-11pm Sat; 🚇1 to 50th St; B/D, E to 7th Ave)

Modern
FRENCH $$$

12 🍽 MAP P154, E2

Shining two (Michelin) stars bright, the Modern delivers confident creations like foie gras tart. Fans of Sex and the City may know that it was here that Carrie announced her impending marriage to Mr Big. (Hint: If you're on a writer's wage, you can opt for cheaper grub in the adjacent Bar Room.) Cocktails are as tasty as the meals. (📞212-333-1220; www.themodernnyc.com; 9 W 53rd St, btwn Fifth & Sixth Aves; 3-/6-course lunch $138/178, 4-/8-course dinner $168/228; 🕐restaurant noon-2pm & 5-10:30pm Mon-Sat, bar 11:30am-10:30pm Mon-Sat, to 9:30pm Sun; 🚇E, M to 5th Ave-53rd St)

NoMad
MODERN AMERICAN $$$

13 🍽 MAP P154, E6

Sharing the same name as the 'it kid' hotel it inhabits, and run by the perfectionist restaurateurs behind Michelin-starred Eleven Madison Park (p135), NoMad

Fine Dining in Midtown 🍽

Savoring Midtown's A-list restaurants without mortgaging the house is possible if you go for the prix-fixe lunch menu where available. Participants include Michelin-starred Le Bernardin, which offers dishes featured in their evening menus. How far ahead you should book depends on the restaurant. It can sometimes be a one-month wait at Le Bernardin, which offers online reservations.

has become one of Manhattan's culinary highlights. Carved up into a series of distinctly different spaces – including an elegant 'parlor' and a snacks-only 'library' – the restaurant serves delicacies like roasted quail with plums, kale and chanterelle. (📞212-796-1500; www.thenomadhotel.com; NoMad Hotel, 1170 Broadway, at 28th St; mains $29-42; 🕐noon-2pm & 5:30-10:30pm Mon-Thu, to 11pm Fri, 11am-2:30pm & 5:30-11pm Sat, 11am-2:30pm & 5:30-10pm Sun; 🚇N/R, 6 to 28th St; F/M to 23rd St)

Totto Ramen
JAPANESE $

14 🍽 MAP P154, C2

There might be another two branches in Midtown, but purists know that neither beats the tiny 20-seat original. Write your name and number of guests on the clipboard and wait your turn. Your

A Brief History of Times Square

At the turn of the 20th century, Times Square was an unremarkable intersection (called Longacre Square) far from the city's downtown commercial heart. Then subway pioneer August Belmont made a deal with *New York Times* publisher Adolph Ochs. Heading construction of the city's first subway line (from Lower Manhattan up to Harlem), Belmont astutely realized that a Midtown business hub would maximize both patronage and profit. Belmont approached Ochs, arguing that moving to Broadway and 42nd St would be a win-win: an in-house subway station would mean faster distribution of the newspaper, plus more sales to the influx of commuters – and convinced Mayor George B McClellan Jr to rename the square. In 1904, both the subway station and the *Times'* new headquarters at One Times Square made their debut.

That New Year's Eve, the *Times* hosted a party, setting off fireworks from its skyscraper rooftop. For safety reasons this was changed in 1908 to a 700-pound ball that was lowered at midnight – a tradition still followed today.

reward: extraordinary ramen. Go for the pork, which sings in dishes like miso ramen (with fermented soybean paste, egg, scallion, bean sprouts, onion and homemade chili paste). (📞212-582-0052; www.totto ramen.com; 366 W 52nd St, btwn Eighth & Ninth Aves; ramen $11-18; 🕙noon-4:30pm & 5:30pm-midnight Mon-Sat, 4-11pm Sun; Ⓢ C/E to 50th St)

Burger Joint

BURGERS $

15 🍴 MAP P154, D1

With only a small neon burger as your clue, this speakeasy-style burger hut lurks behind the lobby curtain in the Le Parker Meridien hotel. Though it might not be as 'hip' or as 'secret' as it once was, it still delivers the same winning formula of graffiti-strewn walls,

retro booths and attitude-loaded staff slapping up beef 'n' patty brilliance. (📞212-708-7414; www. burgerjointny.com; Le Parker Meridien, 119 W 56th St, btwn Sixth & Seventh Aves; burgers $9-16; 🕙11am-11:30pm Sun-Thu, to midnight Fri & Sat; Ⓢ F to 57th St)

Ess-a-Bagel

DELI $

16 🍴 MAP P154, G2

Fresh, toothsome bagels have made this kosher deli a veritable institution. Tell the bagel monger your preference of bagel, then choose from a sprawling counter of cream cheeses and other sandwich fillings. For a classic, opt for scallion cream cheese with lox (salmon), capers, tomato and red onion ($4.55). If the weather's fine, turn right into 51st St and lunch in pretty Greenacre Park. (📞212-980-1010; www.ess-a-bagel. com; 831 Third Ave, at 51st St, Midtown East; bagels sandwiches $3-4.55; ⏰6am-9pm Mon-Fri, to 5pm Sat & Sun; 🚇6 to 51st St; E/M to Lexington Ave-53rd St)

ViceVersa

ITALIAN $$$

17 🍴 MAP P154, C2

ViceVersa is quintessential Italian: suave and sophisticated, affable and scrumptious. The menu features refined, cross-regional dishes like arancini with black truffle and fontina cheese. For a celebrated classic, order the *casoncelli alla bergamasca* (ravioli-like pasta filled with minced veal, raisins and amaretto cookies and seasoned with sage, butter, pancetta and Grana Padano), a nod to chef Stefano Terzi's Lombard heritage. (📞212-399-9291; www. viceversanyc.com; 325 W 51st St, btwn Eighth & Ninth Aves; 3-course lunch $29, dinner mains $24-33; ⏰noon-2:30pm & 5-11pm Mon-Fri, 4:30-11pm Sat, 11:30am-3pm & 5-10pm Sun; 🚇C/E to 50th St)

El Parador Cafe

MEXICAN $$

18 🍴 MAP P154, G5

Back in the day, the far-flung location of this Mexican stalwart was much appreciated by philandering husbands. The shady regulars may have gone, but the old-school charm remains, from the beveled candleholders and dapper Latino waiters to the satisfying south-of-the-border standbys. (📞212-679-6812; www.elparadorcafe. com; 325 E 34th St, btwn First & Second Aves, Midtown East; lunch $10-22, dinner mains $18-32; ⏰noon-10pm Mon, to 11pm Tue-Sat; 🚇6 to 33rd St)

Hangawi

KOREAN, VEGAN $$

19 🍴 MAP P154, E6

Meat-free Korean is the draw at high-achieving Hangawi. Leave your shoes at the entrance and slip into a soothing, Zen-like space of meditative music, soft low seating and clean, complex dishes. Showstoppers include the leek pancakes and a seductively smooth tofu claypot in ginger sauce. (📞212-213-0077; www. hangawirestaurant.com; 12 E 32nd St, btwn Fifth & Madison Aves; mains lunch $11-30, dinner $19-30; ⏰noon-2:30pm & 5:30-10:15pm Mon-Thu, to 10:30pm Fri, 1-10:30pm Sat, 5-9:30pm Sun; 🍴; 🚇B/D/F/M, N/Q/R/W to 34th St-Herald Sq)

John Dory Oyster Bar

SEAFOOD $$$

20 🍴 MAP P154, E6

Anchored to the **Ace Hotel** (📞212-679-2222; www.acehotel.com/ newyork; 20 W 29th St, btwn Broadway & Fifth Ave) lobby, John Dory is a fine spot to sip some bubbles and slurp on an oyster or three. Top billing goes to happy hour (5pm to 7pm weekdays, noon to 3pm on weekends), when both oysters and clams beckon at $2 a pop. Lest you need reminding, brass oyster shells form the handles

Koreatown 🍴

For kimchi and karaoke, it's hard to beat **Koreatown**. Concentrated mainly on 32nd St just off Herald Sq (with some spillover into the surrounding streets south and north), it's a Seoulful mix of Korean-owned restaurants, shops, spas and karaoke places like **Gapoga Karaoke** (Map p154, E6; ☏212-967-5353; www.gagopakaraoke.com; 28 W 32nd St, Korea Town; rooms from $32 per hr; ☐6pm-4am Mon-Sat, 7pm-4am Sun; ⓢB/D/F/M/N/Q/R/ W train to 34th Street-Herald Sq). Authentic BBQ is available around the clock at many of the all-night spots on 32nd St.

on the bar. (☏212-792-9000; www.thejohndory.com; 1196 Broadway, at 29th St; plates $11-55; ☐noon-midnight; ⓢN/R to 28th St)

Drinking

The Campbell COCKTAIL BAR

As swanky as swank can be, the only thing missing at the Campbell (see 1 ◎ Map p154, F4) is elevation – you don't get the sweeping skyline view that some NYC bars have. Instead, you can sip top-shelf signature cocktails beneath a stunning hand-painted ceiling, restored along with the room with touches that make it seem Rockefeller or Carnegie might just join you. (☏212-297-1781; www.

thecampbellnyc.com; Grand Central Terminal; ☐noon-2am)

Bar SixtyFive COCKTAIL BAR

Not to be missed, sophisticated SixtyFive (see 6 ◎ Map p154, E2) sits on level 65 of the GE Building at Rockefeller Center (p158). Dress well (no sportswear or guests under 21) and arrive by 5pm for a seat with a multi-million-dollar view. Even if you don't score a table on the balcony or by the window, head outside to soak up that sweeping New York panorama. (☏212-632-5000; www.rainbowroom.com/bar-sixty-five; 30 Rockefeller Plaza, entrance on W 49th St; ☐5pm-midnight Mon-Fri, 4-9pm Sun; ⓢB/D/F/M to 47th-50th Sts-Rockefeller Center)

Robert COCKTAIL BAR

Perched on the 9th floor of the Museum of Arts & Design (p160), '60s-inspired Robert (see 10 ◎ Map p154, C1) is technically a high-end, Modern American restaurant. While the food is satisfactory, we say visit late afternoon or post-dinner, find a sofa and gaze out over Central Park with a MAD Manhattan (bourbon, blood orange vermouth and liquored cherries). Check the website for live jazz sessions. (☏212-299-7730; www.robertnyc.com; Museum of Arts & Design, 2 Columbus Circle, btwn Eighth Ave & Broadway; ☐11:30am-10pm Mon-Fri, from 10:30am Sat & Sun; ⓢA/C, B/D, 1 to 59th St-Columbus Circle)

Industry GAY

21  MAP P154, C2

What was once a parking garage is now one of the hottest gay bars in Hell's Kitchen – a slick, 4000-sq-ft watering hole with handsome lounge areas, a pool table and a stage for top-notch drag divas. Head in between 4pm and 9pm for the two-for-one drinks special or squeeze in later to party with the hordes. Cash only. (☏646-476-2747; www.industry-bar.com; 355 W 52nd St, btwn Eighth & Ninth Aves; ⏰5pm-4am; ⓢC/E, 1 to 50th St)

Rum House COCKTAIL BAR

22 MAP P154, C3

This sultry slice of old New York is revered for its rums and whiskeys. Savor them straight up or mixed in impeccable cocktails like 'The Escape,' a potent piña-colada for adults. Adding to the magic is nightly live music, spanning solo piano tunes to jaunty jazz trios and sentimental divas. Bartenders here are careful with their craft; don't expect them to rush. (☏646-490-6924; www.therumhousenyc.com; 228 W 47th St, btwn Broadway & Eighth Ave; ⏰noon-4am; ⓢN/R/W to 49th St)

Lantern's Keep COCKTAIL BAR

23 MAP P154, E3

Cross the lobby of the Iroquois Hotel to slip into this dark, intimate cocktail salon. Its specialty is classic drinks, shaken and stirred by passionate, personable mixologists. If you're feeling spicy, request a Gordon's Breakfast (not

The Campbell

SIVAN ASKAYO/LONELY PLANET ©

Midtown Drinking

on the menu!), a fiery melange of gin, Worcestershire sauce, hot sauce, muddled lime and cucumber, salt and pepper. Reservations are recommended. (☏212-453-4287; www.iroquoisny.com; Iroquois Hotel, 49 W 44th St, btwn Fifth & Sixth Aves; ⏱5-11pm Mon, to midnight Tue-Fri, 7pm-1am Sat; ⓢB/D/F/M to 42nd St-Bryant Park)

Top of the Strand COCKTAIL BAR

24 🚇 MAP P154, E5

For that 'Oh my God, I'm in New York' feeling, head to the Marriott Vacation Club Pulse (formerly the Strand Hotel) hotel's rooftop bar, order a martini (extra dirty) and drop your jaw (discreetly). Sporting comfy cabana-style seating, a refreshingly mixed-age crowd and a sliding glass roof, its view of the Empire State Building is simply unforgettable. (☏646-368-6426; www.topofthestrand.com; Marriott Vacation Club Pulse, 33 W 37th St, btwn Fifth & Sixth Aves, Midtown East; ⏱5pm-midnight Mon & Sun, to 1am Tue-Sat; ⓢB/D/F/M, N/Q/R to 34th St)

Russian Vodka Room BAR

25 🚇 MAP P154, C2

Cozy up to Mother Russia at this swank, affable drinking hole, pouring a head-spinning list of flavored vodkas, from cranberry to horseradish. When the room starts spinning, slow it down with stoic grub like borscht, *pirozhki* (stuffed buns), smoked fish and schnitzel. (☏212-307-5835; www.

russianvodkaroom.com; 265 W 52nd St, btwn Eighth Ave & Broadway, Midtown West; ⏱4pm-2am Mon-Thu, to 4am Fri & Sat; ⓢC/E to 50th St)

Rudy's Bar & Grill BAR

26 🚇 MAP P154, B3

The big pantless pig in a red jacket out front marks Hell's Kitchen's best divey hangout, with cheap pitchers of Rudy's two beers, half-circle booths covered in red duct tape, and free hot dogs. A mix of folks come to flirt or watch muted Knicks games as classic rock plays. (☏646-707-0890; www.rudysbarnyc.com; 627 Ninth Ave, at 44th St, Midtown West; ⏱8am-4am Mon-Sat, noon-4am Sun; ⓢA/C/E to 42nd St-Port Authority Bus Terminal)

Entertainment

Hamilton THEATER

27 ⭐ MAP P154, C3

Broadway's hottest ticket, Lin-Manuel Miranda's acclaimed musical *Hamilton*, uses contemporary hip-hop beats to recount the story of America's first secretary of the treasury, Alexander Hamilton. Inspired by Ron Chernow's Hamilton biography, the show has won a flock of awards, with 11 Tony Awards (including Best Musical), a Grammy for its triple-platinum cast album and the Pulitzer Prize for Drama. Book tickets at least six months in advance. Alternatively, head to the online ticket lottery. Winners are able to purchase one or two $10

Theater in New York City

The Early Days
In the early 20th century, clusters of theaters settled into the area around Times Square and began producing popular plays and suggestive comedies, (a movement with roots in early vaudeville). By the 1920s, these messy works had evolved into on-stage spectacles like *Show Boat,* an all-out Oscar Hammerstein production about the lives of performers on a Mississippi steamboat. In 1943, Broadway's first runaway hit – *Oklahoma!* – remained on stage for a record 2212 performances.

The Big Time
Today, Broadway musicals are shown in one of 40 official Broadway theaters, lavish early 20th-century jewels that surround Times Square, and are a major component of cultural life in New York. If you're on a budget, look for off-Broadway productions. These tend to be more intimate, inexpensive, and often just as good.

Beyond Broadway
NYC bursts with theatrical offerings beyond Broadway, from Shakespeare to David Mamet to rising experimental playwrights including Young Jean Lee. In addition to Midtown staples such as Playwrights Horizons (p170) and **Second Stage Theatre** (Tony Kiser Theater; Map p154, C4; ✆tickets 212-246-4422; www.2st.com; 305 W 43rd St, at Eighth Ave, Midtown West; ◷box office noon-6pm Sun-Fri, to 7pm Sat; ⓢA/C/E to 42nd St-Port Authority Bus Terminal), the Lincoln Center (p204) theaters and smaller companies like Soho Rep (p58) are important hubs for works by modern and contemporary playwrights.

front-row tickets. *Hamilton* for 10 bucks? Yes, please! (Richard Rodgers Theatre; ✆tickets 877-250-2929; www.hamiltonmusical.com; 226 W 46th St, btwn Seventh & Eighth Aves; ⓢN/R/W to 49th St)

Kinky Boots   THEATER
28 ⭐ MAP P154, C3

Kinky Boots was adapted from a 2005 British indie film, and is Harvey Fierstein and Cyndi Lauper's smash hit. It tells the story of a doomed English shoe factory unexpectedly saved by Lola, a business-savvy drag queen. Its solid characters and electrifying energy have not been lost on critics: the musical won six Tony Awards, including Best Musical, in 2013. (Al Hirschfeld Theatre; ✆tickets 877-250-2929; www.kinkybootsthemusical.com; 302 W 45th St, btwn Eighth & Ninth Aves; ◷box office

10am-8pm Mon-Sat, noon-6pm Sun;
S A/C/E to 42nd St-Port Authority Bus
Terminal)

Book of Mormon   THEATER

29 ⭐ MAP P154, C3

Subversive, obscene and
ridiculously hilarious, *The Book of
Mormon*, a cutting musical satire,
is the work of *South Park* creators
Trey Parker and Matt Stone and
Avenue Q composer Robert Lopez.
Winner of nine Tony Awards, it tells
the story of two naive Mormons
on a mission to 'save' a Ugandan
village. Book at least three months
ahead for the best choice of prices
and seats, or pay a premium at
shorter notice. Alternatively, head
to the theater 2½ hours before
the show to enter the lottery.
Winners – announced two hours
before curtain – get in for a bargain
$32. Once the winners are called, a
limited number of standing-room
tickets are sold at $27 (subject to
availability). (Eugene O'Neill Theatre;
🎵 tickets 212-239-6200; www.book
ofmormonbroadway.com; 230 W
49th St, btwn Broadway & Eighth Ave;
S N/R/W to 49th St, 1 to 50th St, C/E
to 50th St)

Jazz at Lincoln Center   JAZZ

30 ⭐ MAP P154, C1

Perched atop the Time Warner
Center, Jazz at Lincoln Center
consists of three state-of-the-
art venues: the mid-sized **Rose
Theater**; the panoramic, glass-
backed **Appel Room**; and the
intimate, atmospheric **Dizzy's
Club Coca-Cola**. It's the last of
these that you're most likely to

Carnegie Hall

TV Tapings

Saturday Night Live (www.nbc.com/saturday-night-live) Known for being difficult to get into. Try your luck in the fall lottery by sending an email to snltickets@nbcuni.com in August. Or line up by 7am on the day of the show on the 48th St side of Rockefeller Plaza for standby tickets.

The Late Show with Stephen Colbert (www.showclix.com/event/thelateshowwithstephencolbert) Tickets for this hugely popular late-night show are available online, but they commonly sell out on the day of their release. Check The Late Show's official Twitter account (@colbertlateshow) and Facebook page for release date announcements, usually made one to two months in advance.

Last Week Tonight with John Oliver (www.lastweektickets.com) Tickets to the news recap show of this biting British comedian are available on the website up to 2½ weeks in advance of taping dates (Sundays at 6:45pm).

Full Frontal with Samantha Bee (www.samanthabee.com) Bee offers incisive and utterly hilarious commentary on the politicos and scandal makers hogging the current news headlines. Her late-night shows are taped at 5:45pm on Wednesdays. Go online to get tickets.

visit, given its nightly shows. The talent is often exceptional, as are the dazzling Central Park views. (☏ tickets to Dizzy's Club Coca-Cola 212-258-9595, tickets to Rose Theater & Appel Room 212-721-6500; www.jazz.org; Time Warner Center, 10 Columbus Circle, Broadway at W 59th St; Ⓢ A/C, B/D, 1 to 59th St-Columbus Circle)

Carnegie Hall   LIVE MUSIC

31 ⭐ MAP P154, D1

Few venues are as famous as Carnegie Hall. This legendary music hall may not be the world's biggest, nor its grandest, but it's definitely one of the most acoustically blessed venues around.

Opera, jazz and folk greats feature in the Isaac Stern Auditorium, with edgier jazz, pop, classical and world music in the popular Zankel Hall. The intimate Weill Recital Hall hosts chamber-music concerts and panel discussions. (☏ 212-247-7800; www.carnegiehall.org; 881 Seventh Ave, at W 57th St; ⊙ tours 11:30am, 12:30pm, 2pm & 3pm Mon-Fri, 11:30am & 12:30pm Sat Oct-Jun; Ⓢ N/R/W to 57th St-7th Ave)

Madison Square Garden   SPORTS/CONCERT VENUE

32 ⭐ MAP P154, C6

NYC's major performance venue – part of the massive complex

Broadway on a Budget

The discount **TKTS Booth** (Map p154, D3; www.tdf.org/tkts; Broadway, at W 47th St; ⏱3-8pm Mon & Fri, 2-8pm Tue, 10am-2pm & 3-8pm Wed & Sat, 10am-2pm Thu, 11am-7pm Sun; S N/Q/R/W, S, 1/2/3, 7 to Times Sq-42nd St) in Times Square offers great deals, though rarely to the hottest shows. Many shows – including Hamilton (p166), Kinky Boots (p167) and Book of Mormon (p168) – run lotteries for cheap tickets at the theater several hours before the performance, though spots are limited and in high demand. Some shows (including those above) also offer online lotteries; check the show websites to try your luck.

housing **Penn Station** (W 33rd St, btwn Seventh & Eighth Aves; S 1/2/3, A/C/E to 34th St-Penn Station) – hosts big-arena performers, from Kanye West to Madonna. It's also a sports arena, with **New York Knicks** (www.nba.com/knicks.com) and **New York Liberty** (www.liberty.wnba.com) basketball games and **New York Rangers** (www.nhl.com/rangers) hockey games, as well as boxing and events like the Annual Westminster Kennel Club Dog Show. (MSG, 'the Garden'; www.thegarden.com; 4 Pennsylvania Plaza, Seventh Ave, btwn 31st & 33rd Sts; S A/C/E, 1/2/3 to 34th St-Penn Station)

Birdland   JAZZ, CABARET

33 ⭐ MAP P154, C3

This bird's got a slick look, not to mention the legend – its name dates from bebop legend Charlie Parker (aka 'Bird'), who headlined at the previous location on 52nd St, along with Miles, Monk and just about everyone else (you can see their photos on the walls). Covers run from $25 to $50 and the lineup is always stellar. (📞212-581-3080; www.birdlandjazz.com; 315 W 44th St, btwn Eighth & Ninth Aves; cover $30-50; ⏱5pm-1am; 🛜; S A/C/E to 42nd St-Port Authority Bus Terminal)

Jazz Standard   JAZZ

34 ⭐ MAP P154, F6

Jazz luminaries like Ravi Coltrane, Roy Haynes and Ron Carter have played at this sophisticated club. The service is impeccable and the food is great. There's no minimum and it's programmed by Seth Abramson, a guy who really knows his jazz. A popular jazz brunch ($35) is also an option from 11:30am to 2:30pm on Saturday. (📞212-576-2232; www.jazzstandard.com; 116 E 27th St, btwn Lexington & Park Aves; cover $25-40; S 6 to 28th St)

Playwrights Horizons   THEATER

35 ⭐ MAP P154, B4

An excellent place to catch what could be the next big thing, this veteran 'writers' theater' is dedicated to fostering contemporary American works. Notable past productions include Kenneth Lonergan's *Lobby Hero*, Bruce Norris' Tony Award–winning *Clybourne Park*, as well as Doug Wright's *I Am My Own Wife* and *Grey Gardens*. (📞 212-564-1235; www.playwrights horizons.org; 416 W 42nd St, btwn Ninth & Tenth Aves, Midtown West; Ⓢ A/C/E to 42nd St-Port Authority Bus Terminal)

Don't Tell Mama   CABARET

36 ⭐ MAP P154, C3

Piano bar and cabaret venue extraordinaire, Don't Tell Mama is an unpretentious little spot that's been around for more than 30 years and has the talent to prove it. Its regular roster of performers aren't big names, but true lovers of cabaret who give each show their all, and singing waitstaff add to the fun. (📞 212-757-0788; www. donttellmamanyc.com; 343 W 46th St, btwn Eighth & Ninth Aves, Midtown West; ⏱ 4pm-2:30am Sun-Thu, to 3:30am Fri & Sat; Ⓢ N/Q/R, S, 1/2/3, 7 to Times Sq-42nd St)

Caroline's on Broadway   COMEDY

37 ⭐ MAP P154, D2

You may recognize this big, bright, mainstream classic from comedy specials filmed here on location. It's a top spot to catch US comedy big guns and sitcom stars. (📞 212-757-4100; www.carolines.com; 1626 Broadway, at 50th St, Midtown West; Ⓢ N/Q/R to 49th St; 1, C/E to 50th St)

Midtown Entertainment

Daniel Reichard performing at Birdland

Shopping

MoMA Design & Book Store

GIFTS, BOOKS

The flagship store (see **Museum of Modern Art** 💿 Map p154, E2) at MoMA (p152) is a fab spot for souvenir shopping. Besides gorgeous books, you'll find art prints and posters and one-of-a-kind knickknacks. For furniture, lighting, homewares, jewelry, bags and MUJI merchandise, head across to the **MoMA Design Store**. (📞212-708-9700; www.momastore.org; 11 W 53rd St, btwn Fifth & Sixth Aves; ⏰9:30am-6:30pm Sat-Thu, to 9pm Fri; 🚇E, M to 5th Ave-53rd St)

Grand Central Market

MARKET

38 🔒 MAP P154, F4

It's not all arrivals and departures at Grand Central. The station also harbors a 240ft corridor lined with perfectly coiffed fresh produce and artisan treats. Stock up on anything from crusty bread and fruit tarts to lobsters, chicken pot pies, Spanish quince paste, fruit and vegetables, and roasted coffee beans. There's even a Murray's Cheese stall, peddling milky wonders like cave-aged Gruyère. (www.grandcentralterminal.com/market; Grand Central Terminal, Lexington Ave, at 42nd St, Midtown East; ⏰7am-9pm Mon-Fri, 10am-7pm Sat, 11am-6pm Sun; 🚇S, 4/5/6, 7 to Grand Central-42nd St)

Argosy

BOOKS, MAPS

39 🔒 MAP P154, F1

Bookstores like this are becoming as rare as the books they contain, but since 1925 this landmark has stocked fine antiquarian items such as books, old maps, art monographs and more. There's also an interesting cache of Hollywood memorabilia: personal letters, signed books, contracts and

---

Luxury Fashion

One of the world's fashion capitals, NYC is ever setting trends for the rest of the country to follow. For checking out the latest designs, it's worth browsing some of the best-loved boutiques around town – regardless of whether you intend to spend. A few favorites include Opening Ceremony, Issey Miyake, Steven Alan, Rag & Bone, John Varvatos, By Robert James and Piperlime.

If time is limited, or you simply want to browse a plethora of labels in one go, then head to those heady conglomerations known worldwide as department stores. New York has a special blend of alluring draws – in particular don't miss **Barneys** (www.barneys.com; 660 Madison Ave, at E 61st St), **Bergdorf Goodman** (Map p154, E1; www.bergdorfgoodman.com; 754 Fifth Ave, btwn W 57th & 58th Sts), **Macy's** (Map p154, D5; www.macys.com; 151 W 34th St, at Broadway) and **Bloomingdale's** (Map p154, F1; www.bloomingdales.com; 1000 Third Ave, at E 59th St).

Grand Central Market

autographed publicity stills. Prices range from costly to clearance. (☎212-753-4455; www.argosybooks. com; 116 E 59th St, btwn Park & Lexington Aves, Midtown East; ⊙10am-6pm Mon-Fri, to 5pm Sat Sep–late-May; ⑤4/5/6 to 59th St; N/Q/R to Lexington Ave-59th St)

Drama Book Shop   BOOKS

40 🔒 MAP P154, C4

Nirvana for Broadway fans, this expansive bookstore has taken its theater (both plays and musicals) seriously since 1917. Staffers are good at recommending worthy selections, which also include books on costume, stage design and other elements of performance, as well as industry journals and magazines. Check the store's website and Facebook page for regular in-store

events. (☎212-944-0595; www.drama bookshop.com; 250 W 40th St, btwn Seventh & Eighth Aves, Midtown West; ⊙10am-7pm Mon-Wed & Fri, to 8pm Thu, noon-6pm Sun; ⑤A/C/E to 42nd St-Port Authority Bus Terminal)

B&H Photo Video   ELECTRONICS

41 🔒 MAP P154, C5

Visiting NYC's most popular camera shop is an experience in itself – it's massive and bustling with tech-savvy Hasidic Jewish salesmen. Your chosen item is dropped into a bucket, which then moves up and across the ceiling to the purchase area (which requires waiting in another line). (☎212-444-6600; www. bhphotovideo.com; 420 Ninth Ave, btwn W 33rd & 34th Sts; ⊙9am-7pm Mon-Thu, to 1pm Fri, 10am-6pm Sun, closed Sat; ⑤A/C/E to 34th St-Penn Station)

Explore ◈

Upper East Side

The Upper East Side is one of the ritziest neighborhoods in New York, and it shows. High-end boutiques line Madison Ave, while magnificent Fifth Ave, which runs parallel to the leafy realms of Central Park, is home to the so-called Museum Mile – one of the most cultured strips in New York (and possibly the world).

Start early with a stroll down Fifth Ave's Museum Mile, from around 96th St. You'll pass the Guggenheim Museum (p180) and the Metropolitan Museum of Art (p176), either of which could easily absorb hours of your time. To refuel go to Café Sabarsky (p186) for a slice of old Vienna (followed by a slice of Sachertorte). If you're an art lover, spend your afternoon at the Neue Galerie (p183) or the Frick Collection (p183); for history and culture, try the Museum of the City of New York (p185) or the Jewish Museum (p184). You could also spend the afternoon window-shopping the elite boutiques of Madison Ave – or hitting up a consignment store (p193) to get some bargains for yourself. If you've been able to book well ahead, splurge on sushi at Tanoshi (p185); if not, console yourself with a Michelin-starred French dinner at Café Boulud (p186). Cap off the evening with distinguished cocktails at Bar Pleiades (p189) or Bemelmans Bar (p189), or catch a jazz set at Café Carlyle (p191).

Getting There & Around

S Two train lines serve this area: the 4/5/6 trains run along Lexington Ave, while the Q zooms up Second Ave to its brand-new stations at 72nd, 86th and 96th Sts.

🚌 Crosstown buses at 66th, 72nd, 79th, 86th and 96th Sts take you here through Central Park from the Upper West Side.

Neighborhood Map on p182

Metropolitan Museum of Art (p176) SUSANNE POMMER/SHUTTERSTOCK ©

Top Sight 📷
Metropolitan Museum of Art

This sprawling, encyclopedic museum, founded in 1870, houses one of the world's largest art collections, with more than two million individual objects, from Egyptian temples to American paintings. 'The Met' attracts over six million visitors a year to its 17 acres of galleries, making it the largest single-site attraction in NYC. In other words: plan on spending some time here.

◉ **MAP P182, A3**

☏ 212-535-7710

www.metmuseum.org

1000 Fifth Ave

3-day pass adult/senior/child $25/$17/free; pay-as-you-wish for residents of NY State & students from CT, NY and NJ

🕙 10am-5:30pm Sun-Thu, to 9pm Fri & Sat

Ⓢ 4/5/6, Q to 86th St

Egyptian Art

The museum has an unrivaled collection of ancient Egyptian art, some of which dates back to the Paleolithic era. Located to the north of the Great Hall, the 39 Egyptian galleries open dramatically with one of the Met's prized pieces: the Mastaba Tomb of Perneb (c 2300 BC), an Old Kingdom burial chamber crafted from limestone. From here, a web of rooms is cluttered with funerary stelae, carved reliefs and fragments of pyramids. (Don't miss the intriguing models of Meketre, clay figurines meant to help in the afterlife, in Gallery 105.) These eventually lead to the **Temple of Dendur** (Gallery 131), a sandstone temple to the goddess Isis that resides in a sunny atrium gallery with a reflecting pool – a must-see for the first-time visitor.

European Paintings

Want Renaissance? The Met's got it. On the museum's 2nd floor, the European Paintings galleries display a stunning collection of masterworks. This includes more than 1700 canvases from the roughly 500-year-period starting in the 13th century, with works by every important painter from Duccio to Rembrandt. In fact, everything here is, literally, a masterpiece. In Gallery 621 are several **Caravaggios**, including the expertly painted *The Denial of St Peter*. Gallery 611, to the west, is packed with Spanish treasures, including **El Greco**'s famed *View of Toledo*. Continue south to Gallery 632 to see various **Vermeers**, including *Young Woman with a Water Pitcher*. To the south, in Galleries 634 and 637, you can gaze at several **Rembrandts**, including a 1660 *Self-Portrait*. And that's just the beginning – you could spend hours exploring these many powerful works.

★ Top Tips

o Don't try to see everything – pick a few collections and really immerse yourself.

o Rent a self-guided audio tour in 10 languages (adult/child $7/5) or access excerpts on the Met's free smartphone app.

o Docents offer guided tours of specific galleries (free with admission). Check the website or information desk for details.

✕ Take a Break

The museum's casual **Petrie Court Cafe** sells tasty salads, soups, pastas and hot sandwiches, plus wine and a good selection of tea – all served in an airy setting with floor-to-ceiling views of Central Park.

Far left: Bust of Roman Emperor, Gallery 544

Art of the Arab Lands

In the southeastern corner of the 2nd floor you'll find the Islamic galleries, with 15 incredible rooms showcasing the museum's extensive collection of art from the Middle East, and Central and South Asia. In addition to garments, secular decorative objects and manuscripts, you'll find gilded and enameled glassware (Gallery 452) and a magnificent 14th-century **mihrab** (prayer niche) lined with elaborately patterned polychrome tilework (Gallery 455). There's also a superb array of Ottoman textiles (Gallery 459), a medieval-style Moroccan court (Gallery 456) and the 18th-century **Damascus Room** (Gallery 461).

American Wing

In the northwestern corner, the two-floor American Wing showcases a wide variety of decorative and fine art from throughout US history. These include everything from colonial portraiture to Hudson River School masterpieces to John Singer Sargent's elegantly sexy **Madame X** (Gallery 771; pictured left) – not to mention Emanuel Leutze's massive canvas of **Washington Crossing the Delaware** (Gallery 760).

Greek & Roman Art

The 27 galleries devoted to classical antiquity are another Met doozy. From the Great Hall, a passageway takes you through a barrel-vaulted room flanked by the chiseled torsos of Greek figures. This spills right into one of the Met's loveliest spaces: the airy Greek and Roman sculpture court (Gallery 162), full of marble carvings of gods and historical figures. The statue of a bearded **Hercules** from AD 68–98, with a lion's skin draped about him, is particularly awe-inspiring.

Modern & Contemporary Art

The rooms in the far southwestern corner of the 1st and 2nd floors feature art from the early 20th century onward. Notable names here include Spanish masters Picasso (whose **Still Life with a Bottle of Rum** hangs in Gallery 905), Dalí and Miró, as well as American painters Georgia O'Keeffe and Edward Hopper. Thomas Hart Benton's magnificent ten-panel mural **America Today** takes up an entire room in Gallery 909.

The Roof Garden

One of the best spots in the entire museum is the roof garden, which features rotating sculpture installations by contemporary and 20th-century artists. (Jeff Koons, Andy Goldsworthy and Imran Qureshi have all shown here.) Best of all are the views it offers of the city and Central Park. It's also home to the **Cantor Roof Garden Bar** (☎212-570-3711; 5th fl; ⏰11am-4:30pm Sun-Thu, to 8:15pm Fri & Sat mid-Apr–Oct), an ideal spot for a drink – especially at sunset. It's open from April to October.

Top Sight 📷

Guggenheim Museum

A sculpture in its own right, architect Frank Lloyd Wright's building almost overshadows the collection of 20th-century art inside. Even before it opened, the inverted ziggurat structure was derided by some critics but hailed by others, who welcomed it as a beloved architectural icon. Since its opening, this unusual structure has appeared in countless postcards, TV programs and films.

◎ MAP P182, A1

☎ 212-423-3500

www.guggenheim.org

1071 Fifth Ave

adult/child $25/free, pay-what-you-wish 5:45-7:45pm Sat

🕐 10am-5:45pm Sun-Wed & Fri, to 7:45pm Sat, closed Thu

🚇 4/5/6 to 86th St

A Delayed Beginning

Solomon R Guggenheim was a New York mining magnate who began acquiring abstract art at the behest of his art adviser, an eccentric German baroness named Hilla Rebay. In 1939, with Rebay serving as director, Guggenheim opened a temporary museum on 54th St. Four years later, the pair commissioned Wright to construct a permanent home for the collection. Like most developments in New York, the project took forever to finish. Construction was delayed for almost 13 years due to budget constraints, the outbreak of WWII and outraged neighbors didn't want a giant concrete spaceship in their midst. The museum was finally completed in 1959 – after both Wright and Guggenheim had passed away.

Modernizing an Icon

A renovation in the early 1990s added an eight-story tower to the east, providing an extra 50,000 sq ft of exhibition space. These galleries feature rotating exhibitions from the permanent collection, while the ramps of the Rotunda are occupied by temporary exhibits.

The museum's holdings include works by Kandinsky, Picasso and Pollock, as well as paintings by Monet, Van Gogh and Degas; sculpture by Constantin Brancusi; photographs by Robert Mapplethorpe; and key surrealist works donated by Guggenheim's niece Peggy.

Visiting the Museum

The museum's ascending ramp displays rotating exhibitions of modern and contemporary art; exhibitions are installed from bottom to top. Fans of art and design should stop into the on-site **Guggenheim Store** to browse their excellent collection of books, posters, gifts and homewares.

★ Top Tips

o The ticket line can be brutal at any time of the year. You'll save a lot of time by purchasing your tickets in advance on the website.

o If you have a smartphone, download the Guggenheim's free app, which has info on the building and the collections in five languages.

✖ Take a Break

There are two good on-site food options. **The Wright** (☏ 212-427-5690; mains $23-28; ⏱ 11:30am-3:30pm Mon-Wed & Fri, from 11am Sat & Sun), at ground level, is a space-age-style bistro serving seasonal dishes and classic cocktails. **Cafe 3** (☏ 212-427-5682; sandwiches $10; ⏱ 10:30am-5pm Fri-Wed), on the 3rd floor, offers sparkling views of Central Park, and excellent coffee and light snacks.

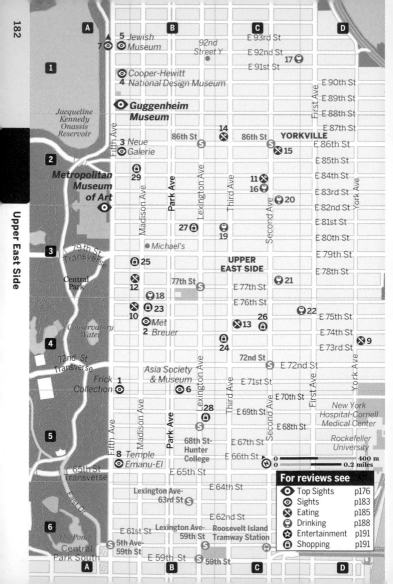

A

5 Jewish Museum
7

92nd Street Y

B

E 93rd St
E 92nd St
E 91st St

17

C

D

Cooper-Hewitt
4 National Design Museum

E 90th St
E 89th St
E 88th St
E 87th St

First Ave

Guggenheim Museum

Jacqueline Kennedy Onassis Reservoir

14

86th St

86th St

YORKVILLE

E 86th St

15

3 Neue Galerie

Fifth Ave

E 85th St

Metropolitan Museum of Art

29

Madison Ave

Park Ave

Lexington Ave

Third Ave

E 84th St

11

16

20

Second Ave

York Ave

E 83rd St

E 82nd St

E 81st St

27

19

E 80th St

E 79th St

Michael's

UPPER EAST SIDE

E 78th St

25

21

12

77th St

E 77th St

Central Park

18

E 76th St

10

23

22

E 75th St

Met
2 Breuer

13

26

9

E 74th St

Conservatory Water

24

E 73rd St

72nd St

E 72nd St

72nd St Transverse

Asia Society & Museum

E 71st St

First Ave

York Ave

Frick Collection 1

6

E 70th St

Second Ave

New York Hospital-Cornell Medical Center

28

E 69th St

Fifth Ave

Madison Ave

Park Ave

Lexington Ave

Third Ave

E 68th St

Rockefeller University

68th St-Hunter College

E 67th St

E 66th St

5

8 Temple Emanu-El

0   400 m
0   0.2 miles

65th St Transverse

E 65th St

East Dr

Lexington Ave-63rd St

E 64th St

6

The Pond

Central Park South

E 62nd St

Lexington Ave-59th St

5th Ave-59th St

Roosevelt Island Tramway Station

59th St

59th St

Sights

Frick Collection

GALLERY

1 ◎ MAP P182, A4

This spectacular art collection sits in a mansion built by steel magnate Henry Clay Frick, one of the many such residences lining the section of Fifth Ave that was once called 'Millionaires' Row.' The museum has over a dozen splendid rooms displaying masterpieces by Titian, Vermeer, Gilbert Stuart, El Greco, Joshua Reynolds, Goya and Rembrandt. Sculpture, ceramics, antique furniture and clocks are also on display. Fans of classical music will enjoy the frequent piano and violin concerts (p191) on Sunday evenings. A worthwhile audio tour (available in several languages) is included in the price of admission. (☏ 212-288-0700; www.frick.org; 1 E 70th St, cnr Fifth Ave; adult/student $22/12, pay-what-you-wish 2-6pm Wed, first Fri of month excl Jan & Sep free; ⊘10am-6pm Tue-Sat, 11am-5pm Sun; ⑤6 to 68th St-Hunter College)

Met Breuer

MUSEUM

2 ◎ MAP P182, B4

The newest branch of the Metropolitan Museum of Art (p176) opened in the landmark former Whitney Museum (p110) building (originally designed by Marcel Breuer) in 2016. Exhibits are dedicated to modern and contemporary art across various media, with sculpture, photographs, video, design and paintings from American and international figures such as Edvard Munch, Yayoi Kusama, Claes Oldenburg, Ettore Sottsass, Dara Birnbaum, Robert Smithson and Mira Schendel. Your ticket gives you three-day admission to the main museum, and medieval exhibits at the Cloisters (p22). (☏ 212-731-1675; www.metmuseum.org/visit/met-breuer; 945 Madison Ave, cnr E 75th St; 3-day pass adult/senior/child $25/$17/free; pay-as-you-wish for residents of NY State & students from CT, NY and NJ; ⊘10am–5:30pm Tue-Thu & Sun, to 9pm Fri & Sat; ⑤6 to 77th St; Q to 72nd St)

Neue Galerie

MUSEUM

3 ◎ MAP P182, A2

This restored Carrère and Hastings mansion from 1914 is a resplendent showcase for Austrian and German art, featuring works by Paul Klee, Ernst Ludwig Kirchner and Egon Schiele. In pride of place on the 2nd floor is Gustav Klimt's golden 1907 portrait of Adele Bloch-Bauer – acquired for the museum by cosmetics magnate Ronald Lauder for a whopping $135 million. The fascinating story of the painting's history is told in the 2015 film *Woman in Gold*. Avoid visiting on weekends (and the first Friday of the month) if you don't want to deal with gallery-clogging crowds. (☏ 212-628-6200; www.neuegalerie.org; 1048 Fifth Ave, cnr E 86th St; adult/student $20/10, 6-8pm 1st Fri of the month free; ⊘11am-6pm Thu-Mon; ⑤4/5/6 to 86th St)

Cooper-Hewitt National Design Museum

MUSEUM

4 MAP P182, A1

Part of the Smithsonian Institution in Washington, DC, this is the only US museum dedicated to both historic and contemporary design. Housed in the 64-room mansion built by billionaire Andrew Carnegie in 1901, the 210,000-piece collection offers artful displays spanning 3000 years over three floors of the building. The beautiful **garden** is open to the public and accessible from 90th St or from inside the museum. **Mansion tours** are at 1:30pm on weekdays, and at 1pm and 3pm on weekends. (☏212-849-8400; www.cooperhewitt. org; 2 E 91st St, cnr Fifth Ave; adult/child $18/free, pay-what-you-wish 6-9pm Sat; ⌚10am-6pm Sun-Fri, to 9pm Sat; Ⓢ4/5/6 to 86th St)

Jewish Museum

MUSEUM

5 MAP P182, A1

This New York City gem occupies a French-Gothic mansion from 1908, housing 30,000 items of Judaica, as well as sculpture, painting and decorative arts. It hosts excellent temporary exhibits, featuring retrospectives on influential figures such as Art Spiegelman, as well as world-class shows on luminaries Marc Chagall, Édouard Vuillard, Modigliani and Man Ray, among others. (☏212-423-3200; www.the jewishmuseum.org; 1109 Fifth Ave, btwn E 92nd & 93rd Sts; adult/child $15/free, Sat free, pay-what-you-wish 5-8pm Thu; ⌚11am-5:45pm Sat-Tue, to 8pm Thu, to 4pm Fri; ♿; Ⓢ6, Q to 96th St)

Met Breuer (p183)

Asia Society & Museum
MUSEUM

6 ◉ MAP P182, B4

Founded in 1956 by John D Rockefeller (an avid collector of Asian art), this cultural center hosts fascinating exhibits as well as Jain sculptures and Nepalese Buddhist paintings. Daily **tours** are offered at 2pm Tuesday through Sunday year-round and at 6:30pm Friday (excluding summer months). (📞212-288-6400; www.asiasociety. org; 725 Park Ave, cnr E 70th St; adult/child $12/free, 6-9pm Fri Sep-Jun free; ⏰11am-6pm Tue-Sun, to 9pm Fri Sep-Jun; S 6 to 68th St-Hunter College; Q to 72nd St)

Museum of the City of New York
MUSEUM

7 ◉ MAP P182, A1

Situated in a Georgian Colonial Revival–style building at the top end of Museum Mile, this local museum focuses solely on New York City's past, present and future. Don't miss the 28-minute film *Timescapes* (on the 2nd floor), which charts NYC's growth from a tiny trading post for Native Americans to burgeoning metropolis. (📞212-534-1672; www.mcny.org; 1220 Fifth Ave, btwn E 103rd & 104th Sts; suggested admission adult/child $18/free; ⏰10am-6pm; S 6 to 103rd St)

Temple Emanu-El
SYNAGOGUE

8 ◉ MAP P182, A5

Founded in 1845 as the first Reform synagogue in New York,

(Almost) Free Museums

The Upper East Side is blessed with many of the finest museums in New York City, though visiting them all can be extremely pricey. Most of them have set admission prices but usually offer specific pay-whatever-you-wish hours once a week, so plan to visit at those times to save some cash. Some also offer completely free admission at specific times, such as the Neue Galerie (first Friday evening of each month; p183) and the Asia Society & Museum (Friday evenings from September to June; p185).

this temple, completed in 1929, is now one of the largest Jewish houses of worship in the world. An imposing Romanesque structure, it is more than 175ft long and 100ft tall, with a brilliant, hand-painted ceiling featuring gold details. (📞212-744-1400; www.emanuelnyc. org; 1 E 65th St, cnr Fifth Ave; admission free; ⏰10am-4pm Sun-Thu; S 6 to 68th St-Hunter College)

Eating

Tanoshi
SUSHI $$$

9 ✖ MAP P182, D4

It's not easy to snag one of the 20 stools at Tanoshi, a wildly popular, pocket-sized sushi spot. The setting may be humble, but the flavors are simply magnificent. Only

The Second Avenue Subway

Nearly a century in the making (and a local in-joke for decades), the Second Avenue Subway finally opened to the public on January 1, 2017...well, the first phase, anyway. Two new miles of track – which took 10 years to build and cost $4.5 billion – now connect an extended Q line to the F train at 63rd St and Lexington Ave, then continue up Second Ave for stops at 72nd, 86th and 96th Sts. With an airy feel and broad, open platforms, the three gleaming new stations feature permanent tile and mosaic installations by artists Chuck Close, Jean Shin, Vik Muniz and Sarah Sze. All the trouble seems to have been worth it: the new line is carrying 176,000 people per day, and morning-rush ridership – and overcrowding – has been reduced by 40% on the formerly beleaguered Lexington Ave 4/5/6 line. Now that the long-awaited line is a reality, the next question is: will the next three sections – extending the line north to 125th and south to the Financial District – ever be built? Only time will tell.

sushi is on offer and only *omakase* (chef's selection) – which might include Hokkaido scallops, king salmon or mouthwatering *uni* (sea urchin). Reserve well in advance. (📞 917-265-8254; www.tanoshisushi nyc.com; 1372 York Ave, btwn E 73rd & 74th Sts; chef's sushi selection $80-100; 🕑 seatings 6pm, 7:30pm & 9pm Mon-Sat; 🚇 Q to 72nd St)

Café Boulud
FRENCH $$$

10 ✖ MAP P182, B4

This Michelin-starred bistro – part of Daniel Boulud's gastronomic empire – attracts a rather staid crowd with its globe-trotting French cuisine. Seasonal menus include classic dish coq au vin, as well as more inventive fare such as scallop *crudo* (raw) with white miso. Foodies on a budget will be interested in the three-course prix-fixe lunch ($45; two courses

for $39). (📞 212-772-2600; www. cafeboulud.com/nyc; 20 E 76th St, btwn Fifth & Madison Aves; mains around $45; 🕑 7am-10:30am, noon-2:30pm & 5:45-10:30pm Mon-Fri, from 8am Sat & Sun; 🍷; 🚇 6 to 77th St)

Café Sabarsky
AUSTRIAN $$

The lines can get long at this popular cafe (see **3** ◉ Map p182, A2) evoking an opulent, turn-of-the-century Vienna coffeehouse. But the well-rendered Austrian specialties make it worth the wait. Expect crepes with smoked trout, goulash soup and roasted bratwurst. There's also a mouthwatering list of specialty sweets, including a divine Sacher torte (dark chocolate cake with apricot confiture). (📞 212-288-0665; www.neuegalerie.org/cafes/sabarsky; 1048 Fifth Ave, cnr E 86th St; mains $18-30; 🕑 9am-6pm Mon & Wed, to 9pm Thu-Sun; 🍷; 🚇 4/5/6 to 86th St)

Two Boots

PIZZA $

11  MAP P182, C2

With the two 'boots' of Italy and Louisiana as inspiration, this quirky, pioneering NYC chain has over 40 original, eclectic pizza flavors – all named after comedians, scientists, musicians, local sports teams and even fictional characters. (☏212-734-0317; www.twoboots.com; 1617 Second Ave, cnr E 84th St; pizza slices $3.50-4.25; ⏱11:30am-11pm Sun-Tue, to midnight Wed, to 2am Thu, to 4am Fri & Sat; ⏷; ⬛Q, 4/5/6 to 86th St)

Sant Ambroeus

ITALIAN $$$

12  MAP P182, B3

Behind a demure facade lies this dressy Milanese bistro and cafe that oozes Old World charm. The long granite counter up-front dispenses rich cappuccinos, pastries and panini; the elegant dining room behind dishes up northern Italian specialties, such as breaded veal chop and seafood risotto. Don't miss its famed gelato. (☏212-570-2211; www.santambroeus.com; 1000 Madison Ave, btwn E 77th & 78th Sts; panini $14-19, mains $26-69; ⏱7am-11pm Mon-Fri, from 8am Sat & Sun; ⏷; ⬛6 to 77th St)

Candle Cafe

VEGAN $$

13  MAP P182, C4

The moneyed yoga set piles into this attractive vegan cafe serving a long list of sandwiches, salads, comfort food and market-driven specials. The specialty here is the house-made seitan. There is a juice bar and a gluten-free menu. (☏212-472-0970; www.candlecafe.

Papaya King (p188)

com; 1307 Third Ave, btwn E 74th & 75th Sts; mains $15-22; ⏲11:30am-10:30pm Mon-Sat, to 9:30pm Sun; 🚇; Ⓢ Q to 72nd St-2nd Ave)

Papaya King

HOT DOGS $

14 🍴 MAP P182, C2

The *original* hot-dog-and-papaya-juice shop, from 1932, over 40 years before crosstown rival Gray's Papaya opened, Papaya King has lured many a New Yorker to its neon-lit corner for a cheap and tasty snack of hot dogs and fresh-squeezed papaya juice. (Why papaya? The informative wall signs will explain all.) Try the Homerun, with sauerkraut and New York onion relish. (☎212-369-0648; www.papayaking.com; 179 E 86th St, cnr Third Ave; hot dogs $2.50-4.50; ⏲8am-midnight Sun-Thu, to 1am Fri & Sat; Ⓢ4/5/6, Q to 86th St)

Schaller & Weber

MARKET $

15 🍴 MAP P182, C2

This award-winning charcuterie and delicatessen is a holdover from when the Yorkville neighborhood was a largely German enclave. It sells over 15 varieties of sausage made at its factory in Queens – German classics like *bauernwurst* and *weisswurst*, chicken bratwurst, cheddar-stuffed brat', Irish bangers, Polish kielbasa and more – alongside imported European goodies: cheese, pickles, condiments, chocolate, wine and beer. (☎212-879-3047; www.schallerweber. com; 1654 Second Ave, cnr E 86th St; sausages from $8 per 12oz; ⏲10am-7pm Mon-Sat; Ⓢ Q, 4/5/6 to 86th St)

Cheap(er) Eats 🍽

The Upper East Side is the epitome of old-school opulence, especially the area that covers the blocks from 60th to 86th Sts between Park and Fifth Aves. If you're looking for eating and drinking spots that are easier on the wallet, head east of Lexington Ave. Third, Second and First Aves are lined with less-pricey neighborhood venues.

Drinking

Caledonia

BAR

16 🍷 MAP P182, C2

The name of this dimly lit, dark-wood bar is a dead giveaway: it's devoted to Scottish whisky, with over a hundred single-malts to choose from (be they Highlands, Islands, Islay, Lowlands or Speyside), as well as some blends and even a few from the US, Ireland and Japan. The bartenders know their stuff and will be happy to make recommendations. (☎212-734-4300; www.caledoniabar.com; 1609 Second Ave, btwn E 83rd & 84th Sts; Ⓢ Q, 4/5/6 to 86th St)

Drunken Munkey

LOUNGE

17 🍷 MAP P182, C1

This playful lounge channels old Bombay with vintage wallpaper, cricket-ball door handles and jauntily attired waitstaff. The monkey chandeliers may be pure whimsy, but the craft cocktails and tasty curries (small, meant for sharing) are serious business. Gin, not surprisingly, is the drink of choice. Try the Bramble: Bombay gin, blackberry liqueur and fresh lemon juice and blackberries. (📞646-998-4600; www.drunken munkeynyc.com; 338 E 92nd St, btwn First & Second Aves; ⏰4:30pm-2am Mon-Thu, to 3am Fri, 11am-3am Sat, to 2am Sun; ⑤Q, 6 to 96th St)

Bar Pleiades   BAR

Next door to Café Boulud (p186), the Bar Pleiades (see 10 ❌ Map p182, B4) serves seasonally created specialty cocktails, along with an upscale bar menu (think oysters, and fennel-and-duck sausage). There's live jazz from 9pm to midnight on Friday nights. (📞212-772-2600; www.barpleiades.com; 20 E 76th St, btwn Fifth & Madison Aves; ⏰noon-midnight; ⑤6 to 77th St)

Bemelmans Bar   LOUNGE

18 🟢 **MAP P182, B3**

Sink into a chocolate-leather banquette and take in the glorious, old-school elegance of this fabled bar – the sort of place where the waiters wear white jackets, a pianist tinkles away on a baby grand and the ceiling is 24-carat gold leaf. The walls are covered in charming murals by the bar's namesake Ludwig Bemelman, famed creator of the *Madeline* books. (📞212-744-1600; www.thecarlyle.com; Carlyle Hotel, 35 E 76th St, cnr Madison Ave; ⏰noon-1am; ⑤6 to 77th St)

Bemelmans Bar

Irving Farm Roasters COFFEE

19  MAP P182, C3

This pioneering New York artisanal coffeehouse – it roasts its own beans in a tiny town 98 miles upstate – serves up full-bodied espressos and single-origin pour-overs, along with a small yet tasty cafe menu. This is the largest of its nine Manhattan locations, with a roomy seating area at the back. (646-861-2949; www.irvingfarm.com; 1424 Third Ave, cnr E 81st St; 10am-8pm Mon-Fri, from 11am Sat & Sun; S 6 to 77th St; 4/5 to 86th St)

Penrose BAR

20 MAP P182, C2

The Penrose, famous for its pickle martinis and fried pickles, brings a dose of style to the Upper East Side, with craft beers, exposed brick walls, vintage mirrors, reclaimed wood details and friendly bartenders. It's packed with a on weekends, but you can usually get a seat along the wall or in the back. (212-203-2751; www.penrosebar.com; 1590 Second Ave, btwn E 82nd & 83rd Sts; noon-4am Mon-Fri, from 10am Sat & Sun; S Q, 4/5/6 to 86th St)

Uva WINE BAR

21 MAP P182, C3

Rustic brick walls, low-lit chandeliers and worn floorboards give this lively eating and drinking spot the feel of an old European tavern. There are dozens of wines by the glass (from $9) plus wine flights (before 7pm), allowing you to sample a range of varietals. In summer,

The Henschel Quartet performing at the Frick Collection

HIROYUKI ITO/CONTRIBUTOR/GETTY IMAGES ©

head for the lovely patio out back. (📞212-472-4552; www.uvanyc.com; 1486 Second Ave, btwn E 77th & 78th Sts; ⏰4pm-2am Mon-Fri, from 11am Sat, 11am-1am Sun; 🚇6 to 77th St)

Seamstress
BAR

22 🚇 MAP P182, D4

This rare uptown gem serves craft cocktails and seasonal pub fare in a screen-free environment that feels much more downtown. Sit at the bar or arrive early and sink into a dark leather banquette. Nibble on oysters, raw field greens or a mutton burger, while sipping complex libations made of rye whiskey, pomegranate liqueur and other unusual spirits. (📞212-288-8033; www.seamstressny.com; 339 E 75th St, btwn First & Second Aves; ⏰5:30pm-midnight Sun-Thu, to 2am Fri & Sat; 🚇Q to 72nd St; 6 to 77th St)

Entertainment

Frick Collection Concerts
CLASSICAL MUSIC

Once a month this opulent mansion-museum (p183) hosts a Sunday 5pm concert (see 1 ⊙ Map p182, A4) that brings in world-renowned performers, such as cellist Yehuda Hanani and violinist Thomas Zehetmair. (📞212-288-0700; www.frick.org; 1 E 70th St, cnr Fifth Ave; $45; ⏰5pm Sun; 🚇6 to 68th St-Hunter College; Q to 72nd St)

Café Carlyle
JAZZ

This swanky spot (see 18 🚇 Map p182, B3) at the Carlyle Hotel draws top-shelf talent. The likes of Judy

92nd Street Y

In addition to its wide spectrum of performances, literary readings and family-friendly events, this nonprofit **cultural center** (Map p182, B1; 📞212-415-5500; www.92y.org; 1395 Lexington Ave, cnr E 92nd St; 🚻; 🚇Q, 6 to 96th St) hosts an excellent lecture and conversation series. Playwright Edward Albee, cellist Yo-Yo Ma, comedian Steve Martin and novelist Salman Rushdie have all taken the stage here.

Collins, Sutton Foster and jazz pianist Loston Harris perform here regularly, and Alan Cumming does cabaret shows. Bring mucho bucks: the cover charge doesn't include food or drinks, and there's a minimum spend. The dress code is 'chic' – gentlemen, wear a jacket. (📞212-744-1600; www.thecarlyle.com; Carlyle Hotel, 35 E 76th St, cnr Madison Ave; cover $95-215, food & drink min $25-75; ⏰shows at 8:45pm & 10:45pm; 🚇6 to 77th St)

Shopping

Diptyque
PERFUME

23 🔒 MAP P182, B4

Come out smelling like a rose – or wisteria, jasmine, cypress or sandalwood – at this olfactory oasis. Parisian company Diptyque has been creating signature scents since 1961, using innovative combinations of plants, woods and flowers. (📞212-879-3330; www.diptyqueparis.com; 971 Madison Ave, cnr E 76th St; ⏰10am-7pm Mon-Sat, noon-6pm Sun; 🚇6 to 77th St)

Flying Tiger Copenhagen
GIFTS & SOUVENIRS

24 🔒 MAP P182, C4

This eclectic Danish design store is an emporium of quirky-yet-useful items. Almost everything is priced under $5 and festooned with bright colors and fun patterns: housewares, art supplies, writing journals, toys and games, accessories etc. Ever wanted a Doodling Robot? You'll find it here. (📞917-388-2812; www.flyingtiger.com; 1282 Third Ave, cnr E 74th St; ⏰10am-8pm Mon-Sat, 11am-6pm Sun; 🚇Q to 72nd St; 6 to 77th St)

Top Shopping for Less

Madison Ave isn't for amateurs. Flagship boutiques from the world's top designers line the stretch from 60th St to 72nd St, including Gucci, Prada and Cartier. A few consignment stores offer pre-loved designer deals: for gently worn top brands such as Louboutin, Fendi, and Dior try Encore (p193) or **Michael's** (Map p182, B3; 📞212-737-7273; www.michaelsconsignment.com; 1041 Madison Ave, btwn E 79th & 80th Sts, 2nd fl; ⏰10am-6pm Mon-Sat, to 8pm Thu; 🚇6 to 77th St).

La Maison du Chocolat
CHOCOLATE

25 🔒 MAP P182, B3

The US flagship store of the famed Parisian chocolatier is a dangerous place for chocoholics. Dark, sweet decadence comes in many forms here, from cocoa-dusted truffles to intensely rich bars made from the world's finest beans. There's a small cafe where you can sink your teeth into crisp macarons and sip a cup of hot chocolate. (📞212-744-7118; www.lamaisonduchocolat.us; 1018 Madison Ave, btwn E 78th & 79th Sts; ⏰10am-7pm Mon-Sat, 11am-6pm Sun; 🚇6 to 77th St)

Ricky's NYC
COSMETICS

26 🔒 MAP P182, C4

One of the many branches of this classic New York beauty shop, Ricky's carries a huge variety of makeup, skincare and hair products from around the world, plus salon-quality accessories and appliances. It also has a range of fun and quirky gifts, and at Halloween time it's a go-to shop for costumes and theatrical makeup. (📞212-988-2291; www.rickysnyc.com; 1425 Second Ave, cnr E 74th St; ⏰9am-9pm Mon-Sat, 10am-8pm Sun; 🚇Q to 72nd St)

Mary Arnold Toys
TOYS

27 🔒 MAP P182, B3

Several generations of Upper East Siders have spent large chunks of their childhood browsing the stuffed shelves of this personable

RICHARD LEVINE/ALAMY STOCK PHOTO ©

Flying Tiger Copenhagen

local toy store, opened in 1931. Check the website for free monthly events, such as scavenger hunts or Lego-making sessions. (☎212-744-8510; www.maryarnoldtoys.com; 1178 Lexington Ave, btwn E 80th & 81st Sts; ☺9am-6pm Mon-Fri, from 10am Sat, 10am-5pm Sun; ♿; Ⓢ4/5/6 to 86th St)

Shakespeare & Co   BOOKS

28 🔒 MAP P182, B5

No relation to the Paris seller, this popular bookstore is one of NYC's great indie options. There's a wide array of contemporary fiction and nonfiction, art and local history books, plus a small but unique collection of periodicals, while an Espresso book machine churns out print-on-demand titles. The small cafe up front

serves coffee, tea and light meals. (☎212-772-3400; www.shakeandco. com; 939 Lexington Ave, cnr E 69th St; ☺7:30am-8pm Mon-Fri, 8am-7pm Sat, 9am-6pm Sun; 📶; Ⓢ6 to 68th St)

Encore   CLOTHING

29 🔒 MAP P182, B2

Upper East Side fashionistas have been emptying out their closets at this pioneering consignment and resale shop since 1954. (Even Jacqueline Kennedy Onassis used to sell her clothes here.) Expect to find a gently worn selection of name brands such as Louboutin, Fendi and Dior. Prices are high, but infinitely better than retail. (☎212-879-2850; www.encoreresale.com; 1132 Madison Ave, btwn E 84th & 85th Sts, 2nd fl; ☺10am-6:30pm Mon-Sat, noon-6pm Sun; Ⓢ4/5/6 to 86th St)

Walking Tour 🥾

Harlem Soul

Harlem: the neighborhood where Cab Calloway crooned; where Ralph Ellison penned Invisible Man, his epic novel on truth and intolerance; where acclaimed artist Romare Bearden pieced together his first collages. Simultaneously vibrant and effusive, brooding and melancholy, Harlem is the deepest recess of New York's soul.

Walk Facts

Start Tom's Restaurant;
S 1 to 110th St

End Shrine; **S** 2/3 to
135th St

Length 4.9 miles;
four to five hours
depending on stops

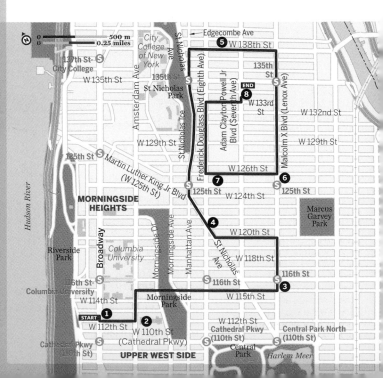

❶ Tom's Restaurant

Down a cuppa joe at Greek American **Tom's Restaurant** (📞 212-864-6137; www.tomsrestaurant.net; 2880 Broadway, at 112th St; mains $8-13; 🕐 6am-1:30am Sun-Thu, 24hr Fri & Sat; 🚇 1 to 110th St), whose exterior and red-neon sign featured on the TV comedy *Seinfeld*.

❷ Cathedral Church of St John the Divine

This epically-scaled and yet-to-be-completed **cathedral** (📞 tours 212-316-7540; www.stjohndivine.org; 1047 Amsterdam Ave, at W 112th St; $10, Highlights Tour $14, Vertical Tour $20; 🕐 7:30am-6pm; 🚇 B/C, 1 to 110th St-Cathedral Pkwy) is the USA's largest place of worship.

❸ Malcolm Shabazz Harlem Market

Trawl this low-key **market** (52 W 116th St, btwn Malcolm X Blvd & Fifth Ave; admission free; 🕐 9am-8pm; 🚻; 🚇 2/3 to 116th St) – run by the mosque where slain Muslim orator Malcolm X once preached – for African jewelry, textiles, drums, leather goods and oils.

❹ Flamekeepers Hat Club

Harlem's Gilded Age lives on at this friendly **boutique** (📞 212-531-3542; 273 W 121st St, at St Nicholas Ave; 🕐 noon-7pm Tue & Wed, to 8pm Thu-Sat, to 6pm Sun; 🚇 A/C, B/D to 125th St) lined with elegant hats. Can't decide? Owner Marc Williamson has a knack for picking the right piece for every face.

❺ Strivers' Row

Ever since ambitious African Americans first moved to **Strivers' Row** (W 138th & 139th Sts, btwn Frederick Douglass & Adam Clayton Powell Jr Blvds; 🚇 B, C to 135th St) in the 1920s, some of Harlem's greatest luminaries have lived in its 1890s town houses, among them blues veteran WC Handy and singer-dancer Bill 'Bojangles' Robinson.

❻ Red Rooster

Taste the 'new Harlem' at **Red Rooster** (📞 212-792-9001; www.redroosterharlem.com; 310 Malcolm X Blvd, btwn W 125th & 126th Sts; mains lunch $18-32, dinner $24-38; 🕐 11:30am-10:30pm Mon-Thu, to 11:30pm Fri, 10am-11:30pm Sat, to 10pm Sun; 🚇 2/3 to 125th St), where chef Marcus Samuelsson gives comfort food a respectful makeover.

❼ Apollo Theater

One of the best places to catch a concert here is the **Apollo Theater** (📞 212-531-5300, tours 212-531-5337; www.apollotheater.org; 253 W 125th St, btwn Frederick Douglass & Adam Clayton Powell Jr Blvds; tickets from $16; 🚇 A/C, B/D to 125th St). The famed Amateur Night takes place every Wednesday.

❽ Shrine

A mainstay on Harlem's nightlife circuit, **Shrine** (www.shrinenyc.com; 2271 Adam Clayton Powell Jr Blvd, btwn 133rd & 134th Sts; 🕐 4pm-4am; 🚇 2/3 to 135th St) hosts an incredible lineup of bands nightly.

Explore ◈
Upper West Side & Central Park

Walking past rows of brownstones on quiet Upper West Side streets will make you feel like you've stepped out of a romantic New York movie. Several world-class cultural institutions are located here, and the neighborhood is bordered by two parks, the smaller Riverside Park and the great verdant expanse of Central Park.

Enjoy a cheap and cheerful breakfast of eggs, bagels and lox at Barney Greengrass (p207), then spend the morning delving into natural science at the American Museum of Natural History (p204) (don't miss the giant whale in the Milstein Ocean Hall, a NYC classic) or local history at the New-York Historical Society (p205). Meander over to Broadway and pick up some picnicking supplies from the gourmet cornucopia at Zabar's (p206), then while away the afternoon on the grass in either Central Park (p198) or Riverside Park (p208). Have dinner at Michelin-starred Dovetail (p205) or the smart bistro Cafe Luxembourg (p206), then take in a performance of opera, ballet or theater at Lincoln Center. Take a cab back up to Cafe Lalo (p207) for dessert and an aperitif to cap off the night.

Getting There & Around

Ⓢ The 1, 2 and 3 lines are good for destinations between Broadway and the river, while the B and C trains are best for museums and Central Park. The A/C, B/D and 1 stop at Columbus Circle and 59th St.

🚌 Crosstown routes at 66th, 72nd, 79th, 86th and 96th Sts go through the park to the Upper East Side, stopping at Central Park West and Fifth Ave – not inside the park.

Neighborhood Map on p202

Top Sight 📷
Central Park

With more than 800 acres of picturesque meadows, ponds and woods, Central Park might seem to be Manhattan in its raw state. But the park, designed by Frederick Law Olmsted and Calvert Vaux, is the result of serious engineering: thousands of workers shifted 10 million cartloads of soil to transform swamp and rocky outcroppings into the 'people's park' of today.

◎ **MAP P202, E4**

www.centralparknyc.org

59th to 110th Sts, btwn Central Park West & Fifth Ave

🕑 6am-1am

🚻

Strawberry Fields

This tear-shaped **garden** (www.centralparknyc.
org; Central Park, at 72nd St on the west side; **S** A/C,
B to 72nd St) serves as a memorial to former
Beatle John Lennon, who lived directly across
the street in the Dakota apartment building
(p205). The garden, which was underwritten
by his widow Yoko Ono, is composed of a grove
of stately elms and a tiled mosaic that reads,
simply, 'Imagine.'

Bethesda Terrace & the Mall

The arched walkways of **Bethesda Terrace** (www.centralparknyc.org; 66th to 72nd St,
Central Park; **S** B, C to 72nd St), crowned by the
magnificent **Bethesda Fountain**, have long
been a gathering area for New Yorkers. To the
south is **the Mall** (featured in countless mov-
ies), a promenade shrouded in mature North
American elms. The southern stretch, known as
Literary Walk, is flanked by statues of famous
authors.

Great Lawn & the Ramble

The **Great Lawn** (www.centralparknyc.org; Central
Park, btwn 79th & 86th Sts; ☉ mid-Apr–mid-Nov;
S B, C to 86th St) is a massive emerald carpet at
the center of the park, surrounded by ball fields
and London plane trees. Immediately to the
southeast is **Delacorte Theater** (www.public
theater.org; Central Park, enter at W 81st St; **S** B, C
to 81st St), home to the annual Shakespeare in
the Park festival (p201), as well as **Belvedere
Castle** (☎ 212-772-0288; www.centralparknyc.org;
Central Park, at W 79th St; admission free; ☉ 10am-
4pm; 🛗; **S** 1/2/3, B, C to 72nd St), a birdwatch-
ing lookout. Further south is the leafy **Ramble**
(Central Park, midpark from 73rd to 79th Sts; **S** B,C
to 81st St), a popular birding destination. On
the southeastern end is the **Loeb Boathouse**
(☎ 212-517-2233; www.thecentralparkboathouse.
com; Central Park, btwn 74th & 75th Sts; boating per

★ Top Tips

○ Try Bike & Roll
(p205) for daily bike
rentals and guided
tours.

○ Avoid the carriage
rides. They're a rip-
off and the horses
lead miserable lives.

✕ Take a Break

Create a picnic from
the assortment of
gourmet goodies
at Zabar's (p206)
or **Whole Foods**
(☎ 212-823-9600;
www.wholefoods
market.com; Time
Warner Center, 10 Co-
lumbus Circle; ☉ 7am-
11pm; **S** A/C, B/D, 1
to 59th St-Columbus
Circle), both a short
hop from the park.

Inside the park
you can dine al
fresco at casual **Le
Pain Quotidien**
(☎ 646-233-3768;
www.lepainquotidien.
com; Mineral Springs
Pavilion, Central Park,
off West Dr; mains $12-
17.50, pastries $4-5;
☉ 7am-7pm; 🛜 🍴 🛗;
S B, C to 72nd St).

Central Park Then & Now

In the 1850s, this area of Manhattan was occupied by pig farms, a garbage dump, a bone-boiling operation and an African American village. It took 20,000 laborers two decades to transform this terrain into a park. Today, Central Park has more than 24,000 trees, 136 acres of woodland, 21 playgrounds and seven bodies of water – and more than 38 million visitors a year.

hr $15; ⏱10am-dusk Mar or Apr–mid-Nov; 🚇; ⑤B, C to 72nd St; 6 to 77th St), home to a waterside restaurant that offers rowboat rentals and gondola rides.

Jacqueline Kennedy Onassis Reservoir

The reservoir (at 90th St) takes up almost the entire width of the park and serves as a gorgeous reflecting pool for the city skyline. Its surrounding 1.58-mile track draws legions of joggers. Nearby, at Fifth Ave and 90th St, is a statue of New York City Marathon founder Fred Lebow, peering at his watch.

Central Park Zoo

Officially known as Central Park Wildlife Center (but no one calls it that), this small **zoo** (📞212-439-6500; www.centralparkzoo.com; Central Park, 64th St, at Fifth Ave; adult/child $12/7; ⏱10am-5pm Mon-Fri, to 5:30 Sat & Sun; 🚇; ⑤N/Q/R to 5th Ave-59th St) is home to penguins, snow leopards, dart poison frogs and red pandas. Feeding times in the sea lion and penguin tanks make for a rowdy spectacle.

Conservatory Garden

If you want a little peace and quiet (as in, no runners, cyclists or buskers), the 6-acre **Conservatory Garden** (www.centralparknyc.org; Central Park, Fifth Ave at 105th St; ⏱8am-5pm Nov-Feb, to 6pm Mar & Oct, to 7pm Apr & Sep, to 7:30pm or 8pm Aug, to 8pm May-Jul; ⑤6 to 103rd St) serves as one of the park's official quiet zones. And it's beautiful, to boot: bursting with crabapple trees, meandering boxwood and, in the spring, lots of flowers.

Summer Events

During the warm months, Central Park is home to countless cultural events, many of which are free. The two most popular are **Shakespeare in the Park** (www.publictheater.org), which is managed by the Public Theater, and **SummerStage** (www.cityparksfoundation.org/summerstage; Rumsey Playfield, Central Park, access via Fifth Ave & 69th St; ⏱Jun-Sep; 🚇; ⑤6 to 68th St-Hunter College), a series of free concerts.

Left: Jacqueline Kennedy Onassis Reservoir

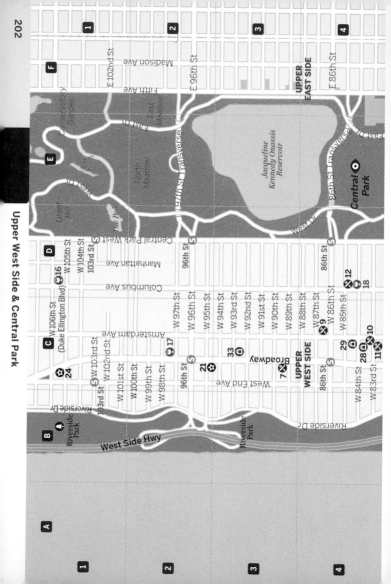

Upper West Side & Central Park

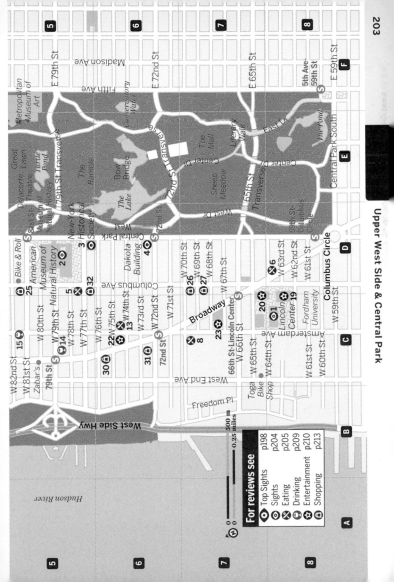

Hudson River

West Side Hwy

Freedom Pl

Zabar's

W 82nd St
W 81st St
79th St

W 80th St
79th St Natural History
W 78th St
W 77th St
W 76th St
W 75th St
W 74th St
W 73rd St
72nd St
W 72nd St
W 71st St
Broadway
West End Ave

Columbus Ave
Amsterdam Ave

66th St–Lincoln Center
W 66th St
W 65th St
W 64th St
W 63rd St
W 62nd St
W 61st St
W 60th St
W 59th St

Columbus Circle

Toga
Bike
Shop

Bike & Roll

American
Museum of
Natural History

New-York
Historical
Society

Central Park
West

Dakota
Building

Fordham
University

Lincoln
Center

E 79th St
Madison Ave

E 72nd St

E 65th St

5th Ave–
59th St
E 59th St

Fifth Ave
Conservatory
Water

Metropolitan
Museum of
Art

Great
Lawn

Delacorte
Theatre
81st St–Transverse

Turtle
Pond

The
Ramble

Bow
Bridge

The
Lake

79th St Transverse

West Dr

72nd St Transverse

Central Dr

The
Mall

Sheep
Meadow

65th St Transverse

Literary
Walk

East Dr

Central Dr

The
Pond

Central Park South

500 m
0.25 miles

For reviews see

◎	Top Sights	p198
⊙	Sights	p204
⊗	Eating	p205
⊗	Drinking	p209
⊗	Entertainment	p210
⊗	Shopping	p213

5
6
7
8

A B C D E F

Sights

Lincoln Center ARTS CENTER

1  MAP P202, C8

This stark arrangement of gleaming modernist temples houses some of Manhattan's most important performance companies: the New York Philharmonic (p212), the New York City Ballet (p210) and the iconic Metropolitan Opera House (p210), whose lobby's interior walls are dressed with brightly saturated murals by painter Marc Chagall. Various other venues are tucked in and around the 16-acre campus, including a theater, two film-screening centers and the renowned **Juilliard School**. (212-875-5456, tours 212-875-5350; www.lincolncenter.org; Columbus Ave, btwn

W 62nd & 66th Sts; tours adult/student $25/20; ⏱tours 11:30am & 1:30pm Mon-Sat, 3pm Sun; ♿; S1 to 66th St-Lincoln Center)

American Museum of Natural History MUSEUM

2  MAP P202, D5

Founded in 1869, this classic museum contains a veritable wonderland of more than 30 million artifacts – including lots of menacing dinosaur skeletons – as well as the **Rose Center for Earth & Space**. From October through May, the museum is home to the **Butterfly Conservatory**, a glasshouse featuring 500-plus butterflies from all over the world that will flutter about and land on your outstretched arm. (212-769-5100; www.amnh.org; Central Park West, at

Lincoln Center

PIO3/SHUTTERSTOCK ©

Cycling Central Park

The best way to cover all 840 acres of Central Park is to rent a bicycle; try **Bike & Roll** (Map p202, D5; ☎212-260-0400; www.bikeandrollnyc.com; 451 Columbus Ave, btwn 81st & 82nd Sts; bike rentals per 2hr/4hr/day adult $28/39/44, child $16/20/25; ⊗9am-6pm; 👫; ⑤B, C to 81st St-Museum of Natural History; 1 to 79th St) and **Toga Bike Shop** (Map p202, C7; ☎212-799-9625; www.togabikes.com; 110 West End Ave, btwn 64th & 65th Sts; rentals per 24hr hybrid/road bike $35/150; ⊗11am-7pm Mon-Fri, 10am-6pm Sat, 11am-6pm Sun; ⑤1 to 66th St-Lincoln Center). Get more information and a map of the park's bikepaths at the Central Park Conservancy website (www.centralparknyc.org).

W 79th St; suggested admission adult/child $23/13; ⊗10am-5:45pm; 👫; ⑤B, C to 81st St-Museum of Natural History; 1 to 79th St)

New-York Historical Society   MUSEUM

3 ◉ MAP P202, D5

As the antiquated hyphenated name implies, the Historical Society is the city's oldest museum, founded in 1804 to preserve historical and cultural artifacts. Its collection of more than 60,000 objects is quirky and fascinat-

ing and includes everything from George Washington's inauguration chair to a 19th-century Tiffany ice-cream dish (gilded, of course), plus a remarkable collection of Hudson River School paintings. However, it's far from stodgy, having moved into the 21st century with renewed vigor and purpose. (☎212-873-3400; www.nyhistory.org; 170 Central Park West, at W 77th St; adult/child $20/6, by donation 6-8pm Fri, library free; ⊗10am-6pm Tue-Thu & Sat, to 8pm Fri, 11am-5pm Sun; 👫; ⑤B, C to 81st St-Museum of Natural History)

Dakota Building   NOTABLE BUILDING

4 ◉ MAP P202, D6

A turreted, gabled building described in 1884 as so far uptown it was in 'the Dakotas,' this sand-colored gem quickly became the epitome of cool, housing Boris Karloff, Rudolph Nureyev, Lauren Bacall and, most famously, John Lennon, who was fatally shot at its gated entrance. (1 W 72nd St, at Central Park West; ⑤B, C to 72nd St)

Eating

Dovetail   MODERN AMERICAN $$$

5 ✖ MAP P202, D5

This Michelin-starred restaurant showcases its Zen-like beauty in both its decor (exposed brick, bare tables) and its delectable, seasonal menus – think striped bass with sunchokes and burgundy truffle, and venison with bacon, golden beets and foraged greens. Each evening there are two seven-course tasting menus: one for

Don't Forget the Bagels 🍽

A bastion of gourmet Kosher foodie-ism, the sprawling local market **Zabar's** (Map p202, C5; ☎212-787-2000; www.zabars. com; 2245 Broadway, at W 80th St; ⏰8am-7:30pm Mon-Fri, to 8pm Sat, 9am-6pm Sun; Ⓢ1 to 79th St) has been a neighborhood fixture since the 1930s. And what a fixture it is! It features a heavenly array of cheeses, meats, olives, caviar, lox (smoked salmon), pickles, dried fruits, nuts and baked goods, including bagels of every flavor and pillowy, fresh-out-of-the-oven *knishes* (Eastern European–style dough-wrapped potato dumplings).

omnivores and one for vegetarians. (☎212-362-3800; www.dovetailnyc. com; 103 W 77th St, cnr Columbus Ave; prix fixe $68-88, tasting menu $145; ⏰5:30-10pm Mon-Thu, to 10:30pm Fri & Sat, 5-10pm Sun; 🍴; Ⓢ B, C to 81st St-Museum of Natural History; 1 to 79th St)

Épicerie Boulud   DELI, FRENCH $

6 ❌ MAP P202, D8

A deli from star chef Daniel Boulud is no ordinary deli. Forget ham on rye – here you can order suckling pig confit, *jambon de Paris* and Gruyère on pressed ciabatta, or paprika-spiced flank steak with caramelized onions and three-grain mustard. Other options at this fast-gourmet spot include salads, soups, roast vegetables, pastry, gelato, coffee...and in the evening, oysters and wine. (☎212-595-9606; www.epicerieboulud. com; 1900 Broadway, at W 64th St; sandwiches $9.50-14.50; ⏰7am-10pm Mon, to 11pm Tue-Sat, 8am-10pm Sun; 🍴; Ⓢ1 to 66th St-Lincoln Center)

Candle Cafe West   VEGAN $$

7 ❌ MAP P202, C3

The wide-ranging menu at this popular, candlelit restaurant is entirely vegan, entirely organic and entirely delicious: with options like spaghetti and 'wheatballs', seitan piccata, chimichurri-grilled portobello steak and lasagna, you will not go hungry. It also has huge salads, fresh juices and smoothies and housemade ginger ale. (☎212-769-8900; www.candlecafe.com; 2427 Broadway, btwn 89th & 90th Sts; mains $17-23; ⏰11:30am-10:30pm Mon-Sat, to 9:30pm Sun, closed 4-5pm; 🍴; Ⓢ1 to 86th St)

Cafe Luxembourg   BRASSERIE $$$

8 ❌ MAP P202, C7

This quintessential French bistro is generally crowded with locals – and it's no mystery why: the setting is understatedly elegant, the staff genuinely friendly, and there's an outstanding menu to boot. The classics – steak tartare, *moules frites* (mussels and fries), roast chicken – are all deftly executed, and its proximity to Lincoln Center makes it a perfect pre-show destination. (☎212-873-7411; www.

cafeluxembourg.com; 200 W 70th St, btwn Amsterdam & West End Aves; mains lunch $19-38, dinner $26-40; ⏰8am-11pm Mon & Tue, to midnight Wed-Fri, 9am-midnight Sat, to 11pm Sun; Ⓢ1/2/3 to 72nd St)

Barney Greengrass DELI $$

9 ✖ MAP P202, C4

The self-proclaimed 'King of Sturgeon', Barney Greengrass serves up the same heaping dishes of eggs and salty lox, luxuriant caviar and melt-in-your-mouth chocolate babkas that first made it famous when it opened over a century ago. Pop in to fuel up in the morning or for a quick lunch (there are rickety tables set amid the crowded produce aisles). (☎212-724-4707; www. barneygreengrass.com; 541 Amsterdam Ave, at 86th St; mains $12-26;

⏰8:30am-4pm Tue-Fri, to 5pm Sat & Sun; Ⓢ1 to 86th St)

Cafe Lalo DESSERTS $

10 ✖ MAP P202, C4

The vintage French posters and the marble-topped tables make this longtime Upper West Side date spot feel like a Parisian cafe. But forget decor – you're here for the mind-blowing array of desserts: choose (if you can) from 27 different cakes, 23 flavors of cheesecake, nine types of pie, a dozen kinds of fruit tart, cookies, pastries, zabaglione, chocolate mousse and more. (☎212-496-6031; www.cafelalo. com; 201 W 83rd St, btwn Amsterdam & Columbus Ave; desserts around $10; ⏰9am-1am Sun-Thu, to 3am Fri & Sat; Ⓢ1 to 79th St; B, C to 81st St-Museum of Natural History)

Barney Greengrass

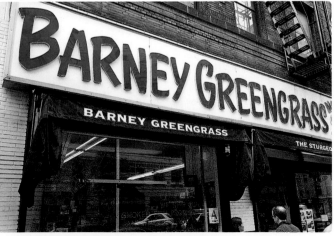

Jin Ramen

JAPANESE $

11 MAP P202, C4

This buzzing little joint off Amsterdam Ave serves up delectable bowls of piping hot ramen. *Tonkotsu* (pork broth) ramen is a favorite, though vegetarians also have options. Don't neglect the appetizers: *shishito* peppers, pork buns and *hijiki* salad. The mix of rustic wood elements, exposed bulbs and red industrial fixtures gives the place a cozy vibe. (✆646-657-0755; www.jinramen.com; 462 Amsterdam Ave, btwn 82nd & 83rd Sts; mains $13-17; ⏱lunch 11:30am-3:30pm, dinner 5-11pm Mon-Thu, to midnight Fri & Sat, to 10pm Sun; 🖊; 🚇1 to 79th St)

Riverside Park

If Central Park feels too crowded for you, head to **Riverside Park** (Map p202, B1; ✆212-870-3070; www.riverside parknyc.org; Riverside Dr, btwn 68th & 155th Sts; ⏱6am-1am; 👪; 🚇1/2/3 to any stop btwn 66th & 157th Sts), a classic beauty designed by Central Park creators Frederick Law Olmsted and Calvert Vaux. This waterside spot, running north on the Upper West Side and banked by the Hudson River from 59th to 155th Sts, is lusciously leafy; plenty of bike paths, playgrounds and dog runs make it a family favorite. Views from the park make the Jersey side of the Hudson look quite pretty.

Kefi

GREEK $$

12 MAP P202, D4

This homey, whitewashed eatery run by chef Michael Psilakis channels a sleek taverna vibe while dispensing excellent rustic Greek dishes. Expect favorites such as spicy lamb sausage, sheep-milk dumplings and creamy sun-dried-tomato hummus. You can also assemble a feast of meze (sharing plates), including crispy calamari, meatballs and tzatziki, and grilled octopus and bean salad. (✆212-873-0200; www.michaelpsilakis.com/kefi; 505 Columbus Ave, btwn 84th & 85th Sts; small sharing plates $8-17, mains $17-28; ⏱noon-3pm & 5-10pm Mon-Thu, noon-3pm & 5-11pm Fri, 11am-11pm Sat, to 10pm Sun; 🖊👪; 🚇B, C to 86th St)

Hummus Place

MIDDLE EASTERN, VEGETARIAN $

13 MAP P202, C6

Hummus Place is nothing special in the way of ambience – about eight tables tucked below street level, fronting a cramped, open kitchen – but it's got amazing hummus platters, served warm and with various toppings, from whole chickpeas to fava bean stew with chopped egg. You'll also find tasty salads, couscous and stuffed grape leaves. Everything here is vegetarian. Great value. (✆212-799-3335; www.hummusplace.com; 305 Amsterdam Ave, btwn 74th & 75th Sts; sandwiches $12-15; ⏱11am-10:30pm Mon-Fri, from 10:30am Sat & Sun; 🖊; 🚇1/2/3 to 72nd St)

ILYA S. SAVENOK/STRINGER/GETTY IMAGES ©

Jin Ramen

Drinking

Manhattan Cricket Club

LOUNGE

14 MAP P202, C5

Above Australian bistro Burke & Wills (www.burkeandwillsny. com) – ask its host for access – this elegant drinking lounge is modeled on the classy Anglo-Aussie cricket clubs of the early 1900s. Sepia-toned photos of batsmen adorn the gold brocaded walls, while mahogany bookshelves and chesterfield sofas create a fine setting for quaffing well-made (but pricey) cocktails. It's a guaranteed date-pleaser. (646-823-9252; www.mccnewyork.com; 226 W 79th St, btwn Amsterdam Ave & Broadway; 6pm-late; S 1 to 79th St)

Irving Farm Roasters

COFFEE

Tucked into a little ground-floor shop, the Upper West Side branch of this popular local coffee chain (see 14 Map p202, C5) is bigger on the inside – beyond the coffee counter the space opens up into a sunny back room. Enjoy a menu of light meals along with your fresh-pulled espresso. (212-874-7979; www. irvingfarm.com; 224 W 79th St, btwn Broadway & Amsterdam Ave; 7am-10pm Mon-Fri, 8am-10pm Sat & Sun; S 1 to 79th St)

Dead Poet

BAR

15 MAP P202, C5

This narrow, mahogany-paneled pub is a neighborhood favorite. It takes its Guinness pours seriously, and features cocktails named after deceased masters of verse, including a Walt Whitman Long Island Iced Tea ($13) and a Pablo Neruda spiced-rum sangria ($12). Feeling adventurous? Order the signature cocktail ($15), a secret recipe of seven alcohols – you even get to keep the glass. (☏212-595-5670; www.thedeadpoet.com; 450 Amsterdam Ave, btwn 81st & 82nd Sts; ⊙noon-4am; ⓢ1 to 79th St)

Bob's Your Uncle
BAR

16 😀 MAP P202, D1

This is the kind of friendly, easygoing neighborhood bar you wish was your local. (We do, anyway.) Beverages focus mainly on craft brews and unfussy, inexpensive cocktails. The exposed brick walls, industrial fixtures and lack of sport-playing TVs feel more Brooklyn than UWS. (☏646-791-5942; www.bobsyouruncle. nyc; 929 Columbus Ave, btwn 105th & 106th Sts; ⊙2pm-2am Sun-Wed, to 3am Thu-Sat; ⓢB, C, 1 to 103rd St)

Earth Café
CAFE

17 😀 MAP P202, C2

This charming neighborhood cafe beckons you inside with its cheery, sunny interior of whitewashed brick walls and the scent of fresh-roasted coffee beans lingering in the air. Order an expertly poured almond latte, take a seat at the street-facing counter behind large French windows and watch the city glide past. (☏646-964-5192; 2580 Broadway, at 97th St; ⊙7am-11pm Mon-Fri, from 8am Sat & Sun; 🛜; ⓢ1/2/3 to 96th St)

Prohibition
BAR

18 😀 MAP P202, D4

This buzzing drinking den features a live band every night on the front-room stage, though decibel levels are low enough that your ears won't bleed. The back room is band-free; for those who prefer a little action, there's a billiard table. (☏212-579-3100; www.prohibition. net; 503 Columbus Ave, btwn 84th & 85th Sts; ⊙4:30pm-2am Sun-Thu, to 3:30am Fri & Sat; ⓢB, C to 86th St)

Entertainment

New York City Ballet
DANCE

19 🌟 MAP P202, C8

This prestigious ballet company was first directed by renowned Russian-born choreographer George Balanchine back in the 1940s. Today, the company has 90 dancers and is the largest ballet organization in the US, performing 23 weeks a year at Lincoln Center's David H Koch Theater. During the holidays the troupe is best known for its annual production of *The Nutcracker*. (☏212-496-0600; www. nycballet.com; Lincoln Center, Columbus Ave at W 63rd St; 👫; ⓢ1 to 66th St-Lincoln Center)

Metropolitan Opera House
OPERA

New York's premier opera (see 1 ◎ Map p202, C8) company is the place to see classics such as *Carmen*, *Madame Butterfly* and *Macbeth*, not to mention Wagner's Ring Cycle. It also hosts premieres and revivals

New York City on Page & Screen

New York has been the setting of countless works of literature, television and film. From critical commentaries on class and race to the lighter foibles of falling in love, these stories are not just entertainment: they are carefully placed tiles in NYC's diverse mosaic of tales.

Books

The Amazing Adventures of Kavalier & Clay (Michael Chabon; 2000) Touches upon Brooklyn, escapism and the nuclear family.

A Tree Grows in Brooklyn (Betty Smith; 1943) An Irish American family living in the Williamsburg tenements in the 20th century.

Down These Mean Streets (Piri Thomas; 1967) Memoirs of tough times growing up in Spanish Harlem.

Invisible Man (Ralph Ellison; 1952) Poignant exploration of the situation of African Americans in the early 20th century.

Manhattan Beach (Jennifer Egan; 2017) Pulitzer Prize–winning author Egan's novel follows a young woman working in the Brooklyn Navy Yard during WWII.

Vanishing New York (Jeremiah Moss; 2017) Delves into gentrification and how NYC has changed in the 21st century.

Films

Taxi Driver (1976) Martin Scorsese's story of a troubled Vietnam vet turned taxi driver.

Do the Right Thing (1989) Spike Lee's critically acclaimed comedy-drama probes the racial turmoil lurking just beneath the surface.

Requiem for a Dream (2000) Darren Aronofsky's unusual tale of a Brooklyn junkie and his doting Jewish mother.

Angels in America (2003) Mike Nichols' movie version of Tony Kushner's Broadway play recalls AIDS out of control in 1985 Manhattan.

Precious (Lee Daniels, 2009) Based on the novel *Push* by Sapphire; an unflinching tale of a Harlem teenager abused by her parents.

Margaret (2015) Kenneth Lonergan's second film explores the devastating effects of an accident on a Manhattan teen.

of more contemporary works, such as John Adams' *The Death of Klinghoffer*. The season runs from September to April. (🎟tickets 212-362-6000, tours 212-769-7028; www.metopera.org; Lincoln Center, Columbus Ave at W 64th St; S 1 to 66th St-Lincoln Center)

Film Society of Lincoln Center
CINEMA

The Film Society (see 1 ⊙ Map p202, C8) is one of New York's cinematic gems, providing an invaluable platform for a wide gamut of documentary, feature, independent, foreign and avant-garde art pictures. Films screen in one of two facilities at Lincoln Center: the **Elinor Bunin Munroe Film Center** (☏212-875-5232; www.filmlinc.com), a more intimate, experimental venue, or the **Walter Reade Theater** (☏212-875-5601; www.filmlinc.com), with wonderfully wide, screening-room-style seats. (☏212-875-5367; www.filmlinc.com; Lincoln Center; ⑤1 to 66th St-Lincoln Center)

New York Philharmonic
CLASSICAL MUSIC

20 ✪ MAP P202, C7

The oldest professional orchestra in the US (dating back to 1842) holds its season every year at David Geffen Hall (known as Avery Fisher Hall until 2015); music director Jaap van Zweden took over from Alan Gilbert in 2017. The orchestra plays a mix of classics (Tchaikovsky, Mahler, Haydn) and contemporary works, as well as concerts geared toward children. Tickets run in the $29 to $125 range. If you're on a budget, see about checking out open rehearsals for only $22. (☏212-875-5656; www.nyphil.org; Lincoln Center, Columbus Ave at W 65th St; ⑪; ⑤1 to 66 St-Lincoln Center)

Symphony Space
LIVE PERFORMANCE

21 ✪ MAP P202, C2

Symphony Space is a multidisciplinary gem supported by the local community. It often hosts three-day series that are dedicated to one musician, and also has an affinity for world music, theater, film, dance and literature (with appearances by acclaimed writers). (☏212-864-5400; www.symphonyspace.org; 2537 Broadway, at 95th St; ⑤1/2/3 to 96th St)

Beacon Theatre
LIVE MUSIC

22 ✪ MAP P202, C6

This historic 1929 theater is a perfect medium-size venue with 2829 seats (not a terrible one in the house) and a constant flow of popular acts from ZZ Top to Wilco (plus comedians like Jerry Seinfeld). A 2009 restoration left the gilded interiors – a mix of Greek, Roman, Renaissance and rococo design elements – totally sparkling. (☏212-465-6500; www.beacontheatre.com; 2124 Broadway, btwn 74th & 75th Sts; ⑤1/2/3 to 72nd St)

Merkin Concert Hall
CLASSICAL MUSIC

23 ✪ MAP P202, C7

Just north of Lincoln Center, this 450-seat hall, part of the Kaufman Center, is one of the city's more intimate venues for classical music, as well as jazz, world music and pop. The hall hosts Tuesday matinees (a deal at $20) that highlight emerging classical solo artists. (📞212-501-3330; www.kaufman-center.org/mch; 129 W 67th St, btwn Amsterdam Ave & Broadway; 🚇1 to 66th St-Lincoln Center)

Smoke
JAZZ

24 😊 MAP P202, C1

This swank but laid-back lounge – with good stage views from plush sofas – brings out old-timers and local faves, such as George Coleman and Wynton Marsalis. Most nights there's a $10 cover (sometimes higher), plus a $38 per person minimum spend on food and drink. On Sundays there's a soulful jazz brunch from 11am to 4pm. (📞212-864-6662; www.smoke jazz.com; 2751 Broadway, btwn 105th & 106th Sts; 🕐5:30pm-3am Mon-Sat, 11am-3am Sun; 🚇1 to 103rd St)

Shopping

Book Culture
BOOKS, GIFTS & SOUVENIRS

25 🔒 MAP P202, D5

The warm aesthetic and friendliness of this neighborhood bookstore belies its size and selection. It caters not just to literary types but to browsers looking for unique gifts, writers stocking up on Euro-style journals and parents desperate to occupy little ones in the large downstairs kids' space, which hosts regular story-time sessions in several languages (check the website for times). (📞212-595-1962; www.bookculture.com; 450 Columbus Ave, btwn 81st & 82nd St; 🕐9am-10pm Mon-Sat, to 8pm Sun; 👫; 🚇B, C to 81st St-Museum of Natural History)

Beacon Theatre

Icon Style

VINTAGE, JEWELRY

26  MAP P202, D7

This tiny gem of a vintage shop, tucked away on a side street, specializes in carefully curated dresses, gloves, bags, hats and other accessories, as well as antique fine and costume jewelry. Half of the shop is covered in a strikingly restored apothecary's wall, with the goods displayed in open drawers. (212-799-0029; www.iconstyle.net; 104 W 70th St, near Columbus Ave; noon-8pm Tue-Fri, 11am-7pm Sat, noon-6pm Sun; 1/2/3 to 72nd St)

T2

TEA

27 MAP P202, D7

Aficionados of the brewed leaf will find more than 200 varieties at this outpost of an Australian tea company: oolong, green, black, yellow, herbals, you name it. But you don't just have to go by smell – the staff will brew samples of anything you care to try. It also carries a selection of tea-related gifts. (646-998-5010; www.t2tea.com; 188 Columbus Ave, btwn 68th & 69th Sts; 10am-8pm Mon-Sat, 11am-7pm Sun; 1 to 66th St-Lincoln Center; B, C to 72nd St)

Magpie

ARTS & CRAFTS

28 MAP P202, C4

This charming little outpost carries a wide range of ecofriendly objects: elegant stationery, hand-painted mugs, organic-cotton scarves, recycled-resin necklaces, hand-dyed felt journals and wooden earth puzzles are a few things that may catch your eye. Most products are fair-trade, made of sustainable

Grand Bazaar NYC

E J WESTMACOTT/ALAMY STOCK PHOTO

materials or locally designed and made. (📞212-579-3003; www.magpienewyork.com; 488 Amsterdam Ave, btwn 83rd & 84th Sts; ⏱11am-7pm Mon-Sat, to 6pm Sun; Ⓢ1 to 86th St)

West Side Kids

TOYS

29 🔒 MAP P202, C4

A great place to pick up a gift for that little someone special, no matter their age. In stock are lots of hands-on activities and fun educational games, as well as puzzles, mini musical instruments, science kits, magic sets, snap circuits, old-fashioned wooden trains and building kits. (📞212-496-7282; www.westsidekidsnyc.com; 498 Amsterdam Ave, at 84th St; ⏱10am-7pm Mon-Sat, 11am-6pm Sun; Ⓢ1 to 86th St)

Barneys New York

DEPARTMENT STORE

30 🔒 MAP P202, C6

An anchor of fashion in NYC, Barneys has a well-curated collection of women's apparel and accessories from luxury brands such as Alexander Wang, Stella McCartney and Band of Outsiders. Prices are high – look for sales. (📞646-335-0978; www.barneys.com; 2151 Broadway, btwn 75th & 76th Sts; ⏱10am-7pm Mon-Sat, 11am-6pm Sun; Ⓢ1/2/3 to 72nd St)

Westsider Records

MUSIC

31 🔒 MAP P202, C6

Featuring more than 30,000 LPs, this shop has got you covered when it comes to everything from funk to jazz to classical, plus opera, musical theater, spoken word, film

soundtracks and other curiosities. (Don't miss the $1 bins up front.) It's a good place to lose all track of time – as is its bookstore further uptown. (📞212-874-1588; www.westsiderbooks.com; 233 W 72nd St, btwn Broadway & West End Ave; ⏱11am-7pm Mon-Thu, 10am-9pm Fri & Sat, noon-6pm Sun; Ⓢ1/2/3 to 72nd St)

Grand Bazaar NYC

MARKET

32 🔒 MAP P202, D5

One of the oldest open-air shopping spots in the city, browsing this friendly, well-stocked flea market is a perfect activity for a lazy Upper West Side Sunday morning. You'll find a little bit of everything here, including vintage and contemporary furnishings, antique maps, custom eyewear, hand-woven scarves and so much more. (📞212-239-3025; www.grandbazaarnyc.org; 100 W 77th St, near Columbus Ave; ⏱10am-5:30pm Sun; ⒮B, C to 81st St-Museum of Natural History; 1 to 79th St)

Shishi

FASHION & ACCESSORIES, CLOTHING

33 🔒 MAP P202, C3

A welcome addition to a fashion-challenged 'hood, Shishi is a delightful boutique stocking an ever-changing selection of stylish but affordable apparel such as elegant sweaters, shift dresses and eye-catching jewelry. It's fun for browsing, and with the enthusiastic staff kitting you out, you'll feel like you have your own personal stylist. (📞646-692-4510; www.shishiboutique.com; 2488 Broadway, btwn 92nd & 93rd Sts; ⏱11am-8pm Mon-Sat, to 7pm Sun; Ⓢ1/2/3 to 96th St)

Walking Tour 🥾

Queens: Astoria

A short hop from Midtown Manhattan, Astoria is a charmingly diverse neighborhood of restaurant-lined boulevards, tree-lined side streets and indie shops and cafes. Come with an appetite, as eating and drinking is an essential part of the Astoria experience. The best time to visit is on weekends, when the neighborhood is at its liveliest.

Walk Facts

Start Socrates Sculpture Park; 🚢 NYC to Astoria; Ⓢ N, W to Broadway

End George's; Ⓢ M, R to Steinway St

Length 1.6 miles; two to three hours depending on stops

❶ Socrates Sculpture Park

Amid cutting-edge installations and wispy birch trees, this picturesque waterside **park** (www. socratessculpturepark.org; 32-01 Vernon Blvd; admission free; ⏰9am-dusk; Ⓢ N, W to Broadway) offers serene views across to Manhattan. It's hard to believe this abandoned landfill was once an illegal dumpsite. On summer weekends, there's often something afoot, including yoga and tai chi, markets and kayaking in Hallets Cove.

❷ King Souvlaki

Follow the plumes of smoke wafting along 31st St to this celebrated **food truck** (☎917-416-1189; www. facebook.com/KingSouvlaki; 31st St, near 31st Ave; mains $6-10; ⏰9am-11pm Mon-Wed, to 5am Thu-Sat, 11am-11pm Sun; Ⓢ N, W to Broadway), one of Astoria's best. Order a pita sandwich stuffed with mouthwatering morsels of pork, chicken or beef, along with a side of feta-topped Greek fries.

❸ Astoria Bookshop

This much-loved indie **bookshop** (☎718-278-2665; www. astoriabookshop.com; 31-29 31st St; ⏰11am-7pm; Ⓢ N, W to Broadway) has ample shelf space dedicated to local authors – pick up a title about the Queens dining scene or the borough's ethnic diversity. A stalwart of the community, Astoria Bookshop also hosts author readings, discussion groups and writing workshops.

❹ Lockwood

You'll find loads of gift ideas in this whimsical **store** (☎718-626-3040; http://lockwoodshop.com; 32-15 33rd St; ⏰11am-8pm; Ⓢ N, W to Broadway), including plenty of intriguing Queens-related objects. Think vintage wall hangings, paper doll books of famous women, skull candles, scented candles, eye-catching flasks and so on. Their stationery store is a few doors up.

❺ Astoria Bier & Cheese

A neighborhood institution, this **deli** (☎718-545-5588; www.astoria bierandcheese.com; 34-14 Broadway; ⏰noon-11pm Mon-Thu, to midnight Fri & Sat, to 10pm Sun; Ⓢ N, Q to Broadway; M, R to Steinway) serves up a wide variety of temptations, including gourmet grilled cheeses, avocado toast and fancy sandwiches stuffed with prosciutto. There's a rotating selection of craft brews, and outdoor seating in back.

❻ George's

Set inside the Kaufman Astoria Studios, **George's** (☎718-255-1947; www.georges.nyc; 35-11 35th Ave; mains $15-33; ⏰4-10pm Tue-Thu, to 11pm Fri & Sat, 11:30am-9pm Sun; Ⓢ M, R to Steinway St) feels like a hidden spot with its low-lit interior and vintage vibe. Order a signature cocktail while taking in a bit of live music and surveying the 1920s interior. A full menu gives American classics a modern twist.

Worth a Trip 🔭
MoMA PS1

The smaller, hipper sibling of Manhattan's Museum of Modern Art, MoMA PS1 hunts down razor-sharp art and serves it up in an ex-school locale. Forget about lily ponds and gilded frames. Here you'll be peering at videos through floorboards and debating the meaning of nonstatic structures while staring through a hole in the wall. Nothing is predictable. Best of all, admission is free with your MoMA ticket.

📞718-784-2084

www.momaps1.org

22-25 Jackson Ave, Long Island City

suggested donation adult/child $10/free, free with MoMA ticket

🕑noon-6pm Thu-Mon, Warm Up parties noon-9pm Sat Jul-Aug

Roots, Radicals & PS 1 Classics

PS1 first hit the scene in the 1970s. This was the age of Dia, Artists' Space and the New Museum – new-gen projects showcasing the city's thriving experimental, multimedia art scene. In 1976, Alanna Heiss – a supporter of art in alternative spaces – took possession of an abandoned school building in Queens and invited artists like Richard Serra, James Turrell and Keith Sonnier to create site-specific works. The end result was PS1's inaugural exhibition, *Rooms.* Surviving remnants include Richard Artschwager's oval-shaped wall 'blimps' and Alan Saret's light-channeling *The Hole at P.S.1, Fifth Solar Chthonic Wall Temple,* on the north wing's 3rd floor.

Saturday Warm Up

On Saturday afternoons from July to early September, rock on at one of New York's coolest weekly music/culture events, Warm Up. It's a hit with everyone from verified hipsters to plugged-in music geeks, who spill into the courtyard to eat, drink and catch a stellar line-up of bands, experimental music and DJs. Featured artists have included acid-house deity DJ Pierre and techno pioneer Juan Atkins.

Sunday Sessions

Another cultural treat is the Sunday Sessions, on Sundays from September to May. Spanning lectures, film screenings, music performances and even architectural projects, the lineup has included experimental comedy, postindustrial noise jams and Latin art-house dance. One week you might catch a symphony debut, the next an architectural performance from Madrid. Upcoming events are listed on the MoMA PS1 website.

★ **Top Tip**

o Check exhibitions online before heading out. Sometimes the museum has limited pieces on display.

o Stock up on MoMA exhibition catalogs, coffee-table tomes and art and design mags at the book-store.

✕ **Take a Break**

The on-site **M Wells Dinette** (☏ 718-786-1800; www.magasinwells.com; 22-25 Jackson Ave, Long Island City; mains $9-14; ☽ noon-6pm Thu-Mon; Ⓢ E, M to 23rd St-Court Sq, G, 7 Court Sq) gives regional ingredients a French-Canadian makeover.

★ **Getting There**

MoMA PS1 is 3 miles straight east of Times Sq, in Queens.

Ⓢ Take the E or M to Court Sq-23rd St, or the 7 to Court Sq.

Explore ◈

Brooklyn: Park Slope, Gowanus & Green-Wood Cemetery

Known for leafy streets and classic brownstones, Park Slope is filled with families and designer dogs, plus great eateries and boutiques. It abuts Brooklyn's most important green space, the 585-acre Prospect Park. To the west is formerly-industrial Gowanus, dotted with shops and nightlife. South lies the beautiful and histori-cally significant Green-Wood Cemetery.

Start at Grand Army Plaza (p225) and grab a breakfast taco from King David (p227), then spend your morning wandering Prospect Park (p224). Head west into Park Slope, along Montgomery Place (p225), before grabbing lunch at Luke's Lobster (p226). Head down to Green-Wood (p224), or poke around some stores, including the massive No Relation Vintage (p230). Grab dinner at Sidecar (p226) and enjoy a cocktail at upscale Lavender Lake (p228) or a brew at dive bar Freddy's (p229), then and go for some live music at Barbès (p229) or Bell House (p230).

Getting There & Around

S Several lines travel along the edges of Park Slope: the 2/3 along Flatbush Ave; the R along Fourth Ave (through Gowanus); and the F and G stopping at Fourth and Seventh Aves along 9th St. The 4/5, B/D and N/Q go to the massive transit hub of Atlantic Ave–Barclays Ctr, at Park Slope's northwestern corner.

Neighborhood Map on p222

Audubon Center Boathouse, Prospect Park (p224)
LITTLENY/SHUTTERSTOCK ©

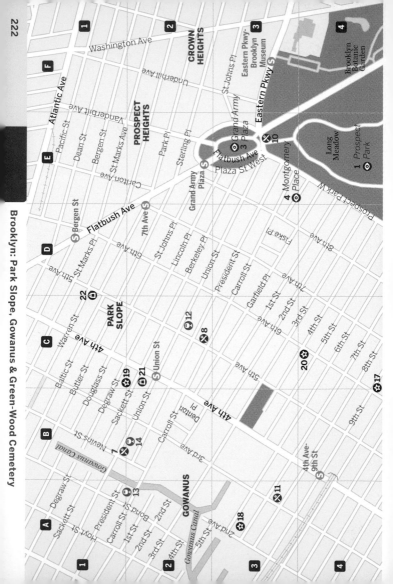

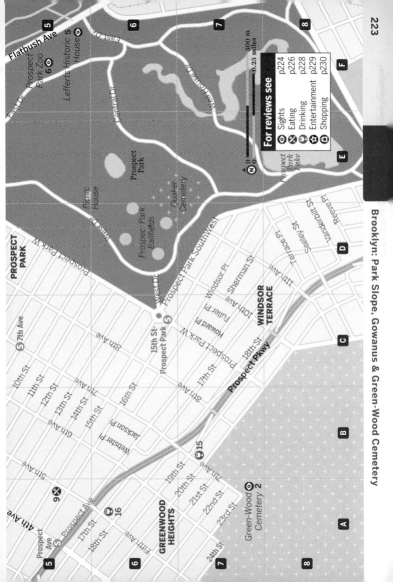

Brooklyn: Park Slope, Gowanus & Green-Wood Cemetery

For reviews see

0 500 m
0 0.25 miles

Flatbush Ave

East Dr

Prospect Park Zoo 6

Lefferts Historic House

Central Dr

Well House Dr

Prospect Park

PROSPECT PARK

Prospect Park W

Picnic House

Quaker Cemetery

Prospect Park Ballfields

West Dr

Prospect Park Lake

7th Ave

15th St–Prospect Park

West Dr

Prospect Park West

Prospect Park Southwest

10th St

11th St

12th St

13th St

14th St

15th St

16th St

7th Ave

8th Ave

Jackson Pl

Webster Pl

5th Ave

6th Ave

7th Ave

8th Ave

Howard Pl

Fuller Pl

Windsor Pl

Sherman St

10th Ave

11th Ave

Terrace Pl

Seeley St

Vanderbilt St

Reeve Pl

WINDSOR TERRACE

Prospect Pkwy

17th St

18th St

19th St

20th St

21st St

22nd St

23rd St

24th St

15

16

GREENWOOD HEIGHTS

Green-Wood Cemetery 2

9

Prospect Ave

4th Ave

5th Ave

Prospect Ave

Sights

Prospect Park

PARK

1 ◉ MAP P222, E4

The designers of the 585-acre Prospect Park – Frederick Law Olmsted and Calvert Vaux – considered this an improvement on their other New York project, Central Park (p198). Created in 1866, Prospect Park has many of the same features. It's gorgeous, with a long meadow running along the western half, filled with soccer, football, cricket and baseball players (and barbecuers), hilly forests and a lovely lake and boathouse on the east side. (☎718-965-8951; www.prospectpark.org; Grand Army Plaza; ⊙5am-1am; ⑤2/3 to Grand

Army Plaza; F to 15th St-Prospect Park; B, Q to Prospect Park)

Green-Wood Cemetery

CEMETERY

2 ◉ MAP P222, A7

If you really want to enjoy a slice of scenic Brooklyn in total peace and quiet, make for Green-Wood Cemetery. This historic burial ground set on the borough's highest point covers almost 500 hilly acres with more than 7000 trees (many of which are over 150 years old); its myriad tombs, mausoleums, lakes and patches of forest are connected by a looping network of roads and footpaths, making this a perfect spot for some aimless rambling. (www.green-wood.com; 500 25th St, at Fifth Ave, Greenwood

Soldiers' and Sailors' Memorial Arch, Grand Army Plaza

NATTYC/SHUTTERSTOCK ©

Heights; admission free; ⏰7am-7pm Jun-Aug, from 7:45am May & Sep, to 6pm mid-Mar–Apr & Oct, to 5pm Nov–mid-Mar; 🚇R to 25th St)

Grand Army Plaza MONUMENT

3 👁 MAP P222, E3

A large, landscaped traffic circle with a massive ceremonial arch sits at the northern end of Prospect Park, where Flatbush Ave meets up with the beginning of Eastern Pkwy. Formally known as the Soldiers' and Sailors' Memorial Arch, the arch, which was built in the 1890s, is a memorial to Union soldiers who fought in the Civil War. (Flatbush Ave & Eastern Pkwy, Prospect Park; ⏰6am-midnight; 🚇2/3 to Grand Army Plaza; B, Q to 7th Ave)

Montgomery Place ARCHITECTURE

4 👁 MAP P222, E3

This shady, one-block street contains a coveted series of beaux-arts row houses, most of which were built by Paris-educated Charles Pierrepont Henry Gilbert in the 1880s. (Montgomery Pl, btwn Prospect Park W & Eighth Ave, Park Slope; 🚇2/3 to Grand Army Plaza)

Lefferts Historic House HISTORIC SITE

5 👁 MAP P222, F5

Inside Prospect Park (p224), this 18th-century Dutch farmhouse of the Lefferts family has old-fashioned toys and tools to play with in period rooms and a working

Brooklyn for Kids

If you're traveling with children, family-oriented Park Slope is a great place to explore, with numerous things geared toward kids: the Prospect Park Zoo, weekend puppet shows at Puppetworks (p230), ice-cream-making classes at Ample Hills Creamery (p226) and kid-oriented events at Lefferts Historic House.

garden. It was moved here in the early 20th century from its original location on Flatbush Ave, in a neighborhood now called **Prospect Lefferts Gardens**. The online calendar lists kid-friendly events; besides its official hours, the house is also open on every NYC public-school holiday. A major restoration is planned for sometime in 2019. (📞718-789-2822; www.prospectpark.org/lefferts; near Flatbush Ave & Empire Blvd, Prospect Park; suggested donation $3; ⏰noon-5pm Thu-Sun Apr-Jun & Sep-Oct, to 6pm Jul-Aug, to 4pm Sat & Sun Nov-Dec, closed Jan-Mar; 👪; 🚇B, Q to Prospect Park)

Prospect Park Zoo ZOO

6 👁 MAP P222, F5

This small zoo (12 acres) is mainly geared toward kids and features a variety of crowd-pleasing animals: Pallas's cats, red pandas, sea lions, Fennec foxes, tamarins, wallabies and a small petting zoo. It's located within Prospect Park (p224) and is accessible from Flatbush Ave or via a park path. (☎718-399-7339; www.prospectparkzoo.com; 450 Flatbush Ave, Prospect Park; adult/child $8/5; ☺10am-5pm Mon-Fri, to 5:30pm Sat & Sun Apr-Oct, to 4:30pm Nov-Mar; 👶; ⑤B, Q to Prospect Park; 2/3 to Grand Army Plaza)

Eating

Ample Hills Creamery

ICE CREAM $

7 🍴 MAP P222, B1

Ice-cream lovers: we found the mother ship. All of Ample Hills' magnificently creative flavors – snap mallow pop (a deconstructed Rice Krispies treat), Mexican hot chocolate, salted crack caramel – are whipped up right here in the creamery's Gowanus factory. Grab a cone and watch the goods being made through the kitchen's picture window. (☎347-725-4061; www.amplehills.com; 305 Nevins St, at Union St, Gowanus; cones $4-7; ☺noon-11pm Sun-Thu, to midnight Fri & Sat, shorter hours in winter; ⑤R to Union St; F, G to Carroll St)

Luke's Lobster

SEAFOOD $$

8 🍴 MAP P222, C2

Each location of Luke's Lobster prides itself on providing fresh, sustainable and mouthwatering seafood at reasonable prices. This is all true of the Park Slope location, which serves Luke's legendary menu in a small, well appointed restaurant complete with a charming backyard patio. (☎347-457-6855; www.lukeslobster.com; 237 Fifth Ave, Park Slope; lobster roll $17, lobster corn chowder $7-10; ☺11am-10pm Fri-Sun, from noon Mon-Thu; ⑤R train to Union Ave.)

Sidecar

AMERICAN $$

9 🍴 MAP P222, A5

Upscale classic American cuisine doesn't get much better than Sidecar. This atmospheric restaurant serves unfussy takes on classics that add a modern touch, such as fried chicken served with a savory root mash and sautéed kale with bacon on the side. Sidecar specializes in cocktails that you can pair with

---

Smorgasburg 🍴

Every Sunday from April through October, Brooklyn's favorite open-air food market **Smorgasburg** (www.smorgasburg.com; ☺11am-6pm Sun Apr-Oct) sets up shop in Prospect Park (south of the boathouse), with dozens of vendors selling an incredible array of goodness: Italian street snacks, duck confit, Indian flatbread tacos, roasted-mushroom burgers, vegan Ethiopian comfort food, sea-salt caramel ice cream, passionfruit doughnuts, craft beer and more.

ALLEN.G/SHUTTERSTOCK ©

Smorgasburg

your meal, or enjoy on their own at the bar. (☏718-369-0077; www.sidecarbrooklyn.com; 560 Fifth Ave, btwn 15th and 16th Sts, Park Slope; mains $14-27; ⏰6pm-2am Mon-Wed, to 4am Thu, 3pm-4am Fri, 11am-4am Sat, to 2am Sun; 🚇R to Prospect Ave)

King David Tacos

TACOS $

10 ✕ MAP P222, E3

Native Texan Liz Solomon found NYC missing one thing: authentic, Austin-style breakfast tacos. So in 2016 she decided to make her own. Her outdoor stand at Grand Army Plaza offers potato, egg and cheese tacos daily, made that morning and ready to go. Options include the BPEC (with bacon), the 'queen bean' (refried beans) and the 'or'izo' (Mexican chorizo).

(☏929-367-8226; www.kingdavidtacos.com; Grand Army Plaza, Prospect Park; tacos $4; ⏰7-11am Mon-Fri, to 2pm Sat, 8am-1pm Sun; 🖋; 🚇2/3 to Grand Army Plaza)

Four & Twenty Blackbirds

BAKERY $

11 ✕ MAP P222, A3

Sisters Emily and Melissa Elsen use flaky, buttery crusts and seasonal, regionally-sourced fruits to create NYC's best pies, hands down. Any time is just right to drop in to their shop for a slice – the plum-strawberry streusel is *divine* – and a cup of Irving Farm coffee. Add a dollop of fresh whipped cream and you'll be in pie heaven. (☏718-499-2917; www.birdsblack.com; 439 Third Ave, cnr 8th

Gowanus Canal 👍

To the east of the subway station at Smith–9th Sts, in a former industrial area, is the gently curving – and highly polluted – Gowanus Canal. Originally a creek (named for Gouwane, a local indigenous chief), the canal was used by merchant ships for unloading goods. Unfortunately, local industrial operations unloaded all kinds of untreated waste here too, leading to a heavy sludge along the bottom and a reddish-purple sheen on the surface (hence its local nickname: 'the Lavender Lake'). The Environmental Protection Agency (EPA) declared it a Superfund site in 2009; a massive clean-up project is currently underway and is expected to finish in 2027.

Despite the canal's toxic status, it frequently attracts intrepid urban explorers wanting moody waterfront pictures. After rezoning efforts in the 2000s, the low-rent area named Gowanus that stretches north to Baltic St and east to Fourth Ave became home to artists' studios and music venues in large, postindustrial spaces. This led to more restaurants and bars, and eventually to new residential developments – making Gowanus one of Brooklyn's most rapidly changing neighborhoods.

St, Gowanus; pie slices $5.75; ⊙8am-8pm Mon-Fri, from 9am Sat, 10am-7pm Sun; 🛜; SR to 9th St)

Drinking

Union Hall   BAR

12 🚇 MAP P222, C2

Anyone looking for an authentically Brooklyn night out should look no further than Union Hall. This bar and event space is located in a converted warehouse and boasts a double-sided fireplace, towering bookshelves, leather couches and two full-size indoor bocce courts. Head to the basement for live music and comedy. (📞718-638-4400; www.unionhallny.com; 702 Union St, near Fifth Ave, Park Slope; drinks from

$7; ⊙4pm-4am Mon-Fri, 1pm-4am Sat & Sun; SR train to Union St)

Lavender Lake   PUB

13 🚇 MAP P222, A2

This little gem of a bar – named for the old local nickname for the colorfully polluted Gowanus Canal – is set in a former horse stable and serves carefully selected craft beers and a few seasonal cocktails, which include ingredients such as jalapeño-infused tequila. The light-strewn garden is a brilliant summery spot. There's good food, too (mains $11 to $23). (📞347-799-2154; www.lavenderlake. com; 383 Carroll St, btwn Bond Sts & Gowanus Canal, Gowanus; ⊙4pm-midnight Mon-Wed, to 1am Thu, to 2am

Fri, noon-2am Sat, to midnight Sun; **S** F, G to Carroll St; R to Union St)

Royal Palms BAR

14 🚇 MAP P222, B2

If you're hankering for some sports but don't want to sweat or drift too far from the bar stool, Royal Palms is for you. Inside this 17,000-sq-ft space are 10 full shuffleboard courts ($40 per hour), plus board games (massive Jenga, over-size Connect Four), draft brews, cocktails and snacks provided by a food truck (a different rotation each week). (🕿 347-223-4410; www.royalpalmsshuffle.com; 514 Union St, btwn Third Ave & Nevins St, Gowanus; ⏱6pm-midnight Mon-Thu, to 2am Fri, noon-2am Sat, to 10pm Sun; **S** R to Union St)

Greenwood Park BEER GARDEN

15 🚇 MAP P222, B7

Around the corner from the leafy Green-Wood Cemetery (p224), this 13,000-sq-ft indoor/outdoor beer hall in an open, industrial setting is a clever reconfiguration of a former gas station and mechanic's shop. (Look for the giant exterior wall made of old pallets.) You'll find more than two dozen beers on draft, plus burgers, salads, wings and other pub fare. (🕿 718-499-7999; www.greenwoodparkbk.com; 555 Seventh Ave, btwn 19th & 20th Sts, Greenwood Heights; ⏱noon-2am Sun-Thu, to 3am Fri & Sat, shorter hours in winter; 🛜 ♿; 🚌 B67, B69 to 18th St. **S** F, G to Prospect Park)

Freddy's BAR

16 🚇 MAP P222, A6

This old-time bar with a fascinating history (read more on the website) is just past the southern fringe of Park Slope. Tip one back at the vintage mahogany bar while admiring the crazy art videos made by co-owner Donald O'Finn. There's also free live music (uke jams, honky-tonk), comedy nights and the odd film screening. A true New York classic. (🕿 718-768-0131; www.freddysbar.com; 627 Fifth Ave, btwn 17th & 18th Sts, Greenwood Heights; ⏱noon-4am; 🛜; **S** R to Prospect Ave)

Entertainment

Barbès LIVE MUSIC, JAZZ

17 ⭐ MAP P222, C4

This compact bar and performance space, named after a North African neighborhood in Paris, is owned by French musician (and longtime Brooklyn resident) Olivier Conan, who sometimes plays here with his Latin-themed band Las Rubias del Norte. There's live music all night, every night: the impressively eclectic lineup includes Afro-Peruvian grooves, West African funk and gypsy swing, among other sounds. (🕿 718-965-9177; www.barbesbrooklyn.com; 376 9th St, at Sixth Ave, Park Slope; requested donation for live music $10; ⏱5pm-2am Mon-Thu, 2pm-4am Fri & Sat, to 2am Sun; **S** F, G to 7th Ave; R to 4th Ave-9th St)

Bell House LIVE PERFORMANCE

18 ⭐ MAP P222, A3

A large, old venue in a mostly barren area of industrial Gowanus, the Bell House features high-profile live performances, indie rockers, DJ nights, comedy shows and burlesque parties. The handsomely converted warehouse has a spacious concert area, plus a friendly little bar in the front room with flickering candles, leather armchairs and 10 or so beers on tap. (☏718-643-6510; www.thebell houseny.com; 149 7th St, btwn Second & Third Aves, Gowanus; ⊙5pm-late; 🛜; ⑤F, G, R to 4th Ave-9th St)

Littlefield LIVE PERFORMANCE

19 ⭐ MAP P222, C1

This performance and art space occupying a 6200-sq-ft former textile warehouse showcases a wide range of live music and other shows, including comedy, storytelling, theater, dance, film screenings and trivia nights. Wyatt Cenac hosts the popular *Night Train* comedy show on Mondays; other regular events include the groan-inducing game show *Punderdome 3000* and embarrassing-story-telling night *Mortified*. No under-21s. (www.littlefieldnyc.com; 635 Sackett St, btwn Third & Fourth Aves, Gowanus; ⑤R to Union St)

Puppetworks PUPPET THEATRE

20 ⭐ MAP P222, C4

In a tiny theater in Park Slope, this nonprofit outfit stages delightful marionette shows that earn rave reviews from pint-sized critics. Catch puppet adaptations of classics like *Beauty and the Beast*, *Goldilocks and the Three Bears* and (of course) *Pinocchio*. Most shows happen on Saturdays and Sundays at 12:30pm and 2:30pm. Check the website for schedules. (☏718-965-3391; www.puppetworks.org; 338 Sixth Ave, at 4th St, Park Slope; adult/child $11/10; ⊙12:30pm & 2:30pm Sat & Sun; 👪; ⑤F, G to 7th Ave)

Shopping

No Relation Vintage VINTAGE

21 🅐 MAP P222, C2

Looking for a sports jersey? What about a piece of vintage designer clothing? There are many thrift stores in NYC, but few have quite

Celebrate Brooklyn

One of Brooklyn's biggest highlights is the summer-long **Celebrate Brooklyn! Festival** (☏718-683-5600; www.bricartsmedia.org; near Prospect Park W & 11th St, Prospect Park Bandshell, Park Slope; ⊙Jun-Aug), a stellar line-up of live music, films, dance and more at the Prospect Park bandshell. Shows are held throughout each week, many with free admission.

The L Train Shutdown

In April 2019, NYC is planning to close the Canarsie Tunnel, which connects Manhattan with Williamsburg, on the L train line, for much-needed repairs. The upcoming closure, slated to last 15 months, has caused much anxiety in north Brooklyn. During its closure, there will be regular L eastward service from Bedford Ave to Canarsie, but no service across to Manhattan, or within Manhattan itself. If planning to visit Williamsburg, be sure to research your options ahead of time: taking an alternate subway line (J/Z or M from Manhattan; G from Queens or south Brooklyn) and walking or taking the bus, cycling via Citi Bike over the Williamsburg Bridge, or going by NYC Ferry (p242). You can get the latest subway updates at http://web.mta.info.

this range. This gigantic vintage shop in the Gowanus area has a staggering inventory (you'll need to spend some time here), with great deals for bargain hunters. No Relation has five shops around Brooklyn and one in the East Village. (☎718-858-4906; https://ltrainvintage.com; 654 Sackett St, near Fourth Ave, Gowanus; ⏰noon-8pm; 🚇R to Union St)

Grand Army Plaza Greenmarket
MARKET

(10) 🔒 MAP P222, E3

Held at the southern edge of Grand Army Plaza every Saturday, this Greenmarket with local and regional produce stalls and fun food trucks is a good spot to grab

a picnic before heading into Prospect Park (p224). (www.grownyc.org; Prospect Park W & Flatbush Ave, Grand Army Plaza, Prospect Park; ⏰8am-4pm Sat year-round; 🚇2/3 to Grand Army Plaza)

Beacon's Closet
VINTAGE

22 🔒 MAP P222, D1

An excellent vintage shop stocked full of shoes, jewelry and bright vintage finds. There's a much bigger branch in Greenpoint, and another one in Bushwick. (☎718-230-1630; www.beaconscloset.com; 92 Fifth Ave, cnr Warren St, Park Slope; ⏰noon-9pm Mon-Fri, 11am-8pm Sat & Sun; 🚇2/3 to Bergen St; B, Q to 7th Ave)

Walking Tour 🥾

Brooklyn: Williamsburg

Once a bastion of Latino working-class life, Williamsburg is the dining and nightlife center of northern Brooklyn. This erstwhile bohemian magnet has seen the starving artists move to Bushwick for cheaper rents, leaving gleaming condos and refurbished brownstones to professionals and hip young families. There's lots to explore, from vintage-cocktail dens to shops selling one-of-a-kind creations from local craftspeople.

Walk Facts

Start East River State Park

End Rough Trade

[S] L to Bedford Ave

(See p231 for information about the L train shutdown from April 2019.)

Length 2.2 miles; three to four hours

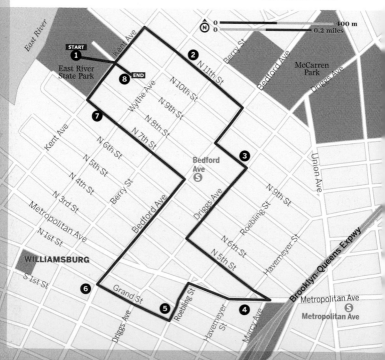

❶ East River State Park

Offering fabulous, waterside Manhattan views, this **park** (☎718-782-2731; www.parks.ny.gov/parks/155; Kent Ave, btwn 8th & 9th Sts; ⏰9am-dusk) is an open green space, with picnicking and occasional concerts in summertime.

❷ Brooklyn Brewery

Williamsburg was once the center of beer-brewing in New York. This **brewery** (☎718-486-7422; www.brooklynbrewery.com; 79 N 11th St, btwn Berry St & Wythe Ave; tours Sat & Sun free, 5pm Mon-Thu $15; ⏰tours 5pm Mon-Thu, 1-5pm Sat, 1-4pm Sun; tasting room 6-11pm Fri, noon-8pm Sat, noon-6pm Sun) not only serves tasty local suds, it also offers tours.

❸ Buffalo Exchange

For a wardrobe with some local flavor, try this popular **resale shop** (☎718-384-6901; www.buffaloexchange.com; 504 Driggs Ave, at N 9th St; ⏰11am-8pm Mon-Sat, noon-7pm Sun) for lightly used, on-trend fashions for men and women.

❹ City Reliquary

This snug storefront **museum** (☎718-782-4842; www.cityreliquary.org; 370 Metropolitan Ave, near Havemeyer St; $7; ⏰noon-6pm Thu-Sun; Ⓢ G to Metropolitan Ave) is packed with artifacts and ephemera from New York's days of yore, including from the 1939 World's Fair.

❺ Fuego 718

A fun little **shop** (☎718-302-2913; www.fuego718.com; 249 Grand St, btwn Roebling St & Driggs Ave; ⏰noon-8pm) that transports you south of the border with Day of the Dead boxes, colorful frames and mirrors, and crafts from Mexico, Peru and beyond.

❻ Maison Premiere

Crank that time machine back at this retro **bar** (☎347-335-0446; www.maisonpremiere.com; 298 Bedford Ave, btwn S 1st & Grand Sts; ⏰2pm-2am Mon-Wed, to 4am Thu & Fri, 11am-4am Sat, to 2am Sun), which features bespoke cocktails, oysters and other treats with a smart Southern vibe.

❼ Artists & Fleas

Browse the aisles of this weekend **shopping warren** (www.artistsandfleas.com; 70 N 7th St, btwn Wythe & Kent Aves; ⏰10am-7pm Sat & Sun) of several dozen booths featuring locally crafted jewelry, art, cosmetics and housewares and vintage records and clothes.

❽ Rough Trade

This American outpost of the legendary UK **record store** (☎718-388-4111; www.roughtradenyc.com; 64 N 9th St, btwn Kent & Wythe Aves; ⏰11am-11pm Mon-Sat, to 9pm Sun; 📶) is a warehouse-sized dream for music lovers, with frequent in-store concerts of upcoming talent. End your stroll with a latte from their cafe.

Worth a Trip 👀
Coney Island

An hour by subway from midtown Manhattan, Coney Island was once New York's most popular beachside amusement area. After decades in the doldrums, revitalization has brought the summertime crowds back for hot dogs, roller coasters, and strolls down the boardwalk. All of Coney Island's sights are concentrated within a seven-block-long strip between the subway station and the beach, so it makes for an easy day trip.

www.coneyisland.com

Surf Ave & Boardwalk, btwn W 15th & W 8th Sts

The People's Playground

A famed working-class amusement park and beach resort at the turn of the 20th century, Coney Island's kitschy charms have had a 21st-century revival after decades of seedy decline. Though not the booming attraction it once was, it still draws crowds of tourists and locals alike for roller-coaster rides, hot dogs and beer on the beachside boardwalk.

Ticket to Ride

Luna Park (☏718-373-5862; www.lunaparknyc. com; Surf Ave, at 10th St, Coney Island; ☉Apr-Oct; ⑤D/F, N/Q to Coney Island-Stillwell Ave) is one of Coney Island's most popular amusement parks and contains one of its most legendary rides: the **Cyclone** ($10), a wooden roller coaster that reaches speeds of 60mph and makes near-vertical drops. The pink-and-mint-green **Deno's Wonder Wheel** (☏718-372-2592; www. denoswonderwheel.com; 1025 Riegelmann Boardwalk, at W 12th St, Coney Island; rides $8; ☉from noon Jul & Aug, from noon Sat & Sun Apr-Jun & Sep-Oct; ⑪; ⑤D/F, N/Q to Coney Island-Stillwell Ave), which has been delighting New Yorkers since 1920, is the best place to survey Coney Island from up high.

Hot Diggity Dog

The hot dog was invented in Coney Island in 1867, and there's no better place to eat one than **Nathan's Famous** (☏718-333-2202; www. nathansfamous.com; 1310 Surf Ave, cnr Stillwell Ave, Coney Island; hot dogs from $4; ☉10am-midnight; ☎; ⑤D/F to Coney Island-Stillwell Ave), established 1916. When thirst strikes, head to **Ruby's** (☏718-975-7829; www.rubysbar.com; 1213 Riegelmann Boardwalk, btwn Stillwell Ave & 12th St, Coney Island; ☉11am-10pm Sun-Thu, to 1am Fri & Sat Apr-Sep, weekends only Oct; ⑤D/F, N/Q to Coney Island-Stillwell Ave), a legendary dive bar right on the boardwalk.

★ **Top Tips**

○ Luna Park rides are à la carte: the higher the thrill, the more it costs. If you want to hit everything, you'll save money with the all-day pass.

○ Note that not all of the rides at Coney Island are part of Luna Park, and thus require separate fees.

○ Go weekdays during the daytime to avoid crowds and lines.

✗ **Take a Break**

For something more substantial than a hot dog, head over to **Totonno's** (☏718-372-8606; www.toto nnosconeyisland.com; 1524 Neptune Ave, near W 16th St, Coney Island; pizzas $18-21, toppings $2.50; ☉noon-8pm Thu-Sun; ✈; ⑤D/F, N/Q to Coney Island-Stillwell Ave), one of Brooklyn's oldest and most authentic pizza joints.

★ **Getting There**

Coney Island is approximately 14 miles southeast of Times Sq.

⑤Take the D/F or N/Q to Coney Island-Stillwell Ave (last stop).

Survival Guide

Before You Go

Book Your Stay

o In general, expect high prices and small spaces. Room rates are priced by availability, not by high- or low-season rules (but major holidays will always cost more).

o Accommodations fill up quickly and range from boxy cookie-cutter chains to stylish boutiques.

o You'll find better-value hotels, hostels and even some B&Bs in Brooklyn and Queens than Manhattan.

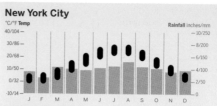

When to Go

Winter (Dec–Feb) Snowfalls and below-freezing temperatures (though days are bright).

Spring (Mar–May) Eager cafes drag their patio furniture out at the first hint of warm weather. One of the best times to explore the city.

Summer (Jun–Aug) Oppressively hot at the height of summer, though there's also a packed lineup of festivals, free outdoor concerts and other events. Locals often leave town on weekends.

Fall (Sep–Nov) Brilliant bursts of red and gold illuminate the city's parks, with still-warm days and cool nights.

Useful Websites

newyorkhotels.com (www.newyorkhotels. com) Self-proclaimed official website for hotels in NYC.

NYC (www.nycgo. com/hotels) Listings from the Official Guide.

Lonely Planet (www. lonelyplanet.com/usa/ new-york-city/hotels) Reviews and online booking service.

Best Budget

Carlton Arms (www. carltonarms.com) An atmospheric art-filled inn just a few blocks east of Madison Square Park.

Bubba & Bean Lodges (www.bblodges.com) A charming Upper East Side townhouse with five modern guestrooms.

Club Quarters World Trade Center (www. clubquartershotels. com/new-york/world-trade-center) Clean rooms at reasonable prices in the Financial District, with lots of guest perks.

YMCA (www.ymca nyc.org) It's fun to stay in recently redesigned rooms with access to a pool and sauna.

Best Midrange

Citizen M (www. citizenm.com) Contemporary, high-tech rooms near the heart of Times Square.

Wall Street Inn (www. thewallstreetinn. com) Comfy beds and colonial-style rooms in the Financial District.

NYLO Hotel (www. nylo-nyc.com)

Boutique hotel on the Upper West Side with plush bedding and roomy bathrooms.

Roxy Hotel Tribeca (www.roxyhotelnyc.com) Downtown hotel with contemporary rooms, plus multiple bars, a cinema and a jazz club all on site.

Yotel (www.yotel.com) Small but cleverly configured futuristic rooms with killer views in Midtown West.

Best Top End

Knickerbocker (www.theknickerbocker.com) A luxurious Midtown option with a fabulous rooftop bar.

Hôtel Americano (www.hotel-americano.com) This designer's Chelsea dream is the boutique sleep of the future.

Greenwich Hotel (www.thegreenwichhotel.com) Individually designed rooms in this downtown standout.

NoMad Hotel (www.thenomadhotel.com) Parisian aesthetics mixed with mod cons in western Midtown.

Mark (www.themarkhotel.com) Plush fittings and marble bathrooms on the Upper East Side.

Arriving in NYC

John F Kennedy International (JFK)

Destination	Best Transport
Brooklyn	**S** LIRR to Atlantic Terminal
Lower East Side	**S** J/Z line
Lower Manhattan	**S** A line
Midtown	LIRR to Penn Station
Greenwich Village	Village **S** A line
Upper West Side	**S** A line
Upper East Side	**S** E, then 4/5/6 lines
Harlem	**S** E, then B or C lines

LaGuardia Airport (LGA)

Destination	Best Transport
Harlem	🚍 M60
Upper East Side	🚍 M60 & **S** 4/5/6 line
Midtown	🚍 Q70 & **S** F, 7 or E lines
Union Square	🚍 Q70 then **S** R line
Greenwich Village	🚍 Q70 then **S** F line
Brooklyn	Taxi

Newark Liberty International Airport (EWR)

○ About the same distance from Midtown as JFK (16 miles), Newark is a hub for United Airlines and offers the only non-stop flight to Havana, Cuba, in the New York City area.

○ Take the AirTrain to Newark Airport train station, and board any train bound for Penn Station ($13).

○ Taxis range from $60 to $80 (plus $15 toll and tip).

Getting Around

Subway

○ The New York subway system is cheap ($2.75 per ride, regardless of the distance traveled), works around the clock and is overall safe and (somewhat) clean.

○ Free wi-fi is available in all underground stations.

○ Ask the station attendant for a free map. Get info online at www.mta.info or download a useful smartphone app (such as Citymapper).

Important Numbers

Local directory	📞 411
Municipal offices & information	📞 311
National directory information	📞 212-555-1212
Operator	📞 0
Fire, police & ambulance	📞 911

◦ Don't wear headphones when you're riding: you might miss an important announcement about track changes or skipped stops.

Taxi

Yellow taxis There are set fares for rides (which can be paid with credit or debit card): $2.50 for the initial charge (first one-fifth of a mile), 50¢ for each additional one-fifth mile as well as per 60 seconds of being stopped in traffic, $1 peak surcharge (weekdays 4pm to 8pm), and a 50¢ night surcharge (8pm to 6am), plus a MTA State surcharge of 50¢ per ride. Tips are expected to be 10% to 15%, but give less if you feel in any way mistreated; be sure to ask for a receipt and use it to note the driver's license number.

Boro taxis Green Boro Taxis operate in the outer boroughs and Upper Manhattan. These allow folks to hail a taxi on the street in neighborhoods where yellow taxis rarely roam. They have the same fares and features as yellow cabs, and are a good way to get around the outer boroughs (from, say, Astoria to Williamsburg, or Park Slope to Red Hook). Drivers are reluctant (but legally obligated) to take passengers into Manhattan as they aren't legally allowed to take fares going out of Manhattan south of 96th St.

Passenger rights The Taxi & Limousine Commission (TLC) keeps a Passenger's Bill of Rights, which gives you the right to tell the driver which route you'd like to take, or ask your driver to stop smoking or turn off an annoying radio station. Also, the driver does not have the right to refuse you a ride based on where you are going – so get in first, then say where you're going.

Private car A common taxi alternative in the outer boroughs. Fares differ depending on the neighborhood and length of ride, and must be determined beforehand (no meters). These 'black cars' are quite common in Brooklyn and Queens, however, it's illegal if a driver simply stops to offer you a ride – no matter what borough you're in. Car services in Brooklyn include **Northside** (www.northsideservice.com, 📞 718-387-2222) in Williamsburg and **Arecibo** (📞 718-783-6465) in Park Slope.

Ride-sharing App-based car-hailing services have taken over the streets of the five boroughs. Now, with nearly five times as many cars as yellow cabs and growing, they're both convenient, indispensable for some, and of course adding to the already terrible traffic problem. Tipping is highly encouraged; drivers may give you a low rating if you stiff them.

Subway Cheat Sheet

Numbers, letters, colors Color-coded subway lines are named by a letter or number, and most carry a collection of two to four trains on their tracks, often following roughly the same path through Manhattan before branching out into the other boroughs.

Express & local lines Each color-coded line (except the L and the G) is shared by local trains and express trains; the latter make only select stops in Manhattan (indicated by a white circle on subway maps). If you're covering a greater distance, you're better off transferring to the express train (usually just across the platform from the local) to save time.

Getting in the right station Some stations have separate entrances for downtown or uptown lines (read the sign carefully). If you swipe in at the wrong one, you'll either need to ride the subway to a station where you can transfer for free, or just lose the $2.75 and re-enter the station on the correct side (usually across the street). Also look for the green and red lamps above the stairs at each station entrance; green means that it's always open, while red means that a particular entrance will be closed at certain hours, usually late at night.

Weekends All the rules switch on weekends, when some lines combine with others, some get suspended, some stations get passed, others get reached. Locals and tourists alike stand on platforms confused, sometimes irate. Check www.mta.info for weekend schedules, or download the MTA Weekender smartphone app. Sometimes posted signs aren't visible until after you reach the platform.

Bus

o Buses can be a handy way to cross town or to cover short distances when you don't want to bother going underground. Rides cost the same as subway ($2.75 per ride), and you can use your Metrocard or pay in cash (exact change required)

o If you pay with a Metrocard, you get one free transfer from bus to subway, bus to bus, or subway to bus. If you pay in cash, ask for a transfer (good only for a bus to bus transfer) from the bus driver when paying.

o Look for the route on the small sign mounted on the pole of the bus stop.

Bicycle

o NYC has hundreds of miles of newly designated bike lanes. The excellent bike-sharing network Citi Bike (www.citibikenyc.com) has kiosks all over Manhattan and parts of Brooklyn and Queens.

o You can get Citi Bike for a 24-hour or three-day access pass (around $12 or $24 including tax) at any kiosk. During that period you can use the bike for an unlimited number of 30-minute periods.

o Helmets aren't required by law, but strongly

How to Hail a Taxi

o To hail a yellow cab, look for one with its roof light lit (if it's not lit, the cab is taken).

o Stand in a prominent place on the side of the road and stick out your arm.

o Once inside the cab, tell them your destination (it's illegal for drivers to refuse you a ride).

o Pay your fare at the end, either with cash or credit card (via the touch screen in back). Don't forget to tip 10% to 15%.

o If you download the smartphone app Curb, you can book a taxi to come pick you up, like any other ride-sharing service.

recommended. You'll need to bring or buy your own.

o Find bike lanes for every borough on NYC Bike Maps (www. nycbikemaps.com). Free maps are also available at most bike shops.

o Most importantly, for your safety and that of others, obey traffic laws.

Boat

NYC Ferry (www.ferry.nyc; one-way $2.75) Operating in the East River, these boats link Manhattan, Brooklyn, Queens and the Bronx. Only $2.75 a ride ($1 more to bring a bicycle on board) and with charging stations and mini convenience stores on board.

NY Water Taxi (www. nywatertaxi.com) Zippy yellow boats that provide hop-on, hop-off services with a few stops around Manhattan (Pier 79 at W 39th St; World Financial Center and Pier 11 near Wall St) and Brooklyn (Pier 1 in Dumbo), plus a ferry service between Pier 11 and the Ikea store in Red Hook, Brooklyn.

Staten Island Ferry (www.siferry.com; Whitehall Terminal, 4 South St, at Whitehall St; ⏲24hr; S 1 to South Ferry; R/W to Whitehall St; 4/5 to Bowling Green) Free-ferry to Staten Island makes constant journeys across New York Harbor (great for the views even if you come right back).

Essential Information

Accessible Travel

o Much of the city is accessible with curb cuts for wheelchair users.

o All the major sites (the Met museum, the Guggenheim, and Lincoln Center) are also accessible.

o Some, but not all, Broadway theaters are accessible.

o Unfortunately, only about 100 of New York's 468 subway stations are fully wheelchair accessible. In general, the bigger stations have access, such as West 4th St, 14th St-Union Sq, 34th St-Penn Station, 42nd St-Port Authority Terminal, 59th St-Columbus Circle, and 66th St-Lincoln Center.

o For a complete list of accessible subway stations, visit http://web. mta.info/accessibility/ stations.htm. Also visit www.nycgo.com/ accessibility.

o All of NYC's MTA buses are wheelchair accessible, and are often a better option than negotiating cramped subway stations.

○ Order an accessible taxi through **Accessible Dispatch** (☎ 646-599-9999; http://accessibledispatch.org); there's also an app that allows you to request the nearest available service.

○ Download Lonely Planet's free Accessible Travel guide from http://lptravel.to/AccessibleTravel.

Business Hours

Standard business hours are as follows:

Banks 9am–6pm Monday–Friday, some also 9am–noon Saturday

Bars 5pm–4am

Businesses 9am–5pm Monday–Friday

Clubs 10pm–4am

Restaurants Breakfast 6am–11am, lunch 11am–around 3pm, and dinner 5pm–11pm; weekend brunch 11am–4pm

Shops 10am–around 7pm weekdays, 11am–around 8pm Saturday, and Sunday can be variable – some stores stay closed while others keep weekday hours. Stores tend to stay open later in the neighborhoods downtown.

Discount Cards

New York CityPASS (www.citypass.com) Admission to six major attractions (including the Empire State Building) for $122, saving around 40% if purchased separately.

The New York Pass (www.newyorkpass.com) One-day access to some 90 different sites for $119. Multiday passes also available (from two to 10 days).

Downtown Culture Pass (www.downtownculturepass.org) Three-day pass ($25) gets free admission (and shop discounts) at a handful of sites in Lower Manhattan, including the Museum of American Finance and the Museum of Jewish Heritage – both locations where you can purchase the pass in person.

Explorer Pass (www.smartdestinations.com) Lets you choose the between three and 10 attractions for discounted admission. You pick the sites from among 63 options, including the MoMA, the Intrepid Museum, Sightseeing cruises and the Top of the Rock. Prices start at $84 for three sites, up to $199 for 10 sites.

Electricity

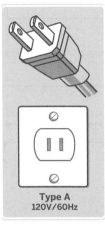

Type A
120V/60Hz

Type B
120V/60Hz

Legal Matters

o If you're arrested, you have the right to remain silent. There is no legal reason to speak to a police officer if you don't wish to – especially since anything you say 'can and will be used against you' – but never walk away from an officer until given permission.

o All persons who are arrested have the legal right to make one phone call. If you don't have a lawyer or family member to help you, call your consulate. The police will give you the number upon request.

Etiquette

Politeness It's courteous to greet nearby staff when entering or leaving a shop, cafe or restaurant.

Greetings Shake hands with men and women when meeting for the first time and when saying goodbye. Female friends are often greeted with a single (air) kiss.

Taboo Topics Although Donald Trump is almost universally reviled in NYC, politics and religion are topics best avoided.

Transport Allow passengers to exit the subway car before entering; don't block the doors.

Gratuity Not optional in restaurants or bars; don't forget to tip.

Internet Access

o Most public parks in the city now offer free wi-fi. Some prominent ones include the High Line, Bryant Park, Battery Park, Central Park, City Hall Park, Madison Square Park, Tompkins Square Park and Union Square Park (Brooklyn and Queens are also well covered).

o For other city hot spots, check out www.nycgovparks.org/facilities/wifi.

o All subway stations now offer free wi-fi as well, including many city buses (some of which also feature USB charging ports).

o LinkNYC (www.link.nyc) is rolling out free internet-connected kiosks across the city, replete with charging stations and wi-fi access. The network aims to install some 7500 of these structures throughout the five boroughs.

o It's rare to find accommodations in New York City that don't offer wi-fi, though it isn't always free.

o Most cafes offer wi-fi for customers, as do the ubiquitous Starbucks around town.

Money

ATMs widely available; credit cards accepted at most hotels, stores and restaurants. Farmers markets, food trucks and some restaurants and bars are cash-only.

ATMs

o ATMs are on practically every corner. You can either use your card at banks – usually in a 24-hour-access lobby, filled with up to a dozen monitors at major branches – or you can opt for the machines in delis, restaurants, bars and grocery stores, which charge service fees that average $3 but can go as high as $5.

o Most New York banks are linked by the New York Cash Exchange

(NYCE) system, and you can use local bank cards interchangeably at ATMs – for an extra fee if you're banking outside your system.

Changing Money

Banks and money-changers, found all over New York City (including all three major airports), will give you US currency based on the current exchange rate. **Travelex** (☎212-265-6063; www.travelex.com; 1578 Broadway, btwn 47th & 48th Sts, Midtown West; ⏰9am-10pm Mon-Sat, to 7pm Sun; Ⓢ N/Q/R to 49th St) has a branch in Times Square.

Credit Cards

○ Major credit cards are accepted at most hotels, restaurants and shops throughout New York City. Certain transactions, such as purchasing tickets to performances and renting a car, can't be done without one.

○ Visa, MasterCard and American Express are the cards of choice here. Places that accept Visa and MasterCard also accept debit cards. Be sure to check with your bank to confirm that

your debit card will be accepted in other states or countries – debit cards from large commercial banks can often be used worldwide.

○ If your cards are lost or stolen, contact the company immediately.

Taxes & Refunds

○ Restaurants and retailers never include the sales tax – 8.875% – in their prices, so don't order a $4.99 lunch special if you have only $5.

○ Several categories of so-called luxury items, including rental cars and dry-cleaning, carry an additional city surcharge of 5%, so you wind up paying an

extra 13.875% in total for these services.

○ Clothing and footwear purchases under $110 are tax free; anything over that amount has a sales tax.

○ Hotel rooms in New York City are subject to a 14.75% tax, plus a flat $3.50 occupancy tax per night.

○ Since the US has no nationwide value-added tax (VAT), there is no opportunity for foreign visitors to make 'tax-free' purchases.

Tipping

Tipping is *not* optional; only withhold tips in cases of outrageously bad service.

Money-saving Tips

○ MetroCards are valid on subways, buses, ferries and the tramway to Roosevelt Island. If you're staying more than a couple of days, buy a 7-Day Unlimited Pass ($32).

○ Browse our list of free attractions (p27).

○ Many museums offer free admission regularly (eg once a week). Check their websites for admission info.

○ Save on theater tickets by buying tickets at the TKTS booth at Times Square or in Lower Manhattan.

○ Stock up on picnic goodies at the many outdoor farmers markets and gourmet grocers.

Dos & Don'ts

o Hail a cab only if the roof light is on. If it's not lit, the cab is taken, so put your arm down already!

o You needn't obey 'walk' signs – simply cross the street when there isn't oncoming traffic.

o When negotiating pedestrian traffic on the sidewalk think of yourself as a vehicle – don't stop short, follow the speed of the crowd around you and pull off to the side if you need to take out your map or umbrella. Most New Yorkers are respectful of personal space, but they will bump into you – and not apologize – if you get in the way.

o When boarding the subway, wait until the passengers disembark, then be aggressive enough when you hop on so that the doors don't close in front of you.

o In New York you wait 'on line' instead of 'in line'; you'll also hear 'quarter of' rather than 'quarter to' for telling time.

o Oh, and it's pronounced 'How-sten Street', not 'Hugh-sten', got it?

Restaurant servers 18–20%, unless a gratuity is already charged on the bill (usually only for groups of five or more)

Bartenders 15–20% per round, minimum per drink $1 for standard drinks, and $2 per specialty cocktail

Taxi drivers 10–15%, rounded up to the next dollar

Airport & hotel porters $2 per bag, minimum per cart $5

Hotel maids $2–4 per night, left in envelope or under the card provided

Public Holidays

New Year's Day January 1

Martin Luther King Day Third Monday in January

Presidents' Day Third Monday in February

Easter March/April

Memorial Day Late May

Gay Pride Last Sunday in June

Independence Day July 4

Labor Day Early September

Rosh Hashanah and Yom Kippur Mid-September to mid-October

Halloween October 31

Thanksgiving Fourth Thursday in November

Christmas Day December 25

New Year's Eve December 31

Safe Travel

New York City is one of the safest cities in the USA but it's still best to take a common-sense approach:

o Don't walk around alone at night in unfamiliar, sparsely populated areas.

o Carry your daily walking-around money somewhere inside your clothing or in a front pocket rather than in a handbag or a back pocket.

o Be aware of pickpockets, particularly in mobbed areas, like Times Square or Penn Station at rush hour.

o While it's generally safe to ride the subway after midnight, you may want to skip going underground and take a taxi instead, especially if traveling alone.

Smoking

Strictly forbidden in any location that's considered a public place, including subway stations, restaurants, bars, taxis and parks. A few hotels have smoking rooms, but the majority are entirely smoke-free.

Toilets

o Public restrooms are available in transport hubs like Grand Central Terminal, Penn Station and Port Authority Bus Terminal, and in parks, including Madison Square Park, Battery Park, Tompkins Square Park, Washington Square Park and Columbus Park in Chinatown, plus several places scattered around Central Park.

o Your best bet is to pop into a Starbucks, a department store or a neighborhood park like Tompkins Square in the East Village or Bleecker Playground (at W 11th & Hudson) in the West Village.

Tourist Information

NYC Information
Center (📞212-484-1222; www.nycgo.com; Broadway Plaza, btwn W 43rd & 44th Sts; ⏰9am-6pm Dec-Apr, 8am-8pm May-Nov; Ⓢ N/Q/R/W, S, 1/2/3, 7, A/C/E to Times Sq-42nd St) There are official NYC Visitor Information Centers throughout the city. The main office is in Midtown.

Explore Brooklyn
(www.explorebk.com) has up-to-date event listings and lots of of other info on this much-loved borough.

Visas

o The US Visa Waiver Program allows nationals of 38 countries to enter the US without a visa. For the up-to-date list of countries included in the program and current requirements, see the US Department of State (https://travel.state.gov) website.

o Citizens of VWP countries need to register with the US Department of Homeland Security and fill out an ESTA application (www.cbp.gov/travel/international-visitors/esta) before your visit. There is a $14 fee for registration; when approved, the registration is valid for two years or until your passport expires, whichever comes first.

o If you hold a passport from a non-VWP country, are planning to stay longer than 90 days in the US or are planning to work or study here, you must obtain a visa from a US embassy or consulate in your home country.

Index

See also separate subindexes for:

🍴 Eating p251

🍸 Drinking p252

✪ Entertainment p253

🛍 Shopping p254

Behind the Scenes

Send Us Your Feedback

We love to hear from travelers – your comments help make our books better. We read every word, and we guarantee that your feedback goes straight to the authors. Visit **lonelyplanet.com/contact** to submit your updates and suggestions.

Note: We may edit, reproduce and incorporate your comments in Lonely Planet products such as guidebooks, websites and digital products, so let us know if you don't want your comments reproduced or your name acknowledged. For a copy of our privacy policy visit lonelyplanet.com/privacy.

Acknowledgements

Cover photograph: Cityscape with the Empire State Building, Francesco Carovillano/4Corners©

Photographs pp34–5 (clockwise from top left): Songquan Deng; Marcio Jose Bastos Silva; Photo Spirit; Jeff Whyte; Michael Urmann/Shutterstock ©

This Book

This 7th edition of *Pocket New York City* was curated by Ali Lemer and researched and written by Regis St Louis, Robert Balkovich, Ray Bartlett and Ali, with contributions by Michael Grosberg. The previous edition was written and researched by Regis and Cristian Bonetto.

Destination Editor
Trisha Ping

Senior Product Editor
Kate Mathews

Product Editors Hannah Cartmel, Shona Gray

Senior Cartographer
Alison Lyall

Book Designer
Mazzy Prinsep

Assisting Editors
Melanie Dankel, Bruce Evans, Jennifer Hattam, Alison Morris, Anne Mulvaney, Kristin Odijk, Christopher Pitts,

Benjamin Spier, Gabrielle Stefanos

Assisting Cartographer
James Leversha

Cover Researcher
Brendan Dempsey-Spencer

Thanks to Mikki Brammer, Victor de Wolff, Liz Heynes, Anne Mason, JT McKay, Karl Micallef, Michael Oanea, Darren O'Connell, Martine Power, Rachel Rawling, Kathryn Rowan

Our Writers Map Included

Ali Lemer

Ali has been a Lonely Planet writer and editor since 2007, and has authored guidebooks and travel articles on Russia, NYC, Los Angeles, Melbourne, Bali, Hawaii, Japan and Scotland. A native New Yorker and naturalized Melburnian, Ali has also lived in Chicago, Prague and the UK, and has traveled extensively around Europe and North America.

Re

Re   ly Planet
titl   ments.
His   ins of
Ka   nesia,
an   w him on
In

R

W   were go-
in   e went to
M   train. He's
n   experiences
t   to report
b   ky.

F

F   decades,
b   parts of
f   ublishers,
                                        n Facebook,
                                       y.kaisora.com

Published by Lonely P
CRN 554153
7th edition – Oct 2018
ISBN 978 1 78657 068 0
© Lonely Planet 2018   Photographs © as indicated 2018
10 9 8 7 6 5 4 3 2 1
Printed in Malaysia

nd Lonely Planet
ble care in preparing
this book, we make no warranty about the
accuracy or completeness of its content and,
to the maximum extent permitted, disclaim
all liability arising from its use.